also by John Sanford

The Water Wheel (as Julian L. Shapiro), 1933
The Old Man's Place, 1935
Seventy Times Seven, 1939
The People From Heaven, 1943
A Man Without Shoes, 1951
The Land That Touches Mine, 1953
Every Island Fled Away, 1964
The $300 Man, 1967
A More Goodly Country, 1975
Adirondack Stories, 1976
View From This Wilderness, 1977
To Feed Their Hopes, 1980
The Winters of That Country, 1984
Williams/Sanford Correspondence, 1984
The Color of the Air, 1985
The Waters of Darkness, 1986
A Very Good Land to Fall With, 1987
A Walk in the Fire, 1989
The Season, It Was Winter, 1991
Maggie: a Love Story, 1993
The View From Mt. Morris, 1994

Clarks, Nebraska, 1907: The Little Sister, with Dan, Bijou, Constance and Pearl.

WE HAVE A LITTLE SISTER

Marguerite: the Midwest Years

John Sanford

We have a little sister,

and she hath no breasts:

what shall we do for our

sister in the day when

she shall be spoken for?

—Song of Solomon 8.8

CAPRA 🐏 PRESS

SANTA BARBARA

ACKNOWLEDGMENT

Bijou Arissa Gustafson was tireless
in recalling family events and generous
in imparting the information, and your
debt to her is great. Quite as much are
you obliged for her lifelong goodness
to your Marguerite, the little sister.

—J.S.

LIBRARY OF CONGRESS CATALOGING-IN-PUBLICATION DATA

Sanford, John B., 1904-
We have a little sister : Marguerite, the Midwest years / John Sanford.
p. cm.
ISBN 0-88496-399-3 (cloth)
1. Roberts, Marguerite, d. 1989—Homes and haunts—Middle West,
2. Roberts, Marguerite, d. 1989—Childhood and youth. 3. Women novelists,
American—20th century—Biography. 4. Women screenwriters—United States—
Biography. 5. Frontier and pioneer life—Middle West. 6. Middle West—Social life and customs.
I. Title

PS3537.A694Z86   1995   95-33054
812'.54—dc20   CIP
[B]

Published by CAPRA PRESS
Post office box 2068, Santa Barbara, CA 93120

DEDICATION

On occasion, it suited her to speak without speech, and in some semi-secret place, you'd come upon a half-hidden note—in a sock or a pocket or under the roller of your Royal. It'd be a mere scrap of paper reminding you of a promise forgotten, or picturing your face on the head of a daisy, or assuring you of what you were sure of—her unfailing devotion. Scraps only, but you prized them one and all, and in time the collection numbered in the high hundreds.

When she died, after a marriage of more than fifty years, she took with her all pleasure, even the small one of finding her stashed embassies. Never again would you be drawn as a dog labeled Best in Show; *never, as* Mag the Hag, *would she present herself as cockeyed and turnip-headed; nor ever, behind the platen of your typewriter, would you find a wish for a good day at the machine or a plea for two peanuts and a tangerine. All the same, you couldn't relinquish the hope that from some hiding-place, you might still bring to light a last artless drawing, a last warm word. Six years after her death, you found what you'd been looking for.*

In her Medical Journal, under the date Nov. 17, 1985, she recorded an appointment for an angiogram, a risky procedure known in some cases to have caused a stroke. To this entry she'd added:

> Dear Jabez, if I don't make it, know that I love you. Please be good to my folks—and to yourself. Mag

ॐ

To Maggie, then, for Maggie

1905-1989

THE SMITH FAMILY

Henry Albert Smith, father 1861-1948

Decky Wells Smith, mother 1866-1954

☙

Pearl Arizona, daughter 1885-1983

Daniel Webster, son 1885-1946

Harry Anson, son 1887-1907

Constance Audra, daughter 1895-1985

Bijou Arissa, daughter 1900-1993

Marguerite Azora, daughter 1905-1989

CONTENTS

FOREWORD

Marguerite Smith, the central character of these pages, was professionally known as Marguerite Roberts, and when you became acquainted with her, late in 1936, she was a screenwriter employed by Paramount Pictures in Hollywood. Likewise were you, but as a novice recently brought out from New York, you'd been teamed by the Company with the experienced Joseph March, and it was he who presented you to Marguerite in a hallway of the Writers Building. There and then began a relationship that lasted until her death in 1989, by which time she'd been your wife for more than fifty years.

An account of her during those years was given in your Autobiography, *Scenes from the Life of an American Jew,* and, with greater particularity, in *Maggie: a Love Story.* As yet, though, little has been told of her earlier years, when, all unaware, she was drifting toward that encounter in a studio hallway. That period of her life, much of it spent in Nebraska and Colorado, is the compass of this book.

– J. S.

BIRTH CERTIFICATE

The document is a white-on-black photostat, and slanting across its face is an overstamp:

To Whom It May Concern: This birth was reported to the State office in 1905. Nebraska did not adopt the U.S. standard form of birth certificate until 1912. Hence the omission of a number of items from this record.

The copy, issued by the State Department of Health at Lincoln, Nebraska, was made from the original filed by *L. Little, M.D.*, the physician in attendance, and only to certain of the numbered queries did he respond:

1. Place of birth: *Clarks, Merrick County*
2. Full name of child: *Marguerite Azora Smith*
3. Sex: *Female*
7. Date of birth: *November 26, 1905*
8. Father's name: *Henry Albert Smith*
10. Color or Race: *White American*
17. Mother's maiden name: *Decky Wells*
19. Color or Race: *White American*

In Dr. Little's report, no date or place of birth is given for the father (9) or the mother (18), nor is the *Nature of his usual occupation* (11) or (16) *the Number of her children at the time of this birth*. Elsewhere only can it be learned that Henry Albert, a sometime Town Marshal, was a mason by trade, and that Decky had four children when Marguerite Azora came into being: the daughters Pearl, Constance, and Bijou, and a son by the name of Dan.

Few other than members of the family would know that Pearl, the eldest, was already a married woman, and that on the same day as her mother, she bore a child of her own. Nor would this have been widely known, that her child died within hours, that anguished by the loss, she bespoke the care of her day-old sister (*for a while, Mama, only for a while*), and that to console her, Marguerite was given into her hands.

But all Clarks and much of Merrick County knew this, that *a while* grew until it was measurable in years, and when Decky at last demanded the child's return, many opined that it was because she'd begun to call Pearl her mother. They were half-right: it was also because she'd begun to call her mother Grandma.

THE VIEW FROM AFAR OFF

1905: Tannersville, N.Y.

At the moment, he's upwards of a thousand miles away. He's on a hotel lawn in the Catskills, and his picture is being taken on a summer's day that time has dulled to ferrous gray. The grass, the shrubbery, the tree he's under, all are sere, as though within the print the season has changed. He's with his father and mother, and his brown-black eyes are fixed on the window of the camera, as if it gave on the wide world outside and beyond. But it does not: it opens on him, on his father and mother, on a summer's day and the foxed and faded greenery of 1905.

Henry Albert Smith, 1861-1948

MARGUERITE'S FATHER

He was born to Jed and Mary Smith at Council Bluffs, Iowa, on the 9th of October 1861—and there and then, at the beginning, the certainties of his origin end. He brought with him into later life no written record of his birth, for his birth had gone unregistered, nor was he laden with souvenirs of his past, the letters, the documents, the photographs of kinsmen and friends, of places he'd known as home. He came from the shadow trailing the gossamer of memory only, and shredding the more with time, it assured him of little but this, that he'd have to create a past by living it.

His papa simply up and vanished one day like a blown-out light, and as for his mama, she being an eighth-part Cree Indian, she too lit out, and the unnatural woman never once looked back. It's anybody's guess who found the boy and brought him up, and mine would be that he nearabout brought himself up—and with hardly a year of schooling, a good job he made of it. He had only half the Indian blood of his mama, but he was twofold the Indian.

He earned his keep in the sweat of his face, and toil made him manly long before he grew to be a man. He had purpose and an air of self-command, and even among his elders, he was a quiet force. He balanced out at somewhere around a hundred and fifty pounds, give or take, but he'd go round-and-round with a bear and come away like as not with the pelt. Nothing daunted him, no man however huge and no beast however fearsome, and in and about his neighborhood everybody knew it; only the foolish few ever tried him more than once.

For all that, he was soft in speech and mild in manner, and with no more than a drawl, he could rule a notional colt or a stubborn child—*That'll be about all, sir,* he'd say, and resistance somehow ended. He was a good shot, good enough to sink nails in a board at twenty feet, but when he wore his Marshal's badge, the only weapons he carried were his fists, and against a sorehead or a souse or a bindle-stiff, they were all he ever needed. There was one hotspur, though, that he rarely could handle—his own son-in-law, the black Irishman John-boy Roach.

John was built solid, like a seed-bull, and he outweighed Daddy by a good hundred pounds. Sober, he was a sweet and peaceable man, but every so often he'd go on a bender that lasted for a week and sometimes for two. When he was fired up, he'd take on anybody or anything, even a train, and no one man could tame him, no team of men—and what they did, they just let him be till he ran out of steam. Once, I recall, they couldn't let him be, on account of he was laying across the U.P. tracks, meaning for the Flyer to grind him to hash and roaring he'd kill whoever tried to foil him. Likely it was Pearl sent for Marguerite, and with the Flyer almost due, she was brung there in a hurry. A kid of five is all she was and small for her age, but she stepped right up to Roach and stomped her foot, saying *You get up now, John-boy, and come on home*—and I'll be bound if the crazy-ike didn't pick himself up and follow her down the road.

Nor was Henry Albert a tea-drinker. He too relished the taste and sting of whisky, but there was this difference between him and John-boy: he could cork the bottle. When he'd had enough, he'd never brawl,

3

he'd never show fight, he'd never sprawl in the public way. He'd simply go home to Decky Wells—*as pretty as a little red pair of shoes*, he thought—and he'd fall asleep while trying to kiss her.

The only union Daddy ever heard of was the Union Pacific. He worked a ten-hour day, and he got a dollar an hour for standing on a scaffold and making plaster stick to the chicken-wire on a wall. That would've come to a pile of money if he could've done it day in and day out, but for three-four months a year, the weather wouldn't allow it. It wasn't the heat that stopped him; it was the cold and the rain and the wind, and it all seemed to come down from the north. Us kids would want to know why that was so, and he'd say *'Pears like Canada got untidy, and the Lord's putting it to rights.*

He came by his hard black hair through his mother; for the rest, he was indebted to the Holland Dutch and a mix from the British Isles, being much, therefore, like many another "White American." He wore a mustache as soon as he could grow one, and he always wore it wide, halfway across his face. What it did somehow was draw attention to his eyes, a pale blue, like the color of a vein; when he was angry, though, the hue deepened and became a gas-flame blue.

But he'd never get angry at us kids. We could carry on something fierce, and he'd pay us no mind at all. He'd be sitting there, reading the papers and smoking, and what we'd do, we'd take a notion to gussy him up. We'd powder his face with flour and dab cinnamon spots on his cheeks (we didn't have any rouge), and then we'd tie a baby-bonnet on him and stand around laughing fit to split. He just kept on sitting there, like it was slick and natural for a doll to be chomping a cigar.

It was a common saying in and around Clarks that the Platte was a mile wide and an inch deep, and for most of the year, the description was true enough for a river that the Indians knew as Nebraska, their word for a shallow stream. But in the late spring, coming down off Colorado with the snow-melt, it was one inch deep no more, nor was it only one mile wide: it was a flood, fast, broad, variable, and dangerous, a vast freshet that fled past with brush torn from the banks, with bridge timbers, and with a steer or a cow that had gone too near and fallen in.

4

The flow cast up sandbars that stranded snags and sawyers, and these trapped fence-rails, barbed wire, and other debris—which sometimes proved to be a man. Henry Albert, known to be the strongest swimmer in Clarks, was always summoned to dive for the body, and he did.

When someone asked Daddy why he took on jobs like that, he said *The Platte don't scare me worth spit, and I guess it does you, sir*—and he was right. He'd get sent for account of he'd take the risk, and the others wouldn't. But just let him pull the drownded man out, and they'd be proud about how they'd've done it if Daddy hadn't. The heck, they would.

Henry Albert was the catcher for the Clarks baseball team. He caught without a glove (once for a pitcher named Grover Cleveland Alexander), and in time he broke every knuckle in either hand.

I can't recall him ever wearing a splint, so I guess he let them set by themselves. The upshot was, he got to be so crookfingered, he couldn't pick a nickel off a table. It didn't stop his work any, but he sure was unhandy with a knife and fork.

The Fire Brigade of Clarks was a twenty-man team that hauled the town's only piece of equipment, a two-wheeled hose-cart. Periodically, it would stage a test-drill against time, and a photograph of one of these shows the men harnessed in pairs, poised for a starter holding a pistol. Henry Albert was the fastest runner and Captain of the team.

I'm so took with that photo that every once in a while I'll bring it out and enjoy it all over again. The men are in uniform, short-sleeved jerseys and knee-length trunks, and you know they're most of them farmers because their legs are pale, and so are their arms to the wrist. Two members of the team are unattached: one's the man toting the nozzle, and the other's Daddy, who's set to run afore and find the fire. There he is, crotched down in the roadway waiting for the gun—and one day it come to me sudden that he's wearing his wedding-ring. I can't rightly say why that excaped me before. It's plain to see. It's shining in the dust.

There was no complexity in Henry Albert Smith, there were no hidden meanings, no slick-sly words and ways. On the contrary, he was an artless man—simple, some might've put it, for when he spoke his mind, he told the whole truth. Being upright, he was now and again diddled by a cheat, but because he was genial after a swindle, he attracted far more friends than fiddlers. He liked people, even the thimbleriggers, and people made him welcome wherever he went.

They simply cottoned to him, it seemed like, all kinds—merchants, cattlemen, back-door peddlers, Indians, tramps off the cars, chippies stomping the high road, and drunks he throwed in the clink. One time, I remember, John Roach blew him to a trip to Omaha, and when he come back, he had a house-guest with him, a wrestler name of Frank Gotch. Trouble was, Gotch had the chicken pox, and we couldn't get red of him for a while.

The saloon in Clarks dealt in tobacco products as well as liquor, and against the wall behind the bar rose columns of cartons and boxes containing cigars and cigarettes. Their gaudy labels composed somehow a mural that patrons would stare at—and stare the more when a few whiskies made the colors and illustrations seem to interweave. After a day on the scaffold with his mortarboard and trowel, Henry Albert Smith, wending home to supper, sometimes paused for a single shot of tonic. The one, generally, was all he'd take, for he was a family man and did not drink his wages; but there were occasions when he'd suspend his own rule, and those were when his wife, *pretty as a little red pair of shoes*, gave birth to a child. For him, then, as for others, the mosaic of labels would come to life, and he'd see the dazzle expand slowly and slowly contract, melt and slide, turn sinuous and glide across the wall. He'd lean against the bar, peering at the intricate gilding, the faces and figures, the lettering, and he'd read the names of the numerous brands when for an instant he caught them standing still.

Gracious life, those names! Over the years, Daddy took five of them home to Mama and insisted that she use them. She'd try to make him back off, saying *But that ain't a child-name, Henry! It's a cigar-name!*, but he was bound and determined, that booze-happy man, and his son got two names from that saloon, Daniel Webster, and each of his daughters got one to wear in the middle: Arissa, Audra, Arizona, and Azora.

On the Nebraska plains, the Indians had flourished once. In great numbers had they dwelt there for many a millennia before the white man came and staked a claim to what not even the red man saw as his own—the earth. The naturals, the simples, soon were most of them gone from that place, evicted, transported, or, at small cost, simply shot, and they that remained were impounded and left to beg or starve.

Many's the time they begged off of Daddy, and they never got turned away. A tramp, he'll sometimes leave a mark on your fence or your mailbox to show you're a soft touch, but Indians, they didn't need a mark for Daddy: they smelt out the Indian in him so easy, it was like he wore a feather in his hair. Another thing, there was pride in their way of begging. They could be perishing for food, but they wouldn't ever ask; they'd just squat there quiet and wait for you to give. Daddy gave every time— and he didn't make them wait, either.

When no work as a mason offered in and around Clarks, Henry Albert Smith sought employment elsewhere, and more often than not, he had to go far afield to find it. Crookfingers and all, he could do many a useful thing with his hands: he could lay pipe, mend harness, and shuck corn in corn-shucking time; he could shingle, paint, cut and haul wood, and string barbed wire; and in dealing with animals, broken or wild, he had the master's touch. But he had no touch at all with machines.

When it came to a gingalory, Daddy was a regalar clunchfist. If it had two parts, it paused him; if the parts moved, it beat him. Dancing around some snorting dingfod, he was like an Indian hearing a clock strike: it had an evil spirit, he thought, and he'd flee lest he be caught in its spell.

It was with esteem that Henry Albert spoke of Theodore Roosevelt; in his hero's headlong life, though his own was vastly different, he must somewhere have caught some aspect of himself. He was obscure and contentedly so, for he was a sure and self-sufficient man and the equal of any other; Teddy, greatly glorious, was vaunting, and though he strode bullying across the world, he was ever daunted by the rich. And yet in that gasconading clap-sword, Henry Albert seemed to sense a correspondence with a small part of his blood, the Cree sixteenth never quite suppressed by the rest. No butcher of birds and beasts was Henry Albert, no fire-eating jingo, no much-man with hair on his body, which an all-Indian would not wear, still did he fancy within Teddy what he felt within himself.

Earthquake, 1906

THE COLOR OF THE AIR

8.3 on the Richter Scale

An Omaha newspaper is spreadeagled on a kitchen table, and huddled roundabout, several members of a small-town family are staring at headlines, at exclamatory stories, at photographic gloom. In far-off San Francisco, all is quiet now, and its fires at last are out, but here in this Nebraska kitchen, there's still the stunning sound of a world coming undone, and the flames—gracious life, they can be seen from the moon! Here the atmosphere is opaque with smoke, here ever-widening fissures appear in the floor, here ceilings fall, and steeples, and walls, and spears of glass—everything falls, as it fell far away....

Beneath the table, a small child sits on a worn rug. Not yet a year old, she's unaware of the all-around commotion, she doesn't hear the planet's underground dissolution, she cannot know of rubble and ash and the dead. She's otherwise absorbed. Her hands, rather like a doll's for size, are fumbling with a plaything, a tawny Teddy Bear, and she eyes it with delight.

Decky Wells Smith, 1866-1954

MARGUERITE'S MOTHER

She knew these things of herself, that her mother had been a Varner from Virginia, and that her father, Daniel David Wells, he too a Virginian, had been a millwright before emigrating westward, where in a caprice he'd abandoned his occupation and become a tailor. Save for such sparse memories, only wisps of her history trailed her out of the past.

Ravelling like mist were places and faces once familiar and their names, and so with her childhood dreams, longings that waking denied her. She seems to come into tangible being only with her marriage to Henry Albert in Sciola, a settlement along the Nodaway River in Iowa. It was then, in 1882, and there, some sixty miles from Council Bluffs, that her known history begins.

Mama and Daddy slept side by side in a double bed for sixty-seven years, and in his sleep one night he died. When we told her that he'd gone, she just said *Shucks* or *Pshaw* or some such double Dutch that all the same was flush with sorrow. They were a pair, those two, but that's not to say they were a matched pair. They were as unalike as roads, he being easy going and she uphill to the end. Some actor-fellow once said he never met a man he didn't like, but Daddy, he never met a man that didn't like *him*. Mama was a sight less simple, and only with her family did she feel secure. She must've got that way early, because I can remember one of her sayings from far back: Never trust a brown-eyed man.

Many such did she find herself among when her husband took her across the Missouri into Nebraska. There the Pawnee dwelt and the Ponca, there too the Omaha and the Ogalalla Sioux, and to the end of her life, she was afraid of them all. Work was scarce, and Henry Albert drifted over the plains to seek it, to Fullerton on the Loup, to Clarks out along the U.P. tracks, and even as far as the Niobrara in the sandhills of the west—but wherever he and Decky lighted for a while, he'd bring home some starving brave to share his food and fire. He loved the Indians, loved them as possibly only another Indian could, but to his wary wife, they were savages, cunning, lightfingered, and treacherous, and, almost as forbidding, they stank.

It wasn't only Daddy's Cree blood talking, though; it was something else as well, something in his nature. He never looked on himself as different to other people. Some might be a little better, maybe, some a little bigger, prouder, meaner, some a little more tightassed than the rest—but taken by and large, he guessed them to be pretty much of a piece. They were all of them just people, white-skinned or red, Scotch-Irish or Winnebago—and he was one of the bunch. It wasn't in his nature to make rules; he had, you might say, a natural nature....Mama was harder to please. The way she saw it, there were two kinds of people, the decent kind and trash—and she thought there was a sight more of one than the other.

Decky Wells had a second aversion, liquor, whereof much was to be found on the fringes of the frontier. It was quite as available there as food and in places quite as cheap, and it might be had on demand wherever two byways crossed and even where they did not—and a mint of cash-money was swilled that could've filled the pot. On his way home from a day of mixing mortar and laying brick, Henry Albert would pause for a refresher, or a restorative, or whatever jawbreaker he used in calling for a swig. He'd call but rarely for more than one, and the rare occasion was the birth of a son or daughter, and then he'd keep on calling without keeping score. When he started for home at such times, the sky would be a great cowl of stars, but his feet would find him the way in the dark. His mind still adazzle with the red-and-gold wall of cigar-boxes, he'd seat himself in a rocker beside his wife's bed, peer at her blurred and variable image, and say *Ma'am, they tell me we got another baby.*

It was Daddy did the naming of us kids, and Mama was always uneasy when the time came, for fear he'd pick out something queersome and stick to it. She told of him once, being a little whiskied, insisting on *Daniel Webster*—he was dead set on *Daniel Webster.* She had to call Dan in to prove he already *had* a Daniel Webster.

For the most part, Henry Albert was a sober hardworking man, adept in all branches of the masonry trade, whether it was laying slabs and sidewalks, constructing chimneys, or setting tiles in a pattern or plain. He'd put in a ten-hour stint for his wages, and sometimes more if material remained in the mixer—but once he reached home, he was done for the day, except for sitting still while his kids tied a bonnet under his chin and played dolly with him....His wife, though, was never done.

Not even in her sleep, it seemed like, because she'd wake up in the morning with the day laid out in her head. Daddy brought in the cash-money for coffee, sugar, salt, and all like that, but lacking Mama, we'd've been dirty, bareassed, and lank. She cleaned house, did the cooking, washed our hair, and made our clothes, and in between, she tended her truck garden, fed the chickens, and scoured the privy—and betwixt the betweens, she put up fruit, she papered, painted, and mended, and out of a mess of silk and cotton scraps, she ran up as beautiful a crazy quilt as you ever saw. All that, mind you, with five kids to manage and coax some use out of. Oh, and one other thing: to earn the $45 dollars that Marg had to pay for business school, Mama took in a neighbor's washing.

Unlike most women in her place and time, she was not a church-goer. Wherever she and her family took up residence, the local preacher tried to persuade her to enter his fold, always to no avail. She'd endure with dignity those visits of the cloth, she'd receive them in her best room, and if the day were warm, she'd even offer what she called *limonade*—but from first to last, she refused every prayer to save her endangered soul.

She was too tender to tell those psalm-singers why, but she told me, and I'll tell you. A long way back, we had a brother name of Harry Anson, as fine a boy as ever was, and rising eighteen, he was took with the quinsy, which in that day and age, you either licked it, or *it* licked *you*— and poor Harry, he was losing. When the doctor gave him up, Mama sent for the preacher to pray over him, but being as the quinsy was so catching, he wouldn't come. After Harry died, Mama swore off church-going—and whilst she was about it, she swore off God too.

In making her division of mankind into two classes, the decent few and the numerous trash, she held the determining factor to be cleanliness, a state so toilsome to maintain that a fall from grace was all too likely. Cease caring for your person, she thought, cease for no more than a day, and you were on the slick way down in station—and so it was with a home and all that the home contained. For self-respecting Decky, therefore, cleanliness was an imperative. The conveniences for achieving it, though, were unavailable to her, and to avoid the downward slide, she made shift with what she had: the wood-burning stove, the coal-oil lamp, water hand-pumped from a cistern, and a jakes out back in the tules.

I don't know that they make the stuff any more, but did you ever see one of those cans of powder with a picture of a woman in wooden shoes chasing dirt with a stick? Dutch Cleanser, it was called. Mama couldn't afford such things, so she didn't use it—and she didn't use a stick, either. She chased dirt with mops and brooms and her own two hands, and she beat the Dutch at it. There was no dirt in any house *she* ever lived in, and there was none on any of us girls at day's end. When we came in from school or chores or sky-gacking, we had to wash up and put on a fresh white apron before we could set to supper, all spick and span like the table we et off of. Gracious life, you could've et off Mama's floor.

Henry Albert's earnings were barely sufficient to feed his family, let alone pay for store-bought clothes. Shirts and pants and dresses and jackets—all were run up on Decky's treasured possession, a sewing machine, and to her daughters, they seemed to flow from under its eye-pointed needle and fall finished to the floor.

How she prized that old thingamaree! Time and again she said if us kids so much as touched it, she'd thump us. Well, we did touch it, but all the thumping we ever got was a tap on the head with her thimble-finger. That machine went along whenever Daddy moved the family, and seeking out work, he moved us often. I don't recall it myself, but Mama tells of sometimes coming to water deep enough to reach the wagon-bed, and Daddy would heist the machine overhead and wade the stream on foot with it. For certain things, though, only hands would do, and watching Mama's was like watching a spider spin a web. Give her a worn sleeve or a torn skirt or a burn-hole, and she'd give it back to you prettier than new.

Her rules of right conduct were strict, but they applied only to family members still beneath her roof; those who'd left it were suffered to govern themselves. Out on their own, they'd fall at times into folly and error—they'd make wrong choices, they'd fail in foresight, they'd take long chances and be easily misled—but by way of reproof, Decky would have nothing to say.

When we were grown enough to be out of the house, she figured, we had to run our own lives. Sad to relate, some of us ran them like foolheads, mostly with the men we picked to marry. Pearlie was one such, tied for a dozen years to an Irish boozer, and Marg was another with that upstuck Leonard Roberts of hers. His people came from the South some place, and they held their chins high—quality, they thought they were, and much too fine for us common stuff. Being down-the-nosed was hard for Mama to bear, being she was a proud little body, but nary a word did we hear from her, not even after Marg got sick of being snooted and sent her feller packing.

Early, even while still a boy, her son Daniel Webster had shown himself to be a rare hand with horses—with horses of all kinds. He was equally successful with three-gaited horses and Clydesdales, with cow ponies, standard-breds, and roadsters. A soft voice matched a light touch, but underlying both was a will of whalebone, and sensing it, an animal seldom held out long. When he was a young man, he traded for a likely-looking pacer, and one day while gypping it in a field, he lost his footing and fell, and with a leg caught in the gyp-rope, he was dragged far before someone brought the frightened horse to a halt. The leg was found to be fractured, there were torn tendons, and in places the flesh was scraped off to the bone.

He was half the year mending, and he wound up with one leg shorter than the other, and he walked gimpy the rest of his life. It was Mama mostly that looked after him when he was laid up, and she got to be specially tender about him—in fact, I think he got to be her favorite. She never said as much or showed it, but we all felt it, and none of us minded: we could stand a son coming first. But being first, he sorrowed her by taking a slummock for a wife. Pearl Cook, her name was, a handsome enough woman, I guess, but the state of Nebraska never saw a bigger slut. She was lazy, she ate slow and steady like a cow, she was a liar, and, worst of all in Mama's eyes, she was dirty in her person and disgusting in her ways. It's disgusting to even tell how disgusting she was: Mama caught her once using a hand-towel to wipe herself after pissing....

On that occasion, Decky enforced her own rule: the act had occurred under her roof, and she condemned the woman to her face. Thereafter, when the daughter-in-law came for a visit, no hand-towel was ever in sight.

13

Reginald Aubrey Fessenden, 1866-1932

THE COLOR OF THE AIR

The First Broadcast

Christmas Eve, 1906

No snow fell that night, and no rain: it was so clear and calm that you could read the constellations in the sea. We were off the Carolinas, not too far from the Stream, and wearing my head-set, I was standing in the doorway of the shack—the eye of a storm, I was, a storm of dots and dashes from other ships and the shore. And then came this that Christmas Eve: *Adore and be still!*

I didn't know the phrase was Gounod's and spoken by a man: for a moment, I suffered the joy of hearing God. *Adore and be still*, I fancied He'd said, and for a moment, for a single moment, I did as I'd been told. I stood where I was and looked upward, and I saw spars write our roll and pitch on the sky, and the wires between them seemed strung with stars.

It turned out to be that fellow Fessenden up at Brant Rock. He'd been singing in an empty room, as God did before the Beginning, but for a moment, for one wondering moment....*

Pearl Arizona Smith, 1885-1983

MARGUERITE'S SISTER PEARL

Within the family, she was affectionately known as "the section boss," or, when more mandatory than usual, as Pill, though still with affection, for she was held in esteem. A small, well-made woman, she pleased the eye without stunning it, but so seemly was she in dress and manner that she detained the eye long. The eye she pleased most belonged to the town saloonkeeper, John Roach, a violent Irishman with a periodic frailty, a fondness for his own wares. While courting Pearl, however, his sole indulgences were sprees of prodigality during which he

*adapted from A More Goodly Country, 1975

14

bestowed diamonds upon her, and gifts of gold, and, on a signal occasion, a spanking turn-out—a lacquered runabout drawn by a high-stepping horse. But it was none of those things that won him his prize: it was the wild nature of the man.

First-born of the Smith children, Pearl was not slow in showing a tendency to assume control and issue orders. In another, the leaning might've led to the making of blunders and a loss of rank, but authority sat well on Pearl, for she seemed always to know more than those she commanded, and under her direction, they did better than the best they'd ever done on their own. For such performances, however, they drew no praise from the section boss. Doing right, she believed, was simply the right thing to do, wherefore it was commonly said of her that she was "not very givey." But if miserly with applause, most readily did she part with her possessions—her earnings, her services, and her time. She who was "not very givey" gave herself.

To console her for the loss of her own baby at birth, Pearl was given the care of her infant sister Marguerite. At no time did she regard herself as the mother, but her husband behaved as though the child had been begotten by him. Both, though, were bewitched by the little girl, and they reared her in a style she could not have found at home— among other advantages, according to sister Bijou, *they had one room off the kitchen that was full of just toys; it was Marguerite's playroom. One Xmas, John bought the toystore out of toys for her.*

"She's only a teeny little thing, John," Pearl said, "but she's your sister-in-law all the same, just like Bijou and Connie. She's not your daughter."

"Well, she's most as good as," Roach said. "We've got the keeping of her."

"Not till the end of the world, we haven't. One of these days, Mama's going to get tired of being called Grandma by her own child, and she'll take Marg away from us."

"Don't say that. Don't even think it."

"I'm only trying to prepare you for what's sure to happen."

"I'm not the kind to face a thing before I have to."

"I know. That's why you're always falling in a hole."

"You sound like you *want* to get red of Marg."

"And you sound like you been drinking some of your redeye. I cherish that child more than you ever could, but only as my sister. I don't lose sight of what's what, and you do."

"She pleasures me, the little squab, and you've gone and spoiled the fun."

"I'm just wasting my breath on you. I swear, you're a weakminded man."

Not him. He was a bullhead, if ever there was one. Let him take a notion, and you'd have to break his skull to get it out of him. He was a lavish man and fine to be with when he left liquor alone; drinking, he was mean, a mean Irish bully. He had four brothers, and if he started to drink, they simply went and got lost. I remember one time when he turned on Pearl and hit her so hard he busted her nose. Daddy come by just then, and seeing what John done to her, he knocked him cold. Another time, John spraddled the U.P. tracks bent on committing suicide, and they had to get Marg out of bed in the dead of night to coax him home. He would just melt to whatever she would ask of him.

In the year 1909, the state of Nebraska enacted a law requiring that saloons be closed between the hours of 8 in the evening and 7 in the morning, thereby all but putting an end to the sale of liquor in single measures.

That John Roach, though, he had the knack of making money. He took over a vacant building in Clarks that used to be a dirty-spoon restaurant, tore everything out, and furnished up a new restaurant with fittings he got from Omaha, very up-to-date. He had a beautiful mirrored soda-fountain, a lunch-counter, and a dining room in back. Pretty near the whole family worked there. Pearl did the cooking, Mama made delicious pies, and Connie waited table. People came there from all around, and the place was a great success.

At the time, Omaha had a population of about one hundred thousand, which made it a city some two hundred times the size of rural Clarks; by no means, though, was it two hundred times as fast. In its liberty, in its tolerance of the unconventional, it was merely Clarks in large; their irregularities differed in number, but not at all in kind. A year or so after the opening of the new restaurant, a druggist by the name of Chester Honnold established himself in Clarks, and in no long while, he and his wife Mildred became friendly with John and Pearl Roach.

"Henry," Decky said, "we've got two girls here at home."

And he said, "Deck, that ain't fresh news. I been seeing Connie and Bijou every day of life."

"Pretty soon, you're going to see three."

"What! You ain't having another baby!"

"You old fool, you. I'm talking of Marguerite, and I say it's high time we took her back from Pearl."

"She's five years away from us. How come you're all of a sudden on fire about it?"

"Yesterday she come visiting, and the child called me Grandma."

"Well, if Pearl's baby had've lived, that's what you'd rightly be."

"The Grandma part don't fret me any, but the visit does. She come to her own home to *visit*. That's got to stop, Henry."

"She's cute as a bug, and I like her around. But so does John Roach, and he's going to be all broke up."

"I ain't thinking of John Roach one bit. I'm thinking of my flesh and blood."

"Pearlie's flesh and blood too."

"She never did think Marg belonged to her. She'll get along."

"That Irishman, there's no telling what he's apt to do. He's been behaving, what with the café and all, but this could send him back to the bottle."

"He ain't never been away. And here's something else: he ain't been behaving, either."

"What's that suppose to mean?"

"Just wait, and you'll see," she said. "But next time Marg comes calling, she stays. I'm her Mama."

The couples, John-Pearl and Chester-Mildred, were much in each other's company, dining and playing cards together, and even joining for an occasional excursion to Omaha on the cars. Privately, they were soon in conjunction in other ways, but Clarks was too small a community in which to conceal those ways long, and when they knew that they were known, they came into the open and exchanged partners, Chester now forsaking Mildred and Roach forsaking Pearl.

For all that it was only a flag-stop, plenty went on in Clarks, but never before a whimwham like that one. It was the talk of Merrick County for years. There were divorces, of course, and then the new pairs got married, but the oddest thing of all was Mama never had a word to say for or against. What happened happened out in the world, not in her house, and far as she was concerned, her son-in-law's name was now Chester. But there was no more restaurant for Pearl and the family to rely on, and we had to find other work, the drug-store being a one-man business.

Surrendered to her mother, Marguerite and her John-boy were never to meet again, but Bijou told her of seeing him twenty years later, saying *Marg, he didn't even recollect your name.*

Once him and Pearl got divorced, he seemed to become a different man. He was never able to earn the good life he had before. It was like he lost the knack, and downhill he went till he was only a fat old fuddlehead with the fire nearly out....Not our sister Pearlie, though. She went to Denver, hocked her diamonds, and took a Beauty School course from a French instructor. Chester gave up the drug-store business, which was never much good, and he followed her to study for a Foot Doctor. He quick got out of that—he was always getting in and out—and he studied how to do permanent waving so's he could go in with Pearl. They set up shop in Greeley, that's above Denver, and they made good money— leastwise Pearl did, because he spent half the time chasing women, getting in and out, you might say. Pearl finally got so fed up that she quit him and took out for Los Angeles. On his own, the do-nothing would've starved in a ditch, so he shut the shop and dogged her to the Coast. Before she softened up, though, he had to do some fancy begging, the randy sponger.

"I wish some of our girls had as good luck as you and me," Decky said.
And Henry Albert said, "Which ones?"
"Well, there's Pearl. First off, she had herself a hard drinker that knocked her about, and now this lady-killer of hers is fixing ladies' hair. I call that bad luck."
"The other three, they're doing all right."
"I ain't so sure of Marg."
"Marg. I thought you kind of liked that Yonny feller hangs around her all the time."
"I ain't so easy in my mind about him."

"Why so?"

"He's a brown-eyed man."

"There's lots of men is brown-eyed."

"But this one's after Marg."

"She can see to herself, you ask me."

"Like she done with that Bob Ives, the Eye-talian? You had to drive him off with a shotgun."

"Well, case of need, I still got the gun."

"This one won't get drove off, I'm afraid. He's gone on Marg."

"What's fretting you, then?"

"Them brown eyes of his. I don't trust a man with brown eyes."

Marguerite Azora Smith, 1905-1989

MARGUERITE

A pretty little blonde with a very feminine body, but with the thoughts of a tomboy.

—sister Bijou

Of the photos taken of her in infancy, only two remain. In one of them, standing beside a spotted dog, she wears a long half-sleeved dress that conceals all of the very feminine body save the minikin forearms. In the other, posed in the same dress and flanked by her three sisters, she sits on the lap of brother Dan. Gazing at the faded prints, you find yourself fancying a miraculous change of place and time, one that transports you to the camera's field of vision and makes you a member of the family group and a companion of the child and her fat old Dalmatian. What inspires your conceit is the desire to have known her from the beginning, to have heard her treble voice and watched her float on hidden feet. You yearn to have been part of her history, and you rue the years you've missed.

What would she have thought if a stranger strangely dressed had suddenly appeared before her green and amber eyes? A little older than she, he'd've been an outlander of a kind seldom seen along the Platte, a stray, perhaps, from some faraway tribe. Still, she'd've spoken, or tried to speak, or, speech failing, wouldn't she have reached for him, as though to make him understand with her hand?....But of course there was no miracle, and the brown-eyed boy did not turn up in those peculiar clothes—the sailor suit and the buckskin shoes—and therefore, with nothing to stare at, she did not wonder who he was or where he'd come from; he hadn't come, he wasn't there at all.

Daniel Webster Smith, 1885-1946

MARGUERITE'S BROTHER DAN

He was a small man—no one in his family was tall—and he was thin-strung, especially in that gimpy leg of his, and though he rarely complained, his health was poor. After the crippling accident, he'd never again been thrifty, exchanging spindling youth for spindling middle age. He was at ease only in the company of his parents and sisters, and he'd sit long with any of them, smoking continuously while listening to the familiar, the safe, the uncensorious; he'd have little to say, little to contribute, but he'd think himself thoughtful and, as nowhere else, a force to be reckoned with. Among others, no similar nicotine fancy was possible, and to drown reality, he relied on alcohol; but liquor made him assertive rather than compelling, and he'd down the more to deaden drink's failure. Save for those of his blood, then, he avoided people and chose lower forms of animal life as his associates, the horse, the dog, and with such he was at his best; they made no demands that he could not meet, and in return for feed and care, they submitted to domination.

But it wasn't the spooky colt that broke his spirit; it was the woman he took for a wife. No one knows where or how he met her, but she came from trashy people, drunks and layabouts, and she was trash herself, and poor Dan, she ruinated him. A handsome enough woman, I'll grant you, but only the way a cow is handsome. She was big and heavy and slow-going, and it seemed like she was forever chomping away at something— a cud, we used to say. Put her in a stanchion, and, gracious life, you could've got a pailful apiece from her tits. If what Dan saw in her was a woman red-hot and ever-ready, he likely was disappointed because she was churchy, one of those Seventh Day Adventists holding that Christ was any day now coming back to slay Satan and all the world's sinners. Part of the rigamarole of her religion was people washing each other's feet, but, shoot, she didn't even wash her own. She was dirty in her person and her habits, her bed was dirty, and the floors, and the toilet, and the kitchen. Mama said she'd have to be a cockaroach to eat in Pearl Cook's house—and even then she'd think twice.

Dan was fascinated by his infantine sister Marguerite. Her whippet size put him in mind of the young of animals, the cub, the calf, the filly foal, and in that kingdom, he found few enemies and suffered few defeats. He'd watch the child tirelessly, enjoying the way she crawled across a carpet, the way she stood uncertainly or sat fumbling with her toys. He'd peer through heaving smoke, he'd hear her high thin voice, and when she came near him, he'd stroke her downed face. *Baby sister*, he'd sometimes say very softly, *baby sister*.

What did she make of the slowly surging air, the whorls she reached for and missed because nothing to touch was there? What did she think of the petal of flame in the coal-oil lamp, of the pattern in the carpet she stood or sat on, of the man in the chair who now and then fingered her face and hair? What she saw and heard no one would ever learn, for she herself was aware only of forms at rest and forms in motion, of sound without meaning, of striving for color, smoke, and light: she was still in the wilderness of an unexplored world.

THE VIEW FROM AFAR OFF

1909: Long Branch, N.J.

From where she stands, in a pasture beside the river Platte, the world runs away to the horizon, a flat expanse on which unknown millions go about the living of their lives. Of these, only one will ever affect her own, and on that day, he's spending it on what seems to be a beach. Dressed in a striped bathing suit, he's seated astride a barrel lying on its side in the sand. Behind him, waves are about to crest and break, and far at sea, a schooner can be seen under sail. But the waves will never break, nor will the schooner ever make its next port of call: they're painted on a backdrop and hanging from a wall.

Constance Audra Smith, 1895-1985

MARGUERITE'S SISTER CONNIE

Everybody used to say that Pearl had the best business-head in the family, but the fact is, Connie did—only it so happened that she never got to prove it. She was apt in school, she had a likely eye for value, and she knew what was going on—I don't mean just in Clarks, but in the what-do-you-call-it economy. With all that, she could've got off to a good start at whatever she put her mind to. But she was just shy of seventeen when she fell for this Tom Schank that worked in the lumberyard, and that's all the further she got with her start. She married him, and he being a German-Irish Catholic, he loaded her up with five kids in six years, and all she ever got of the outside world was a six-month spell in an Omaha sanitarium.

What could she see from where she sat out the days at a window or on a bench in the garden? Did she face a wall or other windows or a barren street, or was the view a long one, across the great bend of the Missouri to the haze of Council Bluffs, or was her gaze on the world within, on the plains and high mountains of the mind? And what did she find there, thoughts of her husband and children and the endless daily round, or was she free there, and only there could she finish what she'd never had the chance to begin?

Bijou Arissa Smith, 1900-1993

MARGUERITE'S SISTER BIJOU

Five years the elder, she was entrusted with the care of Marguerite after the child had been reclaimed from sister Pearl, and like every other in the family, she was enchanted by the pint-size witch.

She just hypmatized us all, the dinky little thing.

None was more bespelled than Bijou. The small being, she thought, was rather like a doll come alive, a plaything that somehow fed itself,

22

dressed itself, and put itself to bed. There was no need for pretense; it spoke, it walked, it actually laughed and cried. What it could not yet do was read, and Bijou, who could, read to her endlessly. She read newspapers and catalogues and almanacs, she read the lyrics from a book of songs, she read *Black Beauty*.

> She wanted to know about those little black bugs on the pages, and I told her they weren't bugs; they were the words that I was saying. And then she said if they were words, why didn't they say themselves. I said....I don't know *what* I said.

What Marguerite could listen to time after time were the stories about Billy Whiskers, a most accomplished goat, a bold, brave, and cunning animal marvelously gifted with the powers of thought and speech. None of these attributes, however, saved him from a long series of capric misadventures, some of them amusing, some astonishing, and not a few calamitous; and to each, Marguerite responded appropriately, with mirth, with wonderment, with tears. So often did she call for those stories that she came to know them by heart, and whenever a tired Bijou left out a part, Marguerite stopped her and supplied the passage from memory.

> I honestly think she knew those stories better than the woman who wrote the book.

But Bijou was far more than a mere governess: without being aware of it, she was acting as a mother, practicing the role in anticipation. In any division she made, of clothing or food or candy, the better or larger share went to her sister, and with rare patience, she endured noise and confusion and the torment of finding a frog or a garter snake in her pocket or her bed. Evidencing the kind of mother she'd one day be in fact, she never became angry or impatient with her charge, never scolded her, never punished her. On the contrary, when Bijou went to work for wages, she spent most of her earnings on her sister. She loved the dinky little thing.

MARGUERITE AND HER FRIENDS

She liked boys' games and climbing trees. No dolls or playing house for her.

—sister Bijou

She also liked animals, loved them, and the love was lifelong. Her first dog was an old Dalmatian, but she didn't know that he was old or even that he was a dog: to her, he was merely another inhabitant of her one-year world, and so far as she was aware, he was little different from herself. True, he turned up day after day in the same mottled suit of clothes, and true too, he still got about on all fours, a method of loco-motion she was inclined to abandon, and also there was this, that nei-ther understood the other's language. But all the same, they were good companions, which spoke well for his forbearance, since she was for-ever trying to pluck those spots from his garments; when she tugged too hard, as she sometimes did, he'd yelp softly, and for a while she'd stop. Although he saw no particular advantage in standing on two legs, he knew that she did, and he helped her by letting her hold his collar as she staggered from here to there and then to somewhere else. So greatly did she enjoy those ambulations that she failed to note his growing reluctance, and she'd wake him from a drowse and take him for a ramble. A day came when she found him in a sleep so profound that she could not rouse him, not even when she scratched his muzzle and stroked his speckled ears. Jack was dead, she was told, and without knowing the meaning of the word, she cried as the dog was carried away.

Other dogs succeeded him. Fizzle was one, Shep another, and spot-less Spot a third, and if she realized by then that they were dogs, not people, she felt, as she had with Jack, a sense of affiliation with them. She could not have explained the relation any more than they could, but among them there was a constancy that all soon came to be certain of: there were no variations of nature and behavior, no changes of mood and affection, and therefore no desires expressed and denied. To her mind, had she sought a word to fit her feeling, dogs were reliable, and they (who can say?) might've thought the same of her. Jack, Fizzle, Shep, and Spot—one would succeed another, and others would succeed them, succeed but never supplant, for who would ever oust a dog, who could think so unthinkable a thing?

Her brother was an ardent horse-trader; he'd trade for anything he fancied more than what he had; he'd trade a black for a sorrel, a pacer for a saddle-bred, a Shetland for a hack; he'd trade up, and he'd trade down. Swapping was his passion, and he ranged the country round-about with whatever he had to offer, but ardor was not always enough, and now and then he'd return to Clarks with less than he'd taken away.

I recall him coming back one time leading as showy a team of Clydes-dales as ever was seen in the county. Only trouble was, they turned out to be so windbroke they couldn't pull hay out of a hayrack. Of course he had to get red of them, but till he found somebody greener than he was, Marg rode the creatures all over the place. There wasn't any saddle would fit them, so she sat them bareback and held onto their manes. She was a sight up there on those monstrous things, but they didn't scare her none. Nothing did.

She'd ride anything on four feet, not only Buck, a cleverly-named buckskin, but cow-ponies also, and stone-horses, and pintos, and mules, and her own bull-calf Bolivar.

In Blanca, we lived near some mines in the Sangre de Cristo Range, and every so often they'd turn loose some burros they had no use for. Dan roped one and brought him home for Marg, and we named him Croppy on account of he'd lost his ear-tips in a blast. A regular-size saddle was all we had, but that didn't matter to Marg; she just climbed aboard and rode the animal over half of Colorado, her feet never once in the sturrups.

She had a tame raccoon that slept in a sideboard drawer; first, how-ever, it would remove the contents and pile them on the floor.

Marg had a bantam hen named Reddy that laid her eggs in the wash-tub. She loved that little bird, and she cried and cried when she found out that Mama, food being scanty, had served it up for supper.

THE VIEW FROM AFAR OFF

1912: New York, N.Y.

Sitting her buckskin pony near the U.P. right-of-way, she seems only to be waiting for a freight train to pass, but her mind is elsewhere, and she hardly sees or hears it come and go. She's unaware that it's the rest of her life that she's waiting for, and of course she doesn't know what it has in store—the New York Jew she's due to marry. He's eight years old and just then posing for a tintype in a Harlem park, and his mind too is somewhere else, he too is in the dark.

MARGUERITE AT THE RIVERBANK

To make some extra money one time, the family started a little dairy business in Clarks. Daddy did the milking, Mama washed the bottles, and Dan made the daily deliveries off a cart that looked like a chariot. Marg's job was bringing the cows in every afternoon, and she'd saddle Buck, stuff her pockets with soda crackers—provisions, she called them— and trot off to the pasture down by the Platte. Nine times out of ten, she'd come back quick enough, herding our half-dozen head like a cow-hand. But the tenth time, the tenth time...!

She'd ride out as usual for the roundup, but somewhere along the way, her errand would be forgotten. Among the willows at the riverside, she'd dismount, tie Buck to a branch, and then, sprawled in the grass, she'd watch the water slowly pass. It ran low at times, and here and there an island of sand would split the current, and at such partings, a weir would form of brush and sticks and trash. So still would she lie that sometimes a flight of mallards would drop down for a landing, and along the sheer bank, swallows would veer and wheel. There were flowers all about her, and there were butterflies like flowers flying, but she had no eyes for these nor ears for insect-sound and the song of birds. Her mind was on the water flowing past her feet.

A fleet of leaves floated by, and with them a feather and a sprig of chokecherry, and she saw them swirled by an eddy and then taken again by the stream. It was a moving road, she thought, and she could

follow it only so far before it vanished around a bend. What lay beyond, she may have wondered, what would be found behind the file
of cottonwoods and the rim of distant hills? Was there only more of
the same, more coulees, more trees, another line of hills—or did the
world end where sight ended, was there nothing more to see? A new
flotilla came on the current, borne toward the bend at the end of the
visible world.

1910

BLANCA, ALT. 7,870, POP. 252

*Daddy won a prize in a raffle, a couple of lots in Colorado, and next
thing we knew, we were on our way to Blanca in the southern part of
the state. It turned out to be a hamlet with one store, a makeshift
school, and a pool hall. Daddy's lots were out in the sagebrush, the
only greenery for miles and miles around, and our house was a tar-
paper shack that looked for all the world like a box-car without wheels.
Poor Daddy, that was some prize he won.*

—sister Bijou

The lots were on the plains near the base of Blanca Peak (14,363
ft.), and few were the days when no wind came off the slopes to blow
some of the prize away. If no wind blew, then rains fell, or snow, or cold
set in, and no tree would grow there, no crop, no flower, nothing save
the gray-green sage. Of the tar-paper shack, only a single photo sur-
vives. In it appear two women and two young girls—Decky, her daughters Bijou and Marguerite, and her daughter-in-law Pearl. All four in
white, they stand on a small and balding lawn, worn-down weed, really,
and against the studded black wall behind them, their spick-and-span
dresses glare. No one else can be seen, no dog or horse for once, no
well or wire, no still machine. Except for the four and their black back-
ground, the scene is empty. Even the sage is sparse, as if thinned by the
weather and exhausted by the wind.

I disremember how long we lived in Blanca, but it was long enough
so's we went to that mishrable school, us girls. This comes back clear,

enough, though: we had a burro to ride. He was running loose in the brush, living on God knows what, and Dan roped him and brought him home. Croppy, we called him.

There exists a photo of Croppy under saddle. He's well-fed now, his belly bulging slightly where the girths are cinched. The two sisters bestride him, Marguerite next to the pommel and Bijou against the cantle. Standing alongside the schoolhouse wall, the burro seems to be suffering with comfort: he's asleep on his feet.

One day, sister Pearlie came down from Nebraska to inspect what we were up to. All she needed was one look at that shanty out there in the middle of nowheres, and she took and drug us all back to Clarks—and to hell with the prize that Daddy won in the raffle.

1910

PURDY'S CAFÉ, JOHN ROACH, PROP.

He kept the old name, nobody knows why, but it was John's place now, and you can lay odds it wasn't the same old Greasy Spoon. Far from it. It would've done credit to Omaha, which is where John got his fixtures and a lot of his fancy foods.

In the Platte, and in the lesser streams around Clarks—the Prairie, the Silver, and the Loup—only catfish could be found, and carp, and a small-size bass known as crappie, but the Roach café offered no such ignoble fare. Shipped in refrigerator cars, salmon arrived from the Pacific and rainbows from the rivers of Idaho, and out of the east came halibut, and pickerel, and Delaware shad, these last along with their sacs of roe; Blue Points came in barrels of ice, and Little Necks, and Cherrystones, and mention should be made of grouse and venison, of patés and artichokes, of Decky Smith's pies.

Save for the pies, nobody in Clarks ever saw eatables like those before, but the Chicago drummers did, and the railroad bigwigs, and his nibs the District Judge, and pretty soon the locals got wind of what they

Blanca, Colorado, 1910: Decky Smith with her daughters Bijou and Marguerite and her daughter-in-law Pearl Cook, Dan's wife. In front of tarpaper shack where they lived.

Blanca, CO, 1910: Bijou and Marguerite on the burro Croppy.

Clarks, NE, 1910: John Roach, Pearl Smith's husband, standing before his restaurant; with him are Marguerite and her friend Teddy Simmons.

Central City, NE, 1912: Marguerite at the Merrick County Fair.

Pilger, NE, 1916: Marguerite.

Greeley, CO, 1922: Marguerite.

Hollywood, CA, 1928: Marguerite.

Big Bear, CA, 1931: Marguerite with her Airedale puppy Minnie the Moocher.

Hollywood, CA, 1931: Marguerite entering the Writers Building at Fox-Western on the first day of her first assignment as a screenwriter.

Kernville, CA, 1934 Marguerite on location for a film written for Fox-Western.

were missing, and they began coming in from all the way to Central City and Columbus, from outside the county, even. John made a mass of money in that café.

To the passing stranger, it seemed to promise little. The horse-rack before it was broken, its cross-bar lying anyway in the road. Crude lettering on the left-hand window proclaimed MEALS AND SHORT ORDERS, and ICE CREAM and COLD DRINKS on the other, and the screen-door between them, for all it revealed of the interior, might've been painted on a wall. A tacked-up square of tin near the entrance spoke of BULL DURHAM THE OLD RELIABLE SMOKING TO-BACCO. If these signals caused no juices to flow in the passing stranger, he went further and fared far worse.

Gracious life, you should've seen that place on a Saturday night!

1910

BABY SISTER

You know how she learned to read? By watching. Watching, I said, and I'm not codding you. I read to her night after night, and what she liked best was a book of stories about the goat Billy Whiskers. I must've gone through it twenty times over, but she never got tired of it, and after a while I noticed she was watching as much as listening. The bright little puckachee, she was matching the words I was saying against the words on the page—and a day came when she took ahold of the book and began to read to *me!*

I love Billy, but he's so naughty, always getting into a scrape and always coming to grief.

But no, not always, because sometimes he shows how smart he is, or how dare-devilish, and sometimes he does something so funny I just have to bust out laughing.

But he really truly is naughty, jumping over fences and excaping whenever he takes a notion. Mama says I'm like Billy; I light out too, and she never can find me.

29

Wouldn't it be a caution if me and Billy lit a shuck at the same time and met somewheres in the road?

I would ask him to come home with me, and when we got there, maybe he would let me ride him like my calf Bolivar does.

I would ask him to stay, but of course Mama wouldn't let him in the house. I would fix him a place in the barn where he could sleep and be out of the rain.

As soon as I did that, I would tell Teddy Simmons, and he'd come around, and we'd have lots of fun with Billy.

He'd be real, not just a picture in a book.

We didn't have a theater in Clarks, but there was a nickelodeon in an empty store, and Marg would go with a bunch of the kids and sit way down front on the first bench, and none of the others being able to read, she'd rattle off the words for them when they came on the screen. *Came the dawn*, she'd say, and *I have you now, my beauty*. Between you and me, some of the older people couldn't read, either.

from 1910

BIJOU, a.k.a. MIDGET

After Marguerite had been reclaimed from Pearl and John Roach, she was placed in the care of Bijou, some five years her elder. Ten at the time, she relished the role, for of the two, she was much more feminine than the schoolyard brawler and climber of trees—and she performed instinctively, knowing without knowledge that she was playing Mother against the day when a mother in fact she'd be.

She spent most of her earnings on Marguerite, she bathed her and washed her hair, she was always on hand to caution her, to join her in a game, to bring her in when the call came from the kitchen door. In addition, she read to her, not only from Black Beauty and Billy Whiskers, but also from the fascinating horrors of a book called *Great Disasters,* which contained accounts and vivid illustrations of the Chicago fire, the Galveston and Johnstown floods, and the San Francisco earthquake. But of more enduring worth than all these services was the warmth of her nature, her freedom from envy, and her forbearance.

Marguerite's attachment to Bijou was deep and everlasting, very much as though they were truly mother and child, but in those early times, it suited her to requite kindness with a dead snake coiled on Bijou's chair, or with a frog stealthily dropped into her pocket. Forbearance was needed indeed.

1911

THE OUTSIDE WORLD FROM INSIDE MARGUERITE

It was a wet day, and standing at her bedroom window, she gazed at the barnyard below through rills of rain meandering down the pane. Her pony, craning into the open from his stall, seemed to be enjoying the bad weather; her bull-calf grazed between his sudden crazes; and Reddy her bantam hen pecked at grains in the gravel, unmindful of her sodden plumage.

I said Midgie if they can be out there why can't I be out there too
and she said because you'll get soaken through
and I said why don't Buck and Reddy and Bolivar get soaken through
and she said how can they Margareet they got fur and feathers
and I said well I got skin and I don't get soaken through when I take a
bath do I

His eyes half-closed with pleasure, Buck dozed in the fringe of rain that hung from the eaves; Bolivar lipped at pompons of clover; and Reddy paused to preen and then fell again to picking over trifles.

she said Margareet how about if I read you another disaster a typhoon
a shipwreck
and I said I wouldn't get any wetter than Reddy is getting

1911

A SHORT COURSE IN BIOLOGY

While walking toward town with her mother one day, Marguerite saw two dogs fighting in a field, and at once she made for an opening in the fence, bent on intervening.

"Come back here, Marg," her mother said.
"I have to stop the fight"
"Just do as I tell you, child."
"But, Mama, the littler one is getting beat!"
"Not so."
"The big one is got the underholt. It'll kill—!"
"It won't do nothing like it."
"But it's plain as plain!"
"Plain to you ain't plain to me. Them dogs ain't fighting."
"What're they doing, then?"
"If they was fighting, they'd be snapping and snarling and foaming and faunching. What they're doing is making baby dogs."

Making baby dogs, Marguerite thought, and after walking on for a way in silence, she said, "Is that how people make baby people?"

And her mother walked a little further before saying, "Yes."

1912

GRADE SCHOOL, CLARKS, NEBR.

What's your name?
My name's Jack Brown:
Ask me again,
And I'll knock you down.
    —schoolboy rhyme

It was a two-story building of red brick, with a three-step stoop leading into a dark central hallway. From the town and roundabout, several

32

dozen boys and girls attended, among them Marguerite Azora, then seven years of age.

> I like school, and I'm never tardy. In winter, I sometimes can't go at all account of the snowdriffs, but when I do go, I always get there before the bell.
>
> I can do sums and spell pretty good and I know the capital of nearly every state, and acourse I can read like sixty...but *sewing!*
>
> Why should I study a thing like that? What do I care about darning and mending and hemstitching? I'm not going to be a seamstrix. *Sewing!*
>
> Bijou Arissa, she just loves that kind of stuff, cooking, ironing, redding up—but no housework for me. Playing with horses and dogs has it beat all hollow, and so has running and rassling and climbing trees. Sewing! I *hate* sewing!

The boys and girls in her classroom, how were they arranged? Were they seated alphabetically or simply by size, the smaller up front and the taller at the rear? Did she observe faces, dress, and manners, did she note the color of someone's hair and eyes? Did she admire this girl's graces and that one's poise, or was it the other way 'round, they prizing her ability to read, ride, run swiftly, and rival the boys at their games in the yard? Were some her friends, and would she, in the days to come, recall their names, their hopes, their personal ways, or would they all be lost to the future in the maze of the past?

> He got fresh, and I punched him, and the teacher sent me home with a note for Mama. Mama wanted to know what the boy did, and when I told her, she said next time I saw him I was to give him a punch for her.

BUSSY

Bussy was a small white dog, one of the strays brought home from time to time by Marguerite Azora. He was an ill-favored animal, being short in the leg and long in the barrel, and taken with his screw tail and his shag coat, he bespoke his blood of many breeds. But for Marguerite, he glowed with the greatest of virtues: he was a dog. That alone was enough to win him the run of the premises, a license he enjoyed throughout his reign in the household.

In one of his periodic efforts to save the souls of the Smith family, to snatch them as brands from the burning, the minister had come out from town to renew his exhortation, thus far fruitless. At the hour he'd chosen for the visit, no one was at home but Marguerite, who, knowing he was entitled to respect, showed him to the parlor, an area rarely used. At her gracious invitation, he accepted a chair, under which lay Bussy *dormant*, and then, the proper hostess, she seated herself nearby. There, alas, her command of the amenities was lost, and she sat facing the minister in silence.

No sound was to be heard save the ticking of the clock on the mantel, and with the shades drawn, the parlor was dim. Marguerite knew that she ought to be making pleasant conversation, but however she cast about, she could not settle on a suitable subject. As for the minister, he may well have fancied himself alone in the room. Whatever he thought of Marguerite—a child, a girl, a minor being—he was remiss in overlooking Bussy, who wasn't a being at all.

Still tongue-tied and agonizing, Marguerite saw the dog yawn, stretch, creep from under the chair, and inhale the delights on the minister's shoe, after which he doused it with a delight of his own, a drench of urine. Only then did the minister become aware of what had happened—and only then did Marguerite find her suitable subject.

"Don't mind Bussy," she said. "He peepees a lot."

THE MERRICK COUNTY FAIR

The fairgrounds were at the county seat, Central City, a town some fifteen miles to the west of Clarks, and Marguerite had been invited to the carnival by her brother Dan. At sun-up of a midsummer's day, he called for her in his buckboard, and after she'd been wrapped in a lap robe against the morning chill, they set out on the long drive, drawn by a spanking road-horse, a mare named Laura K. Beyond the last of Clarks, the way lay through a vast main of grain surging toward the sky, and in a vain pursuit of the shadow it cast, the buckboard ground over the sand and gravel road.

"Dinky," Dan said after a time, "how about you lay hold of the lines?"
She stared at him, saying, "Dan-boy! You really don't mean it!"
"I wouldn't never cod you, baby sister. Here, take 'em."

To get Laura K., Dan had swapped horse for horse and given a pocketful of boot, and knowing how much he prized her, Marguerite could hardly believe, even while holding the reins, that the mare had been put in her hands. But they were soft hands, as Dan was well aware, and gently she held the mare to the crown of the road, where the going was best.

He don't have to tell me to be light on her mouth. He knows I know she's an easy goer, and she's willing too, and I amire how she holds her head high, like she's proud of what she's doing.
And why shouldn't she be? I'm proud of what *I'm* doing, driving Dan-boy's Laura K.
I wonder who she's named after. Somebody's girl, maybe, and maybe she once was Dan's.
Laura K....

He struck a match on the splashboard, and a pale and fragrant veil of tobacco smoke drifted away to be shredded by the wind.

"I'm going to tell you something," she said. "But you got to promise to keep it a secret."

"I promise, baby sister."

"You're my favorite."

"More favorite than Pearlie and Connie and Midge?"

"More favorite than anybody!"

"Why? What did I ever do?"

He'd done nothing. He'd never, like John-boy Roach, been spectacular with gifts, he'd never shone in company, he'd never been dominant, worse, he'd never been heeded, and worse yet, he'd seldom been noticed when there. But not by deeds or gifts or ascendancy had his sister been stirred: it was for their lack that she loved him; she loved him for his nothing.

❦

She did not drive the rig all the way to Central City; a mile or two only, and she was put in a dazzle for the day. And she was kept so by the crowds, the calliope, the interweaving spiel; and the corn-popper world she seemed to be in was sped up by the slide and the swing, the ride on the wheel, the crazy-quilt Indians in the still brilliant plumage of dead-and-gone birds; and there were these things too, the shots in the gallery, the side-shows, the smell of sweat and beer and fried meat, the never-ending outcry....

❦

On the road homeward, she did not drive at all. Not yet for her had the turmoil died, but it was in slow motion now, and she sat beside Dan in a daze a dull delight. Again the sun was behind them, this time going down, and again they were on the heels of their unattainable shadow. She was tired, but it had been too fine a day for her to let go of—fine, she thought, because of Dan. He'd done nothing, won nothing, given nothing; he was only good, and she loved him. And drowsing in the late light and the rhythm of the mare's gait, she heard him say,

"Baby sister, I got a secret too. You been my favorite from the day you was borned."

Laura K., she thought, and she fell asleep against his arm.

Theodore Roosevelt, 1912

THE COLOR OF THE AIR

The Bull Moose

Under no circumstances will I be a candidate for or accept another nomination.

–T.R., November 8, 1904

When the polls closed that night, he became President in his own right and not by reason of the pistol-shots that killed McKinley. In victory, he grew expansive, but alas!, he expanded too far and made the statement that he'd rue the day for. *Under no circumstances*, he'd said, bold words that he'd later have to eat. Never in his life would he have his fill of the limelight, and if he didn't know it when his term began, he damn well would when the four years ended.

His thirst for it slaked, as he may have thought, he took himself off to East Africa, where he shot whatever moved and often what did not, after which the craving returned, and he boarded ship for home. In all, he'd had seven years in the White House, but they weren't quite enough, and he burned for another four. When they were denied him, he broke with his party and ran against its fat nominee. They both got beaten by some-one named Wilson, a schoolmaster, it was said, cold, stiff, something of a stick, really....

1913-14

MARGUERITE'S VERY FEMININE BODY

Among her many gifts from John Roach was a toy wagon known as an Irish Mail. Steered by a singletree, it was used by her to transport this or that from here to there, and often its burden was a dog trying to look dignified as she took it for a ride. When it occurred to her that they might well change places, her brother Dan fashioned a harness, and she became the driver and the dog the driven. Shep, his name was, and clearly he enjoyed his new role in the game.

Alongside the roadway to Clarks, there had been laid a concrete walk some four feet wide, and over its level surface, the rubber-tired wagon would smoothly pass. Whenever Marguerite was sent on an errand, she'd hitch Shep to the Irish Mail and start for a store or the post-office or her father's place of work, and Shep, her willing tractor, would carry her there at a trot. Other girls would watch from their dooryards, and now and then a boy would give chase and ask to be taken on, but the pace was swift, and never a stop was made.

Never, that is, but once.

Marguerite's mother had put up a basket of vegetables from her garden, and they were being shipped by dog-cart to her daughter Pearl, who lived half a mile away. With Marguerite happily at the reins, Shep was moving along at his smart clip when he shied at a shadow or a sudden sound or at nothing at all, and the wagon, veering sharply, overturned. Marguerite was sent sprawling into the road, and all sprangled out, she slid along the rough edge of the sidewalk, tearing her underclothes and raking her thighs.

Bleeding and too badly hurt to ride, she made her way home, leading Shep and the wagon. She was kept from school for a few days, her mother saying, "The child injured her privities."

from 1910

A TEDDY-BEAR NAMED TEDDY

He was given to Marguerite by her father, whose idol Roosevelt was, and no closer did she ever come to owning a doll, nor in truth did she ever desire one: what were dolls but make-believe babies that girls played with until the day for playing ended? It was not that she disliked babies; on the contrary, she was entertained by their futile motion, their jibber-jabber, and their power to destroy whatever they could reach. Rather was it that she did not think of herself as an incipient woman, nor even, it may be, as a girl.

When her father brought him home from Omaha, Teddy was a glistening figure of tawny velour, with black stitching to represent claws and black glass beads for eyes. But much time has passed since then, and his expression, if it was fearsome once, has given way to one of innocence, as if along with his shag, he's shed his bestial nature, and it's absent too from the shoe-buttons that replace his missing eyes. He's rising ninety now, his pelt of plush thinned almost to baldness, and his legs, so firm of yore, so stiff it seemed with force, are limber and loose-jointed, withered within.

Taken everywhere by Marguerite, sometimes borne in her arms, sometimes dragged by his head, running with her when she ran, falling when she fell, and not seldom left out in the rain, Teddy was far from being regarded as a plaything; in Marguerite's mind, he was one of her pets, quite as alive as the living, and he grew only the dearer as he aged. A day came when, because of his infirmities, she relieved him from joining in her hurry-skurry and made him a pensioner for life, free then to watch from a shelf or a corner as she jumped and darted and fell from a tree by herself.

His filling of sawdust long since lost, he's stuffed now with rags, and he's a thing of lumps and welts and unnatural bulges, but he lives on, outlasting all her pets, outlasting even her, his two-legged friend.

1911

CONCERNING MARGUERITE'S VERY FEMININE BODY

Is *very* the word that Bijou used? Wherefore *very?*

True it is that her sister's a small creation, that she's rather like an objet d'art, a frictionless thing of china, say, or of convoluted glass. And true too that she's delicately made, delicacy being a property of hers, like the size and shape of her hands and the color of her eyes.

But is she *very*, meaning extremely, meaning in a high degree, meaning more than most?

She's at home with all creatures and at a loss with all machines. Indoors she does nothing useful. Out in the open, she's the focus of a crowd—dogs, cats, Clydesdales, a bull-calf, and a Rhode Island Red—and usually her dress and drawers are drabbled, and her shoes wear shoes of mud.

Very, did Bijou say?

from 1910

THE SEWING MACHINE

It was a White, a popular and less expensive make than the Howe or the Singer or the Willcox & Gibbs, but for Decky Smith it performed quite as well as the costlier brands, and with it she performed her bib-and-tucker miracles. So often was she seated at its oak and iron table that she seemed to be part of the machine—or was the machine a part of her?

Cash-money was scarce in the Smith family, and only for husband Henry Albert were store-clothes bought. For her two young daughters, goods by the yard were run up by Decky on her magical machine—and what wonders flowed from its copious needle and cascaded to the floor! Cottons and woolens and a now-and-then ell of silk became body clothes and smalls, became jumpers and singlets and camisoles, marvelously became shifts and smocks and dresses and drawers—things of ging-ham, of flannel, worsted, and calico, of rep and mull and drill and serge.

As the elder of the girls, Bijou was given first choice of the piece goods, but time and again she'd defer to little Marguerite and pass the choice to her—and like as not, Marguerite would shrug it back, for between the two sisters the green eye did not exist. Both were the envy of others, though, for the sorcery of their mother and her wizard ma-chine. Her patterns were hardly the last word in fashion, and they'd've found no favor with the bon ton of Omaha, but Clarks had never seen the like of her skill with decoration, her art in the use of buttons and embroidery, of frogging and braid and florets, through all of which the common was made over into the rare—and most happily did the daugh-ters wear their transformations.

THE VIEW FROM AFAR OFF

1913: Pine Brook, N.J.

The little village takes its name from a stream that feeds the Passaic. Fewer than thirty miles from Manhattan, even so it's untouched by the metropoli-tan frenzy, and in the sun and shade of a summer's afternoon, it drowses in the stillness. In the outskirts, a small hotel can be found, but no one is on its roundabout verandah. On the lawn, though, a family of four—a father and mother, a daughter, and a nine-year-old boy—are posing for a photo. All but the boy simply return the camera's gaze. He alone seems to see something more, but if so, it's dimmed by distance and the blear of time.

1914

MARGUERITE ASTRIDE HER BUCKSKIN PONY

Standing not quite fourteen hands, he was a "gilding" according to her brother Dan, and his color was a grayish yellow, rather like soiled chamois. He was good for a few slow gaits, a walk, a trot, and a clumsy canter, but when put to a gallop, he quickly played out. Still, he was Marguerite's particular pet, and he could not have pleased her more had he been a noble Arabian and able to run a hole in the wind.

Grasping his mane to stay on, sometimes she'd ride the pony bareback, and with her feet adangle, she'd bounce around the yard, her own mane streaming. When she meant to range, Dan would cinch the saddle for her, and she'd set out for wherever she was minded to go. Often she had no end in view save the going itself, and she'd let the pony make the pace and pick the way.

The main east-west road was a wide swath across the plains, a convex of gravel that dipped to a deep run-off ditch at either side. It was a poor place to ride and a poorer to be ridden, and given his head, the pony would trend into a fork at the first junction it came to. Almost always this would be a lane through a vast of wheat where horse and rider passed between walls of watching sunflowers, like crowds at a parade. Here grew volunteer oats that whispered when disturbed by the pony's feet, and here too were burdock and thistle, and where they were dense, now and then there'd be a sudden whirring, and a ringneck would hurl itself from cover and whirl itself away.

What thoughts did the little girl have on those expeditions? Was she thinking of what she saw and heard—a thrush on a fence rail, a lark, a prairie dog regardant on a prairie-dog hill—or was she turned inward to the sights and sounds in her mind? And what were those thoughts, what could they have been? She was eight at the time, going on nine, and she might've dwelt on things peculiar to a world of rising nine—a world of the near and the known, of familiar faces, forms, colors, of places where she belonged, of the certainty of safety among the presences always found there. Or she might've strayed to the infinite expanses of fancy, where all was new and strange, where nothing was true, nothing sure—a world of days not yet come.

They'd reach rolling ground, where the lane wound down into a draw, and at the bottom, scarlet against the slope, shrubs of buffalo berry grew, and a cottonwood or two throve in the damp. And then, mounting the far side of the break, the pony would make his way among the sunflowers again, and they'd sway as he passed, as if somewhere in the parade, music were being played, music that only they could hear.

1914

MARGUERITE'S ROOM

Was it hers alone, or did she share it with Bijou, and if shared, was there a single bed for each or a double for the two? Was the space a spare one sparsely furnished—a chair, a table, and little more—or were there rugs on the floor and pictures on the wall, was there a tilted mirror that contained a tilted world? Were the windows shuttered or curtained, or were they bare glass open to the passing eye? And what was the view from inside—a locust tree from which a snow of yellow blossoms fell, or the camber of a landscape empty to the sky? Did she dream there in that place, and were the dreams confined to the images of her age, or did she strain toward a further time and another place and try to find them with her tethered mind?

1913

THE PERIODIC SMITHS

Work at his trade was not always to be had in Clarks or Pilger or Fullerton or wherever else he happened to make his home, and now and again Henry Albert had to fare far and wide to find it, and poorly it paid when he did. His earnings of ten dollars a day yielded only modest provision for the family he'd soon be sending for—lodgings invariably in disrepair, distant from the nearest neighbor and even further from a store. To one such after another was his little clan summoned, but never a complaint did he hear from Decky, however long it took her to paper over water-stain and paint the worse for wear.

For Bijou and Marguerite, school too was usually distant, but save when a snowfall blocked the way, they'd set out together each day, trailed by Shep or Spot or Rover until the dog was scolded and told to stay. These excursions were much the same, a departure at morning and a return in the afternoon, but a day came that differed from the others in this: the elder sister, for a reason withheld from the younger, remained at home.

Trudging alone toward school, Marguerite pondered what she'd seen on awakening—a blot of blood on Bijou's night-shift and blood on the bedsheet she'd risen from. Bijou had fled at once to her mother, and seeking to follow, Marguerite had been barred from the room. Ahead of her, two classmates scuffed through the sand at the road edge, but she did not try to overtake them: she was wondering what had happened to Bijou.

It'd been plain as plain, of course, that Bijou had cut herself, but how she could've done that hadn't been plain at all. It was hard to get cut while you were laying in bed, and it was empossible, she thought, to get cut while you slept. Oh, you could scratch yourself, maybe, but a scratch would never bleed the way Bijou did—a regular slosh of blood, it was, like she went and had a hemrich.

But here's a funny thing—how come Bijou didn't know about the cut till she woke up? How come she slept right through it, the cut and the bleeding and all, and didn't find out till she got out of bed? A cut like that, you just had to feel it, you just had to be in pain. And here's another funny thing—a cut is only a cut, whether you got it in bed or playing a game, so why did Mama shut the door like this one was a shame?

How could a cut be shameful? It was a accident, and you cleaned it out, you dabbed something on it like Mama always does, echinacea or methylene blue, and you forgot it—but not this time. When she shut you out, you knew something else was going on in there, something you weren't supposed to see.

What?, she wondered. What had she not been allowed to see? She was near the school now, and along with many another, she was heading for the doorway as though some force within were ingesting them all. The first bell rang as she disappeared.

During the next several nights, Bijou slept in a spare room, but she gave no reason to Marguerite, nor did their mother. Indeed, so taciturn were they that the accident to Bijou (what accident?) seemed not to have occurred. But it *had* occurred, and all three knew it; only two, though, were aware of its nature.

At supper one evening, Marguerite said, "I want to know why Midgie left off sleeping in our room."

"Child," Decky said, "just you pass your Daddy that dish of greens."

"I got a right to know, Mama."

"You got a right to pass them greens, and that's about all of it."

"I'm being left out, and I don't like it a bit."

"Supposing you hush up, now."

Henry Albert said, "You'll have to tell her some time, Deck. Might as well be now."

"I'll pick the time. You stay out of it."

"I'm out, ma'am. I'm out."

Marguerite turned to Bijou, saying, "You tell me, then."

But Bijou rose and ran from the room.

In bed later that evening, Henry Albert and his wife lay side by side in the dark, he staring at a windowpane, a square of lesser dark, she at a memory of Marguerite. In it, her daughter, barely able to stand by herself, was posed for a photo in a long white dress, but somehow expunged from the recall was the spotted dog Jack.

"You and me, Mama," Henry Albert said. "We thinking the same?"

"That child," Decky said. "That child."

"She's got to be told some—"

"But she's only eight years old! It's too soon to tell her!"

"Better from you to what she'll get some place else."

"She's such a happy little chick, I hate to spoil things."

"What come to Midget'll sure as life come to Marg, and she'll be all the scareder if she ain't ready for it."

"I know you're right, Daddy, but she won't be a little girl after."

When Marguerite returned from school the next day, her mother followed her to a small field behind the barn, her bull-calf's private pasture. The girl, her mother found, was holding the animal by his halter and rubbing him down with a feedsack, and his buff coat shone. Now and again she'd break off to hug his head and kiss his moist muzzle.

"Marg," her mother said, "that gentleman's gussied up like he was getting married."

"He loves for me to fool with him, Mama."

"Does he? Why you hanging onto him, then?"

"Oh, I don't have to. He'd stay."

"I think not, if you let go the halter."

When Marguerite did so, the calf merely nosed at her hand.

"Appears you got him broke better than I knew," her mother said. "Come to me, child, and we'll have a good old foot-washing."

The calf following, Marguerite joined her mother at the fence. "What about, Mama?"

"Midget."

"You mean you're going to tell me!"

"I wouldn't but for Daddy," her mother said. "Careful—you're getting betwixt that creature and the rails."

"Oh, Bolivar wouldn't ever hurt me. We're friends."

Her mother reached through the fence for a feel of the calf's coat; glossed by the ragging-down, it twitched at her touch, as for a fly. After a moment, she said, "Your sister Midget's a woman now."

Puzzled, Marguerite said, "Wasn't she a woman before?"

"She was a *girl* before, like you."

"Did she get to be a woman account of cutting herself?"

"That blood you seen, it wasn't from a cut. It was from...well, the privities."

"I got privities, and *I* don't bleed."

"You will some day, and then you'll be a woman, like Midget."

"She don't look any different to what she did."

"She's different inside. She can have babies now."

"Midgie's going to have a baby!"

Smiling, her mother said, "Not just yet."

Her mind drifting, Marguerite made a few idle passes with the feedsack, and then she said, "Is Midgie all done sleeping in our room, Mama?"

"Only till her monthlies is over."

"Monthlies! Is this going to happen every month?"

"Every month."

"For how long?"

"The most part of her life."

"Why isn't once enough?"

"It's the way of nature, child," her mother said, and then she walked away toward the house.

☙

When she undressed that night, Marguerite examined her privities, but found no sign of what she was looking for. *I'm not a woman*, she told herself, unaware that, even as her mother had said, she was no longer a child.

1913

EVERY FOURTH PHASE OF THE MOON

In time, Bijou returned to the room she shared with her younger sister, and save for some reserve, she seemed no different from the Bijou of old—to others, but not to Marguerite. However slight the outward change, she was aware at once of the stranger who'd come in Bijou's guise, and knowing that the same was in store for herself, she sought forgetfulness in the out-of-doors whenever household duties loomed. Her performance of them had always been slapdash and sporadic, but now she abandoned them altogether for the company of her animals, her calf, her dogs, her beloved buckskin pony.

Housework! You never got any the further with housework—it didn't stay done. Dishes only get dirty again. Beds get tore up every night of life. Dust, and next day you dust where you dusted before. It's simply redicalus. Bijou, she's cheery about donkey-work—cooking, cleaning, redding up—but that's account of she being a woman.

Well, I ain't a woman yet, so I'm going to ride and run—and then run and ride some more.

Go where she would, with her went the knowledge that soon she'd be what Bijou already was, and no matter how far or fast she rode or ran, she could not shake it off. Impending was the drudgery of the housekeeper, the daily reorganization of disarray, but having none of Bijou's nesting instinct, none of her delight in the many stints of the home, never could she have said, as Bijou once had, *When I grow up, I want to be a washwoman....*Never!

Marguerite did not know, did not even know *of*, any other girl who felt as she did. All she'd ever encountered were Bijous in the making and impatient with the slow flow of time. They could hardly wait for the start of the endless round, but why the haste?, she wondered. Let them be ever so late, and the grease and grime would still be there, the smears and crumbs, the scars of passing traffic. How much better it was to be outside! With or without the animals, how much better! Anything was better, she thought.

Mexico, 1914

THE COLOR OF THE AIR

Our Sacred Honor

We have gone down to Mexico to serve mankind.
                                                    —Woodrow Wilson

That's what he said at the funeral of the nineteen marines shot dead in the streets of Veracruz, and being a high-minded man, he may have believed the claim a valid one. All the same, it was not. The Fourth and Fifth Divisions of the Atlantic Fleet were in Mexican waters far less to serve mankind than to serve Wilson, who was maddened by a thug named Victoriano Huerta. Grafter, drunkard, and whoremaster, he'd plotted the assassination of President Madero, after which he'd grabbed the office for himself—*El Presidente Vic!*

That the creature merely lived was enough to addle Wilson's brains, and he longed for some excuse to drive him out of Mexico and drown him in the Gulf. He found it, finally. A few sailors from the gunboat *Dolphin* had been sent ashore for supplies. There they were detained for an hour or two and then released with an apology for the interference.

A nothing-incident, for a fact, but it was all Wilson needed, and before it ended, he almost pumped it up into a war. Admiral Mayo, in command of the Fifth Division, demanded that Mexico atone for its affront to our honor by firing a twenty-one-gun salute to the American flag. It was a humiliation that Mexico would not consent to suffer, and nineteen marines died trying to make it say *Uncle Sam*. It never did, but it said something else. It said (how did the Mexican papers put it?) that we were the pigs of Yanquilandia.

1914

MARGUERITE SOLITAIRE

She cared little for the society of other girls, and when it was forced upon her, as at school, she endured being one of their number, but she never became one of their kind. Far from her own were their concerns and further still their turn of mind: they were sly, they were spiteful and small (chintsy, she called it), and their talk, when not about boys, was a gush of fiddle-faddle. She preferred the more generous nature of her pony and her dogs: girls had no honor, she thought, and animals had no guile.

All us girls had girl-friends, but not Marg. She wasn't stuck-up, just choicy, and never a one come along that fit her fancy. I used to keep an eye on her for Mama, and many's the time I seen her out by the barn playing some game all by herself—and she was happy, the little thing, ducking and dodging like she was up against a team.

Bijou wasn't with her, though, when she rode out over the plains, but even so, she may have been observed. The Pawnee were gone now, but their shades were still there, still hunting on the bluffs above the river, and, who's to say otherwise?, they may have seen her come and go, a bold little paleface on a swaybacked pony. And, spirits admiring spirit,

48

they may have willed her away from snake-holes and pitfalls while her gaze was on a brace of quail she'd flushed from the grass. She was never quite alone.

1914

MARGUERITE AND THAT WHICH SHE FED ON

In Henry Albert's trade, work was hard to come by during the winter months, and he was largely idle until the thaw set in. The family larder, therefore, derived from his warm-weather earnings, usually enough to provide, in addition to staples, a butchered hog and a side of beef. Bought late in the year, the meat was hung out-of-doors on a screened porch, where, safe against predators, it was exposed to the cold. At best, it was a limited store only, and it was made to last by the rationing imposed by Decky, manager and machinery of the Smith household.

She cooked up bacon and flapjacks for breakfast every day of life, but I never once seen Daddy pour 'em with longlick. What he'd do, he'd roll a cake around a rasher and eat it like a sossage. We didn't regalar see meat twiced in the day, but when Mama took a notion, she'd saw off a sliver of round steak and fry it up for the juice. She'd stir some flour into it, and we all had sop for our corn bread and beans.

"Sop's most as good as meat," Henry Albert said.

Bijou and Marguerite laughed at the quip, but laughter required muscular effort, and Decky was too used-up for more than a smile. She was not too weary, though to speak with affection.

"Hank," she said, "you was borned jokey, and you only get more so with age."

"You give a man enough sop, and he clean forgets meat. That's a Godamighty fact."

"You know when I forget meat?" Marguerite said. "When there's eggs."

"You like eggs, do you?" Henry Albert said.

"Better than anything in the world!"

"I didn't know you was so partial."

But he did, the guileful man.

When that child seen a dish of eggs, you could keep the rest of the meal for all she cared. I remember her eating six in a row and ready for more if there was any. I never did know what was so wonderful about eggs. She might've liked the shape, or the way they laid there looking up with that big yellow eye—but whatever, they was her favorite eating. Only thing, they had to be what she called *fried crispy*, so's the bottom was brown and the eye solid. And you know what she done every time? Picked the eye out with a fork and et it first.

Pearl and Connie had married, and only four were at table now, the elders and their two younger daughters, and eggs were often the main course for supper, eggs fried crispy as Marguerite liked them. On a platter this night lay a dozen of them, and they were portioned out three to all but Marguerite, who was given only two. Being the smallest at the board and the slowest eater, she was the last to finish her share, after which, chin-high to the cloth, she fixed longing eyes on the platter and the lone remaining egg.

Henry Albert, guileful man, indicated the leftover, saying, "Shame to let that there one go abegging. Guess I'll have to down it m'self."

He made as though to take it, but his wife was no longer watching him, and neither was Bijou; they were watching Marguerite, whose round face had sagged with yearning. Her mouth, downturned at the corners, seemed freighted with the sorrows of the world, and her lips were in a pout, as if she were about to cry.

"Well," Henry Albert said, "seeing as how nobody else wants it...."

She did not cry, nor, though deprivation was imminent, did she say a word to stay it as Henry Albert, guileful man, speared the egg and brought it toward his plate—only to veer and deposit it on Marguerite's!

On that occasion, his wife was not too tired to laugh.

1914

AS WAS SAID IN EDEN

In the sweat of thy face
–Gen. 3.19

Intermissions in the household round were seldom offered, but in her rare moments of found time, Decky maintained a kitchen garden in the half-acre area between the orchard and the barn, and there amidst her plantings, she spent the spare hour. Small of stature, she was hard to locate behind her cornstalks or her trellised vines, but every so often, she'd straighten to review a weeded row or a channel dug for irrigation, and then it would be seen that the fate decreed in another garden was suffered even in this. Grayed though not yet fifty, drained dry and gaunt, she was a worn-out woman. For all that, though, she was still the equal of any and superior to most at inducing seed to sprout and green to grow, and for her hand, as for a wand, a store came forth for summer's plenty and more for winter's lack. Lining the walls of her cellar and shining in the lessened light were the jars of cherries and apricots she'd put up, the canned pears, crab apples, and melon rind, and along with these were a score of jelly-glasses and another score of preserves....

Shall mention be made of the milking-stool, the butter-churn, the mushroom bed in the barnyard cave, or shall it simply be said that she was endlessly weary and nearly dead on her feet?

"Mama," Pearl said, "every time I come to visit, I find you slaving."

"Well, somebody's got to do it."

"Why does it have to be you? Why not them no-account girls?"

"You sure like to run things. No wonder Daddy calls you the Section Boss."

"I'm only looking after you, Mama."

"You want to run things? Run your own."

"I'm doing that."

"And not too good, the way I get it."

"If you're going at that druggist-man, there ain't nothing twixt him and me."

"You're a growed woman, Pearl, and you're married and out of my

51

house. What you and him are up to is none of my business. See you keep out of mine."

"All I'm out for, Mama, is to stop you working yourself to a nubbin. What's wrong with me telling you to get after them girls?"

"Let the girls be."

"Mooning around—that's all they're good for."

"And don't ever call 'em no-account so's I hear you. In my house, *I'm* the Section Boss, and I say let 'em be."

1914

DECKY, MAID-OF-ALL-WORK, two scenes

1.

Josephine Smith, spoken of in the family as Jos, was the daughter of Mary Wells Clopton, a sister of Decky's, and Fred Anson Smith, a half-brother of Henry Albert's. Her home lay only a few miles from Clarks on the road to Central City, but she herself lived far further from the affections of her kin. Her name, on the rare occasion when she became a topic, was invariably accompanied by a qualifier in apposition: *Jos the draggletail*, Decky would say, *Jos the slump*. No one could've been less to her liking: the woman was rank in her person and a sloven in her ways, and with a slew of urinous children, she dwelt in stink and soil and disarray.

"Jos the slummock," Decky said. "She's trash."

"Seeing the names you put on her," Henry Albert said, "how come you're there every Sunday with your hair in a braid?"

"How many times do I have to tell you? If that child of hers don't get to bathe, she'll die of the itch—and it won't take her no seven years to do it."

"Me, I wouldn't go there for high wages."

"Nobody asked. Just you put Lady to the buggy, and I'll go by myself like always."

"Whatever that kid of hers is got, it marvels me you don't carry it home to Midget and Marg."

"I would, I guess, except I stop on the way and wash off with carbolic."

"Which you get from that druggist-man."

She glanced at him, saying, "What do you—?"

"I ain't the fool you think I am."

"Well, you *are* kind of simple sometimes."

"Just once."

"When was that?"

"The day I married you."

She gave him a soft push as she said, "Get along, and hitch me that buggy."

One of Jos' twelve children, a young girl named Edna, was plagued with scabies, a parasitic skin disease caused by the itch mite. It had not yet been passed along to the other eleven, and Decky hoped to ward off that calamity by curing Edna. In such surroundings, amid disorder and filth, the hope was more a desire than an expectation, but she persisted even so, and Sunday after Sunday she made the drive from Clarks. This Sunday was no different from any other.

On arriving, she tethered Lady in a shaded place and entered the dingy and flyblown kitchen. There she put up water for Edna's bath, using for the purpose a wash boiler that had seldom held wash. Then began the painful work of peeling away the only clothing that Edna wore, a stained shift that was stuck to her body with a glue of pus and serum, some of it hardened and some still seeping from scratched-open blisters. Now a laundry tub was filled with hot water, and while Edna sat soaking her torn and suppurating skin, Decky did what was possible to put the kitchen to rights (*A sty*, she thought. *How do you redd up a sty?*). At last she turned to Edna, and after drying her thoroughly, she smeared the child's body, from her throat to her privities, with sulphur ointment—and her labors completed, she left for home.

Somewhere along the road, she spoke aloud to no one in particular, saying, *Jos the slob. Sat there the whole time like I'm her hired girl. I ought to've stomped out.*

Seated on the steps of the back porch, Henry Albert was awaiting her. After helping her down, he was about to lead Lady away to be ragged off and grained when Marguerite came racing in from the orchard to greet her mother.

"Stand clear, child, till I change my clothes."

"What's that funny smell, Mama?"

"Carbolic," Henry Albert said. "Something you get from the druggist-man."

"What's carbolic?"

"A kind of medicine," Decky said. "You can run along now, Marg."

And Marg ran. She rarely walked; she ran.

"The druggist-man," Henry Albert said. "That's where the sulphur salve come from too."

"Henry," his wife said, "I name you an old fool. What you really are is a *sly* old fool."

"Not much gets past me."

"Go put up that mare, mister."

2.

Even during the spring and summer months, employment was not always to be found in Clarks, and Henry Albert had to fare far for his pay, so far at times that returning to Clarks at the end of the day was impossible. Obtaining work in Fullerton, say, or Genoa, or Beatrice, he'd rent a dwelling there and send for his family, and when Decky had made arrangements for transport, they'd set out to follow him to their new home.

His wife did not expect to find it new in the physical sense; on the contrary, she expected it to be old—and, worse than old, hard-used and in poor repair. Heading for Beatrice or Genoa, for Fullerton or Stromsberg or Osceola, she well knew what a daily wage of ten dollars could provide—only a roof over a ruin, and a ruin is what she never failed to find at journey's end. She did not whine, though, she did not scold, she did not cry quits and sit staring at squalor. Trash so behaved, and she was quality. Boarding her children with a neighboring family, she set herself at once to the work of transforming the ruin into a residence.

At her labors, she was ever put in mind of Jos. It was as if the woman and her baneful brood had been there before her, done their worst, and moved on, leaving the harm they'd wrought for Decky to undo. Decline was everywhere about her, in the curling wallpaper and the scarred woodwork, in the missing windowpanes, the broken stair, the water-stains—it was even in the air. She patched plaster, mended screens, and unblocked drains; she swept, scrubbed, and painted rooms, and she scoured the privy with lye; she hung curtains, she washed the dinge from cupboards and doors, she plugged rat-holes—she even revived the air. And only then, when the house was habitable, did she send for her children.

"Mama," Marguerite said, "I smell that funny smell again."
"It's that carbolic," her father said. "Always makes me think of Pearl and the druggist-man."
"You can go outside now, Marg," her mother said.
"I just got in."
"Come in after—when your Daddy ain't so fritter-minded."

Once more out-of-doors, Marguerite merely wandered about, wondering the while why whenever there was mention of the "druggist-man," her mother sent her away.

What's he got to do with anything but ice-cream combs and pascriptions?
Him and Pearl, anybody'd think they was a pair; speak of her, and there he is.
Why not John-boy? Him and Pearl, there's your pair.
Next to Daddy and Dan, John-boy's my favorite. When I was little, I used to even live in his house, but now I guess I won't get to see him much. We're in—what do they call this place? Pilger! All I've seen of it so far is one hog-farm after another, so it must be good for hogs, but I don't know as it'll be good for me. Not with John-boy back in Clarks with Pearlie. With Pearlie and that druggist-man.
Baby pigs make good pets, most as good as dogs. Maybe Daddy'll get me one. I'll call it Porkus.
I miss John-boy.

THE VIEW FROM AFAR OFF

1914: New York, N.Y.

From where she stands (in Pilger, is it, or Clarks?), the earth ripples away like a vast rucked-up rug, and it seems to end where it seems to meet the sky. She knows, though, that more must lie beyond the limits of vision, and standing there (in Genoa? in Fullerton?), she confronts distances, as if waiting for them to reveal what they contain.

There is no revelation. She doesn't see the ten-year-old boy whose mother has just died, nor is she shown any of the nine million due to die in the war now beginning; she can't sense the sorrow that has come to one or the sorrows on the way to many. Unknown to her then the boy and never to be known the multitudes, but they're there, they're somewhere in the surrounding world.

One day long later, she and that boy will stand together in the dreadful quiet, the gloom of Belleau Wood.

1915

CLOTHESLINE

Head-high and stretched taut across the back yard was a strand of heavy wire. It ran from the trunk of a cottonwood to a corner-post of the barn, and on it Decky hung her washing out to dry. On a certain day of the week, it would fly in the warmth of the sun, and the yard would be aglare with sheets, shirts, towels, and underwear, and the air would carry a scent of freshness as compelling as perfume. But there were days of the week when the yard was bare of its flags of laundry, and then it was that the wire might be put to other uses—and one of these, as now, was play.

Rope-walking: the art of walking, dancing, and performing tricks of equilibrium on a rope or wire....
                                                                —Encyc. Brit.

Accompanied by two of the boys in her class, Bijou had ambled home from school. Following far behind, Marguerite saw them enter the driveway that led past the house to the yard, and by the time she arrived, one of the boys, having placed a ladder against the barn, had climbed it to try his skill on the wire. Steadying himself with outspread arms, he managed a walk of only a few feet before losing his balance and jumping off onto a bale of straw.

"Bijou," he said, "you're next."
"No such thing," she said. "I like it here on the ground."
"Ah, come on. Don't be a panty-waist."
"But I *am* a panty-waist."
"I'm not," Marguerite said.
"You!" the boy said.
"I ain't a scaredy-cat. If you can do it, I can do it."
"Marg, don't you dare!" Bijou said. "You'll fall!"
"I've fell from higher up, and I never even got skinned."
"Don't, I tell you...."

By then, from the topmost rung of the ladder, Marguerite was edging out along the wire, and being smooth in her movements, she made her poise last longer than the boy's, and only when she was well out along the wire did it start to sway.

"Jump, Marg!" Bijou said.

Instead, Marguerite strove to stabilize the wire, but it was beyond her control, and she fell, not on a cushion as the boy had done, but on the hard-packed ground of the yard.

The doctor, summoned from town (Monroe, was it, or Silver Creek?), set her broken arm and put it in a splint of fruit-crate slats.

"Child," Decky said after he'd gone, "as an acrobat, you're some genius."
"I was only out to show that boy."
"Show him what?"
"That I could stay on longer—and I did."
"Yes, and you showed how to land harder."
"Aren't you going to scold me?"

"A broke arm is scolding enough. Midget, though, I give it to her good."

"What for?"

"For letting you."

"She tried to stop me, Mama."

"Trying ain't stopping."

1915

O, THOSE GOLDEN-RULE DAYS

At school, the noontime bell had rung, and carrying her lunch, Marguerite had left the building and taken a seat in the shade of the wall enclosing the yard. Others, those living nearby, had gone home, but many remained on the grounds, and without conscious purpose, she watched them from a distance, watched girls coquetting and boys showing off, and she was hardly aware of the judgments being pronounced by her mind.

Among the boys, there was almost no repose. They dodged and darted, they rose for no reason and for no reason sat down; they made headlong starts and sudden stops; they bragged and brayed, and snatching a slowpoke's apple, they played a game of catch. They had the whickwhacks, she thought, they were full of beans; they were pell-mell, she thought, they were lackbrained, and their tongues were slung in the middle. But they were bald about their donkey doings, they hung themselves out for all to see, like flags: they had no guile. She found herself thinking the word *true*: boys were *true*.

Girls, she thought, were nothing like. They were sly, they were suck-egg spiteful, they were skinching and scheming, and they were liars born; they were choosy and prideful, but mean in spirit and dirty in their ways; they were pickthank friends, they tittered and tattled, and their jibber was only jabber about boys. Girls were *small*, she thought; they weren't like boys at all.

Still in a splint, her arm ached a little, but the bone was knitting, and one day soon, she'd be free to race and wrestle, to throw a ball and climb a tree—and to punch anyone who dared to get fresh, even a girl....

Bijou was coming toward her across the yard. "Setting by yourself?" she said. "Why not with some of the girls?"

"I don't like girls."

"What've you got against girls?"

"They're meeching."

"What about boys?"

"I like boys better."

"Why?"

"They're most as good as animals," Marguerite said. "Like sop's most as good as meat."

1915

A SHORT COURSE IN DOMESTIC RELATIONS

It was suppertime, and the Smith family was seated at the kitchen table, Bijou facing Marguerite across the middle of the board and their mother and father at the ends.

"Marg," Decky was saying, "if you come home when school let out, you'd've missed the rain."

"I stopped by Pearlie's, Mama,"

"You're suppose to come straight on home. That way, I know where you're at."

"I wanted to see John-boy. I waited and waited, but he didn't ever get there." About to feed herself a spoonful of corn bread and beans, she paused to say, "But somebody else did, just as I got up to go," and when no one asked who the somebody else was, she said, "That druggist-man."

A clock ticked. In the stove, a stick squibbed. On the floor, a dog flicked lazily at an ear. But no one spoke.

"What was he doing in John-boy's house?" Marguerite said.

Gazing at nothing, Henry Albert seemed to be thinking aloud when he said, "Ain't it about time she knowed?"

"I guess maybe so," Decky said, and she turned to Marguerite. "No use you seeking after John-boy at Pearl's. He don't live there no more."

"Where *does* he live?"

"Over to the other side of town."

"Why isn't Pearlie with him?"

Cutlery screeched on crockery. A coffee-pot belched. Under the table, a dog yipped twice in his sleep.

Marguerite said, "I want to know what that man is doing in John-boy's house."

"He lives there," Decky said.

"I thought he lived in his own house, with that what's-her-name Mildred."

"She lives with John-boy now, and the druggist-man lives with Pearl."

Marguerite stared at Bijou, at her father, and then at her mother. "I didn't know people could do a thing like that!"

"Truth to tell," Decky said, "I didn't neither."

Marguerite dabbed at her corn bread, softening under its topping of boiled beans. "How ever can I see John-boy now?" she said.

"I'll show you his house," Bijou said.

"But that Mildred woman won't be Pearlie."

"That's a Godamighty fact," Henry Albert said.

"And you ask me," Decky said, "that druggist-man ain't any John-boy."

"Why did they switch, then?" Marguerite said.

No one knew what to say. No one spoke.

1915

WHAT GOD HATH JOINED TOGETHER

At the Merrick County Courthouse in Central City, two of the divorces recorded that year were granted to Pearl Roach and Mildred Honnold. Soon thereafter, each having married the former husband of the other, they became Pearl Honnold and Mildred Roach. By the time Marguerite called at the house that her John-boy had removed to, he'd removed still further, to the main-line town of Columbus, thirty-some miles to the east of Clarks.

"Getting divorced, mama," she said. "What does it mean?"

Her hair was being washed by her mother, and, bent over a basin of lathered water, she'd spoken the question into rising steam. When no reply was made, she spoke it again.

"It's when married people don't want to be married any more," Decky said. "Like Pearl and John."

"Why did Pearlie not want to be married any more?"

"Stoop your head, child. The soap's dreening down your neck."

"Why didn't she, Mama?"

Henry Albert was seated at the kitchen table, and through the newspaper he was holding, he said, "Account of she had her full of him. Couple of drinks, and he was off on a razee."

"Pshaw," Decky said. "She could've put up with that. It was the other thing drove her."

"What other thing?" Marguerite said.

"That ain't for you to know."

Henry Albert lowered the paper, saying "What's the big secret? Everybody in Clarks knows John chased after that Mildred till he got her."

"Why did he chase her?" Marguerite said. "What did she do?"

As her father began to raise the paper again, her mother said, "The child asked *you*, Henry. Being you're the genius here, *you* tell her."

"It's a woman's place to do that."

"If that's so, then just you let me pick the time."

Marguerite said, "Is it like those dogs we saw, Mama? One was chasing the other."

"I guess maybe it is. Just like the dogs."

"She's no foolhead," Henry Albert said.

Taking dipperfuls from a bucket, Decky was now rinsing Marguerite's hair with cold water, and when the runoff was clear, she said, "Raise up, Marg, and I'll dry you."

The towel had been draped before the stove, and it became a warm hood whereunder Marguerite spoke, saying, "Mama, did you ever want to be not married to Daddy?"

There was a silence that ended with her father's laugh. "You're the genius now, Deck. You tell her."

And Decky did. "I been married to him rising thirty years. I wouldn't know what to do without the old fool."

1916

LEVITICUS 15.24

For some little time, Marguerite had noted a reserve in Bijou and on occasion a disinclination for her company: she'd become quieter than usual and less active, she'd turn away when dressing, and for nights on end she'd sleep in a separate room—and then, the withdrawals unexplained, the intimacy would resume, and the sisters would be sisterly as before. It took Marguerite long to recognize that the intermissions were regularly spaced and to associate them with what the girls at school called *the curse*. She'd heard other terms for the condition, one of them being *off the roof*, which struck her as revolting, but the worst, she thought, derived from the Bible. The minister's daughter had discovered the reference and, copying it out, she'd brought it to school and read it to a few pop-eyed and prurient classmates in the yard: *And if any man shall lie with her at all, and her flowers be upon him*....Flowers, for God's sake! Flowers!

Her face was covered with a fine, faint, almost microscopic down, and when the sun was behind her, she seemed to be aglow. She'd been told of the effect, but seeing it only when confronting a mirror, she was largely unconscious of it and went her sprightly way delighting others. She was aware, however, that her body was quite free of the floss, and therefore on undressing one night, she was surprised by a glint on an area below her navel. Moving nearer the lamp to examine herself, she found that there too down had appeared, sparse as yet, but equally fine and no less silken to the touch.

Naked, she gazed at the slight haze spun of the filaments. Would it stay as it was, she wondered, hardly more visible than the shadow of a web, or would it grow, would it darken, would it lose the feel of silk? And why was it only now showing, and what did it mean, and was the meaning good or ill? And did it, she wondered, have to do with becoming a woman, as had happened of late to Bijou...?

MAY 7, 1915

At four o'clock every afternoon, the westbound Union Pacific flyer passed through Clarks. To an outsider, the event would've been a minor one and, save for its sound, ignored. To the community of five hundred, though, no event was minor, and a handful of townspeople were usually at the depot for the occurrence. The flyer was a crack train, and according to the local joke, it went so fast that it took two men to see it, one to say *Here she comes* and one to say *There she goes*. As it sped by, a bundle of newspapers, the Omaha *World-Herald*, would be flung from the baggage-car, and moving at a speed of eighty miles an hour, it would skid across the platform until brought up short by the depot wall.

On this day, the routine was different. As the train bore down on the station, the baggageman could be seen wigwagging from the open door of his car, and in the instant between coming and going, he pointed at a bold headline on the outermost paper—and then, tossing the bundle, he was gone.

Henry Albert, town marshal at the time, was among the bystanders that day, along with Dr. Leo Little, lawyer Warren Morris, Vince Hilliard, the barber, and Ames Campbell, proprietor of the variety store. All five hastened to the twine-tied bundle and stared down at a bold five-inch banner line and the lesser headings below it:

LUSITANIA SUNK
Torpedoed Without Warning
Heavy Loss of Life Feared
Many Americans Aboard

It was Hilliard who reached for a copy of the paper, but holding it before him, he seemed unable to unfold it and read further than the blasting black type of the Extra.

"Give it here," the doctor said, and without waiting for it to be given, he took it, and opening it to the full, he began to read the dispatch aloud:

Liverpool, May 7 (by Reuter's)—Off the Head of Old Kinsale to-day, the Cunard liner *Lusitania* was struck by two torpedoes and sank in twenty minutes. As yet, no accurate tally of survivors is available, but she carried some two thousand passengers, and a large number of these are still unaccounted for; they may have gone down with the ship. More than a hundred U.S. citizens are among the missing....

"God damn the Heinies!" the shopkeeper said.

"They ain't nothing but murderers," the barber said.

"They made an enormous big mistake," the lawyer said. "It's going to cost them the war."

"Drowning's a bad way to die," the doctor said.

And Henry Albert, town marshal, said....

But just then a small soft hand was confided to his, broken-knuckled and rough, and he looked down to see Marguerite's green-brown eyes looking up, and he had a flash remembrance of the night she was born. Azora, he thought—where had he gotten the name Azora?

"Supper's near ready," she said, "and you're to come right on home."

"Then, little daughter, home I'd best go."

And hand in hand, they moved off along the platform.

"Daddy," she said, "why were those men so terrible excited?"

Thinking of Teddy Roosevelt, he said, "Account we're going to have to fight the Germans."

"Why?"

"It's what Teddy would do."

Teddy, she thought, but the name brought the image of a different Teddy—a small plaything of flaxen velour, a bear in effigy with shoebutton eyes and a sharp muzzle, all of it misshapen now, bulging here and sunken there, worn where too much handled, half-dead, really, and saved from total dying by retirement from use, but even so still her prize posses-sion—and she said, "His stuffing's coming out."

Flanders, 1915

THE COLOR OF THE AIR

A Green -Yellow Fog

The first German gas-attack took place on the Ypres front on April 22, 1915.

–Encyc. Brit.

At five o'clock in the afternoon, a bombardment was opened against the four-mile arc of trenches between Steenstreet and Poelcapelle, a sector held by two French divisions, the 87th Territorial and the 45th Algerian. Within moments, a cloud began to form over their lines, and lazily it drifted on the wind. It was strange in color, some say, and strange too in the way it clung to the ground, as if it were heavier than the air that bore it, a thing more material than vapor. Slowly it came on, a great churning mass, a monumental presence turning from green to blue as it passed through Langemarck and Pilckem and Kitchener's Wood. Those who saw it from a distance lived; those it enfolded died where they stood, or, gasping for breath, ran pell-mell from death. Abandoning their positions, flinging away whatever impeded flight, both divisions fled for the rear, the cloud of chlorine following, gassing all it overtook, gassing the already dead.

For some reason, it didn't quite do the trick. It wasn't quick enough to act, or was it too fast? or did a few of the gassed survive?—but whichever, better results would soon be gotten with phosgene, chloropicrin, mustard, and particularly with cyanogen (instant death in concentrations of 1 in 1,000).

The High Command advised troops to wear mouthpads doused with hyposulphate of soda (obtainable at any drug-store), but piss was handier, and it was piss that saved many a stampeding soldier. Just soak a sock, an old sergeant said, and fix it across your face....

1916

CONCERNING MARGUERITE'S BUTTONS

One of them had come loose from her jacket, and she'd brought it to her mother to be sewn back on. Deftly had a needle been threaded, and as if by sleight-of-hand had a knot been tied, but while admiring the skill, she was quite indifferent to the work: sewing, she thought, was only sewing.

"Mama," she said, "I think I'm getting fat."
"You don't look it to me."
"I can feel it."
"Where?"
"Up here."
"Open your shirt and show me."

Marguerite bared her breasts, still scarcely more than pink buttons set in russet rounds—and yet more there was, her mother saw, two excrescent mounds, small as yet, but undeniably there.

"That ain't fat, child," she said.
"What is it, then?"
"It's where babies get fed."
"Titties!" Marguerite said. "I've got titties?"
"Where'd you lay hold of that word?"
"At school. I heard girls saying it."
"That don't give *you* a call to say it," Decky said, and then for a moment, she continued her unerring performance, absently, though, as if it demanded little of her mind. At length, she looked up at her daughter, saying, "Now and again, I'm apt to call Daddy a fool. Do you suppose I mean it?"
"Oh, no, Mama. Just the opposite. It's like when he plays like he's going to eat the last egg himself."
"You got a head on you, child—and so has he. He's a wise one, and don't ever think not....Which brings me to what he's been after me about the best part of a year. He wants I should explain you a thing or two."
"About what, Mama?"

66

"About—well, about life, I guess is the way to put it."

"What's to explain about that?"

"More than I know how to handle." With her thimble-finger, she touched her daughter, first on the left breast and then on the right, each time ever so gently. "These'll be showing more and more now, and pretty soon you'll have to wear something to stop them bouncing around."

"What's that got to do with life?"

"Just this: where I touched you, you're not to let anybody else touch you, specially a boy."

"Why specially a boy?"

"Remember the dogs in that field? Well, a boy's a lot like a dog."

"I don't see what touching's got to do with it."

"A girl being touched, she might get excited and let the boy do a bad thing to her."

"Bad like what?"

"Like those dogs was doing."

"I only know a couple of boys to call friends, Teddy Simmons and Vern Cassell, and they never tried to touch me. If they did, they would get a punch in the face."

"I don't know you'll have to do much punching. A girl like you, a boy'd think twice about getting fresh."

"What if he thought twice and *then* got fresh?"

Decky laughed. "Kick him in the shins," she said. "He won't be looking for that, and it'll smart like fire....Button your shirt now."

1916

FROM PILGER TO OLYMPUS, a round trip

The excursion began in a classroom.

The afternoon bell had rung, and all but one of the pupils had made for the door and fled, some to play in the schoolyard and some to the roadway that led them home. Still at her desk and unaware of their going, Marguerite Azora was absorbed in a drawing that lay before her. She was also unaware of her teacher, who'd come to stand beside her in the aisle.

"Why, Marguerite!" she said. "I never knew you had a talent!"

Marguerite glanced at the teacher (Miss Culbertson? Miss Slaught?) and then turned back to the drawing, tilting her head slightly as if for a better view of the work.

"It's nobody particular," she said. "I thought up the face, but I didn't get it down on paper."

"Maybe yes, maybe no," the teacher said. "But you're the only one in this class that ever *reached* for something. I like that."

Marguerite took up the drawing, a pencil-sketch of a man's head in profile, and holding it at arm's length, she studied it with a cold eye, as if it were the creation of someone else.

"I don't think it's so good," she said.

"I'm not a critic," the teacher said. "What we ought to get is somebody's professional opinion."

"Here in Pilger?"

"Pilger! All they know in Pilger is hogs!"

"Where, then?"

"The Museum of Art in Chicago."

"Oh, I couldn't go that far!"

The teacher laughed. "You stay in Pilger. The *drawing* goes to Chicago in the mail."

Marguerite rose suddenly, saying, "I'm sorry, Miss Slaught (Miss Culbertson?). I didn't mean to be sitting and you standing."

But having risen, she made no move toward the door. Instead, she gazed through a window at the trees in the yard, at the wall, at the plains beyond, dimmed by distance.

The teacher took up the sketch. "I'll send it out tomorrow," she said. "Maybe we'll find we have an artist in Pilger after all."

Marguerite said, "I don't know as I want to be drawing pictures all my life."

"What *would* you want to do?"

"It's easier to say what I *wouldn't*."

"And what's that?"

"Housework."

After a tick of time, the teacher said, "What if you get married?"

"What if I don't?"

"You're a determined one, aren't you? But first let's see what Chicago has to say...."

Marguerite had been frank about her uncertainty: she was *not* irresistibly drawn to the making of pictures as a lifetime work. Thus, once her sketch had been sent off, it sank below the surface of her mind, and for some weeks thereafter, its existence was almost forgotten. A day came when her teacher asked her to remain after the dismissal of the class, and when the bell rang, she watched at her desk as they converged on the door.

The teacher waited for the last of them to leave, and then, taking an envelope from a drawer, she said, "Marguerite, I'm afraid I have a disappointment for you."

"About the picture, you mean?"

"The picture."

"What did they say about it in Chicago?"

The teacher hesitated. "That it showed the talent of the average twelve-year-old."

Marguerite said nothing.

The teacher eyed the envelope (the messenger), but she had to turn away to an object less distressing—a sepia photo of Niagara that seemed to pour down one of the walls. "I feel bad," she said. "I got your hopes up, and look what's happened."

"I didn't have any hopes."

"You're very kind, but I blame myself all the same."

"I think I will go home now," Marguerite said, and as she passed the desk, she indicated the envelope. "Is the picture in there?"

"Yes, it is. You'd better take it with you."

"Thanks for what you did," Marguerite said, and picking up the envelope, she moved toward the door. There she paused long enough to say, "I'm only eleven."

And the excursion ended where it had begun, in a classroom.

THE FAST MAIL TO POINTS WEST

Marguerite's sister Constance Audra was a redhead, eager, ardent, and high-strung, and when scarcely seventeen, she married Tom Schank, a Catholic of German-Irish descent. Well within a year, they had their first child, a daughter named Freda, and soon thereafter they removed from Clarks to Kersey, Colorado, where a second child was born to them, this time a son.

Of the four sisters, Connie was the most tightly wound. *She's always on the bit*, her brother Dan would say, but in truth she was less like a creature and more like a storm: where she'd been, she left a freshened world behind, charging the air and making one aware of the pleasure of breathing. For her mother, she was a renewing presence, the revival of her own early self, young and unwearied, and she declined when Connie departed, taking with her the sense of a bygone time.

"Henry," she said one day, "I'm thinking to look in on Connie."

"Four hundred miles is a longsome walk," he said.

"It's longsome aplenty on the cars."

"Which they don't stop in Clarks. They don't even whistle."

"They stop in Central City, and that's where you'll be driving us."

"Us! I'm square in the middle of a plaster-job."

"Us is me and Marg."

"How come that little pullet gets to go?"

"Bijou can't look after her. She'll have her hands full seeing to you."

"I wish I could be along. I got me a grandson, and I ain't never set eyes on the gentleman."

"I'll be away maybe a week. You suppose you can manage without me?"

He filled his pipe from a can of tobacco, and then he spoke through smoke, saying, "I never could."

"Tell me so, and I'll stay."

"I'll live out the week, I guess. Go, and say I send hello."

"You know, you're kind of a well-meaning old man."

"I ain't old yet." he said.

She laughed and said, "And maybe not so well-meaning."

Dan allowed them the use of Laura K. for the drive to Central City, and there, as Henry Albert put the travelers aboard the westbound Fast Mail, he handed Marguerite a brown-paper sack and a silver dollar.

She untwisted the neck of the sack and said, "Lemon drops! But what's the dollar for?"

"For when you run out of drops." And then to his wife, he said, "You change cars at Julesburg. Forget, and you'll find yourself in Cheyenne."

As the train began to move, Decky said, "Marg, your Daddy is a nice old man."

To Marguerite, it was the station that was moving and her father who was going away. "Oh, he's not old, Mama!"

"That's what he thinks," her mother said.

On the way to Blanca seven years before, Marguerite had traveled the track of the River Platte division, but for all she could recall of the earlier journey, it might've been made in the dark: the world she saw now was new to her, a flatland that spread away to the bottom of the sky. The gradient of the roadbed was steadily upward, but so gradual was the rise that it hardly affected speed. On the vast expanse at either hand, farmhouses floated miles apart, like a scattered fleet, and it was long before grainfields gave way to rolling range, a great rumpled rug of grass where toy cattle grazed on toy-store hills.

"Look, Mama!" Marguerite said.

"What at? I seen enough Herefords to do me a lifetime."

"Not them, Mama. That thing far away."

On the horizon, seen between the telegraph poles and the festoons of wire, a cresting comber seemed poised at the break and about to flood the earth.

"That thing," Decky said, "that thing is the Rocky Mountains."

"It looks like a wave in the ocean."

"You never seen a ocean."

"I saw a picture in a book."

"Maybe some day you'll get to see a real one."

It was past midnight when the Fast Mail reached Julesburg. The

71

Denver accommodation wasn't due for another three hours, and Marguerite, who'd slept for part of the way thus far, now lay on a depot bench, and with her head on her mother's lap, she slept some more. The only light in the waiting room was a low-watt bulb above the ticket-window, and there were black corners and dim spaces, and lackluster were the posters on the walls. Had there been no light at all, though, still would Marguerite have been defined in her mother's mind. Even in the gloom, she'd've seen the blonde hair, the round face, the downed skin, the green-brown eyes....

She's different to the other girls, like she wasn't even a Smith. Pearl, she's one bound and determined woman, and she'll come out topside-up no matter what—always has and always will. Connie with that business head of hers, which I don't know where it come from, she'd've done good at most anything she put her mind to. Like me, Bijou never did want anything but a man, a family, and a house to look after. But Marg, now—something sets her apart. It's hard to say just what she's fitting for, but one thing's sure: she ain't the kind of a hairpin to stay out her life in Clarks. It won't hold her, it ain't big enough, all Nebraska ain't big enough, and one of these days, she'll go....

and in her head, she seemed to hear her daughter say *I've got gooseberry eyes!*

❧

There was only one business enterprise of consequence in Kersey—the Boise-Payette Lumber Company. For the rest, the town, smaller than Clarks, was made up of a few stores for the local trade and a strew of houses, all of it surrounded by dry-land farms in a mesh of irrigation-ditches. Employed by the Company, Tom Schank came from the lumberyard long enough to greet Decky and Marguerite at the depot and direct them to his house, which was no great way from the tracks.

Connie had heard the train come and go, and with her daughter Freda beside her, she was waiting on the porch as her mother and sister neared along a pathway between a ditch and the road.

"Connie looks like she got fat," Marguerite said.

And Decky said, "She's blowed up, all right, but not with food."

"What with, then?"

"Pshaw," Decky said, but she was speaking to herself.

There were embraces and a rush of talk, and there was admiration for the little girl and praise for the newly-arrived gentleman, named after Connie's dead brother Harry Anson, and then Freda wanted to play and show her toys, but Marguerite, for all her spells of sleep along the way, had been wearied by the journey, and she was sent off for a nap in an upstairs room.

No sooner was she out of sight than Decky scanned Connie, saying, "What in the world are you doing to yourself? Three kids in three years!"

"It isn't me doing it. It's him. I can't keep him off of me."

"Then do like I showed you how."

"He won't allow it. He says it's against his religion. *My* religion now, I guess."

"That's some religion—on your back all night and on your feet all day. You ain't hardly twenty yet, and look at you—two kids on the floor and number three in your belly. Keep this up, and you'll regret your life."

"I never thought it'd be like this, Mama."

"You were wild to be married. What did you think it was like—a story in a book?"

"I guess I did."

Decky turned away from her once-turbulent daughter, subdued now, quenched, and again she said, "Some religion."

"You had *no* religion, Mama, but you had a lot of kids too."

Turning to her daughter again, Decky said, "Yes, but I wanted 'em, one and all. There wasn't none shoved into me with gospel."

Neither of them was aware that their voices had carried up the stairwell and that Marguerite had heard every word.

Early 1917

UN BEL DI VIDREMO

On her way to school each day, Marguerite passed the residence of the local banker. It was the finest in Clarks; its grounds, two or more acres, were enclosed by a wrought-iron fence, and from the gate, a long straight driveway entered an arcade of trees. When these were in leaf, the house at the end was hidden from view. In the winter, as now, they were merely scrawls on the sky, and a great pile of filigreed woodwork was exposed, a thing of turrets and balconies alive with fretwork, all of it held together by a wrap-around verandah.

As Marguerite drew near one morning, she found several people standing outside the gate and gazing through it at the house, from which, muted by the snow-covered lawn, a singing voice could be heard. She listened along with the others, but she couldn't understand the words of the song, and when it ended, she went on her way. On her return later in the day, a small group was again at the gate, and the same voice was singing the same song.

"It's one of them talking machines," someone said.
"They must only have one record," someone else said.

Among the last to leave classroom on the following day, Marguerite stopped at the teacher's desk.

"Yes, Marguerite?"
"I wanted to ask, Miss Voight, do you know what's going on at the big house?"
"Everybody knows."
"I don't. There's always people at the gate, and somebody in the house is singing a song."
"It's an aria from opera. Do you know what that is?"
"It's where actors sing instead of talk."
"That's right."
"But why sing the same thing over and over?"
"It's a long story," the teacher said, "and a sad one. I'd sooner you heard it elsewhere."

74

"Can't you even tell me a little?"

From her desk, the teacher drifted toward the window-wall. It was as if in the yard below and the distance beyond lay release from her obligation to reply, to explain—to teach. But she found no freedom there, and she turned back to Marguerite.

"There's a young woman in that house, and she's in love with a certain man."

"That isn't sad."

"It is," the teacher said. "Because the man isn't in love with her."

"Why not?"

"Who can say? You either love a person, or you don't."

"It must be her favorite music if she's all the time playing it."

"It's her father who's playing it."

"Why him?"

"She can't, Marguerite. She can't, but she wants to hear it."

"Why can't she? What's the matter with her?"

Again the teacher seemed to seek escape from her responsibility. She looked away at the empty seats, at the framed photos above the blackboard (the Statue of Liberty, Niagara Falls), at a dingy bust of Lincoln, but there too she found no absolution.

"She took poison," the teacher said, "and she's dying."

Obtained at last, the information was unwieldy, and Marguerite's mind fumbled with it, strained at it, dwelt on it, but in the end, it was still too much for her to fathom.

When Miss Voight spoke again, it was more to herself than to Marguerite. "The music is from *Madame Butterfly*, and the aria is being sung by Geraldine Farrar." And then after a pause, she said, "I have the record myself, but I'll never play it again."

Two days later, the banker's daughter died.*

*This episode was foreshadowed in Scene 30 of *A Very Good Land to Fall With*, Black Sparrow Press 1987.

75

April 6, 1917

WAR

God helping her, she can do no other.
                    –Woodrow Wilson

Henry Albert sat facing his son across the kitchen table. Outspread between them was the front page of a newspaper, the upper third of which was blackened by three huge letters. To Marguerite, who was standing beside her brother, they made more sound than sense, and a roar seemed to fill the room.

"Looks like we're in it for fair," Dan said.

"And high time, you ask me," his father said.

"What wonders me is we didn't get in sooner."

"We would've been if Wilson had Teddy's guts. Just as soon as they sunk that big boat."

"There's going to be hell to pay before it's over."

"Shucks," his father said. "Once we show up, it'll be a turkey-shoot."

Occupied at the stove, Decky spoke without turning. "Them German turkeys shoot back."

"Anybody can lick the frogs or the Great British. We don't run to Mama so quick."

"You ever been a soldier, Henry?"

"No, but if I had my age back, I damn sure would be."

"*I* still got my age," Dan said.

In the sink, water dripped into water; in the stove, air-pockets exploded in the firewood; and moved by the wind, a bare branch fingered the siding of the house. But for a moment, no one spoke.

And then Decky said, "You thinking about joining up?"

"Somebody's got to," Dan said.

"With that game leg of yours," Henry Albert said, "you wouldn't get past the door."

"What door?" Marguerite said to her father.

"There's a place over to Grand Island where a man can sign to be a soldier."

"A soldier? Dan-boy's going to be a soldier?"

"He thinks. He'll be back the same day."

"Why?"

"Account of his leg wouldn't never hold up."

Dan rose and left the room.

"You went a little strong there, Henry," his wife said.

"Strong? I didn't say nothing strong."

"You made too much of the boy's leg. It took him down. It made him different to the rest of us."

"I only said what they'd see soon as he pulled up his pants-leg."

"Sure, but you should've give him a chance to pull it up."

"I didn't mean the boy no harm."

"There's times harm comes of blatting instead of thinking."

The Influenza Pandemic, 1918-1919

THE COLOR OF THE AIR

The War at War's End

They came to the battlefields from all over the world, and there they killed each other to the tune of nine million, give or take a slew, and then they went back to Auckland, to Arizona, to Bombay and Aberdeen, and with them unbeknownst went a non-filterable enemy, the *bacillus influenzae* Pfeiffer.

It killed them in numerous numbers, and it also killed their children and their wives, and most swiftly did it kill the old. The attacks opened with catarrh and congestion of the membranes of the eye, supported by headache, lassitude, and fever, none of these a menace in itself; but within hours all too few, they were followed by intense toxemia and, in twenty million cases, death. Postmortems revealed acute affections of the respiratory system, in particular broncho-pneumonia and hemorrhagic edema, which is to say "wet" or "dripping" lungs.

There were no trenches in Denver, no wire and ruination could be found in Odessa, and no yellow clouds turned inside-out in Montreal. There was only the antagonist within, dormant and harmless in solitude, but awake and outrageous in a crowd—and unable to fight what they couldn't see, what they didn't know was there, the luckless sat still and let it kill them. And kill it did, that bacillus; it killed more of them than the war did....

Or was it the self-same war all the time?

1918

A SEPARATE ROOM

Bijou was now a young woman of eighteen, and her concerns were those of her age. She was no longer little Marguerite's keeper: she'd ceased to be a climber of trees, a sit-behind rider on a burro, a reader of children's stories to a child. Long since gone was that day, and though she loved her sister still, she looked beyond the near and the known, seeking the strange and sensuous far. The better to savor its delights, she asked her mother for privacy, and she was granted a room of her own.

It was Marguerite who was moved, though, to a small chamber across the hall, and with her went her clothing, her accumulation of truck, her Teddy Bear (retired), and her several well-worn books. But no possession, no thing however cherished or familiar, would take the place of Bijou, and it was long before loneliness diminished and died away. Die it did, finally, when she awakened one morning to find that she'd bled in the night, staining the sheet and the bed.

Her mother said, "You ain't as ascared as Bijou was."

"I'm not scared at all. I'm discusted."

"Why's that, child? Only you ain't a child any more."

"I'm discusted because now I've got to watch out every month to see I don't bleed all over the place."

"It goes with being a woman. You ought to be happy you're growed up."

"I was happy the way I was. Now there's this lumpy bandage I've got to wear."

"Just till the bleeding stops. Three-four days, maybe."

"It bulges my dress. And when I have to pee...."

"You'll get used to it. We all do."

"Not me. With this crupper around my tail, how am I going to run around and ride and do summersets?"

"Thirteen's kind of old for summersets."

"Why does this thing have to happen?"

"So's women can have babies."

"Why can't we have them without the mess?"

"If it was up to me, I'd do it different."

"It's discusting," Marguerite said.

The door opened, and Henry Albert started to enter. "We're talking," Decky said, and Henry Albert withdrew.

Officer Michael J. Connolly, 1920

THE COLOR OF THE AIR

On the Brockton Streetcar

They sat in silence, the two Italians, taking in the fragrance of the night. Here and there, lights shone across a field, and in the distance, a town smoldered at the bottom of the sky. It was late in the evening, and the thoughts of both men were of home. Neither would live to see it again, though seven years of their lives remained.

In Bridgewater some months earlier, two gunmen had attempted to hold up the payroll truck of a shoe company. They were driven off by the armed guard.

When Officer Connolly boarded the car, he saw the dark-skinned pair at once, and at once his aversion to their kind overcame him. They were all the same, he thought—black hair, black eyes, black clothes, and they smelled black too. Why weren't they playing *boccie* somewhere and drinking *grappa,* he wondered, why weren't they in bed with their wives? The word *suspicious* picked its way through the thicket of his mind.

> *Eye-witnesses to the attempted holdup had described the gunmen as dark-complected and wearing dark clothes; they were foreign-looking, it was said, they were Italians.*

Officer Connolly was little concerned with lights in distant windows and the glow of distant towns, and he cared nothing for the aromas of the night. His brain was merely fumbling with *suspicious, suspicious characters*, polysyllables in the grinder of his head, but no transformation took place—the words did not become the flesh across the aisle. All his mind could deal with was dark skin, dark hair, dark dress—dark was death, he may have thought, and it may have been fear that impelled him to arrest the two Italians.

Whatever underlay the notion, it tripped the timer of their lives: their last seven years on earth began to run.

1917-1921

FROM THE SMITH FAMILY ANNALS

Dan Smith rode a horse to Central City and tried to enlist in the Army. Required to strip for a physical examination, he was summarily rejected when the doctor saw his leg. As soon as he was dressed, he rode his horse back to Clarks.

ॐ

Within a month of the declaration of war, the druggist-man Chester Honnold joined up. On the strength of his professional experience, he soon thereafter applied for a commission in the Medical Corps, and it was granted.

ॐ

In order to be nearer Connie, the Smiths moved from Clarks to Kersey.

ॐ

In 1918, a fourth child was born to Connie.

ॐ

Returning from France, where he'd served with the A.E.F., the one-time druggist-man opened a Beauty Shop in Greeley. Pearl dressed hair, it was said by some, and he undressed the women.

🐿

Marguerite now attended Kersey High School and played on the girls' basketball team. There were nine other players: Hazel King, Wilma Rissman, Anna Huff, Edna Bacon, Helen Pritchard, Emma Plumb, Ellen Jergens, and the twins Vera and Ann Dix. Their uniforms were not uni-form: they wore what they happened to possess—bloomers, skirts, sweaters, dresses, and assorted middy-blouses (Marguerite's had the striped collar and cuffs of a seaman in the Navy).

🐿

In 1920, a fifth child was born to Connie.

🐿

Five children in seven years put Connie in an Omaha sanitarium for a prolonged stay.

🐿

A cross was burned on Tom Schank's lawn.

🐿

A quiet young man named Vernon Cassell began to turn up in Marguerite's vicinity, and on occasion he was permitted to walk her home from school.

🐿

In 1921, Bijou married Edward Amos Gustafson, a farm-boy from a family of Swedish Methodists in Platte County.

🐿

Henry Albert moved from Kersey to Greeley, some six miles away, and set himself up as a builder. Gustafson was invited to join him, and his father-in-law taught him the trade.

🐿

Upon her graduation from high school, Marguerite took a job with the Greeley Five-and-Dime. At a wage of $1 a day, she stood behind the candy-counter dealing out measures of sticky sweets that came in many shapes and many colors, all combining in an emanation that pervaded her hair and her clothing and long remained in her mind.

🐿

On coming home from Woolworth's one day, Marguerite found her mother in the yard hanging wash out to dry. She failed to recognize the inflated shirts, the flying gingham, the underwear jigging on the air.

"Whose wash is that, Mama?" she said.

"Belongs to a neighbor," Decky said. "Mrs. Gilliard."

"What's the matter with her? Is she sick?"

"Sick nothing. I'm doing it for the money."

Marguerite stared. "You're taking in wash for money! For God's sake, Mama!"

"God ain't in it. It's for *your* sake—if you're still bent on going to business college."

"I sure am—but not on your sweat!"

"Do it on your own, and you'll be a old woman first."

"My Mama's not going to wash clothes for my tuition! I won't go!"

"You *will* go," Decky said. "I'm doing this so's you get your chance. Connie never did, and we don't need another like her, shelling out kids like they was so many peas. You don't belong, wiping up after a bunch of piss-willies. You'll take the money, and you'll go to business college like you been honing to."

The Peace Treaty, 1919

THE COLOR OF THE AIR

The Hall of Mirrors

When this treaty is accepted, men in khaki will never have to cross the seas again....
                                        —Woodrow Wilson, Sept. 1919

In Europe, he was given a welcome that only a come-again Jesus would've gotten when he came. Indeed, he may well have seemed the Christ to many in the multitudes who greeted his ship, his train, his transit along the streets. For them, his cutaway coat may have vanished, and with it the stovepipe and even the tight man in the hard collar, and what passed their eye may not have been a man at all, but a radiance, a splendor clad in lamb-white robes. Certain it is that some were seen to bow their heads and make the sign of the Cross. The rank and file adored him.

Another kind awaited his arrival at Versailles, and when he got there, Savior or not, they picked him clean. Aye, they undressed him: piece by piece, they divested him of his clothing, the cutaway, the silk hat, the high shoes of vici kid. How strange, then, that in the all-around glass, he stood fully covered and they bare to the ass and vile!

1922

GREELEY BUSINESS COLLEGE

Stenography and Typing Taught in Three Months! Tuition-fee $45.
—ad in the Greeley *Tribune*

The school was located in a loft above the offices of the Home Gas & Electric Company. A partition divided the area into a pair of rooms, one of which was equipped with a score of Underwood typewriters and the other with desks facing a ruled blackboard used for the demonstration of stenographic signs. So old were the machines that the lettering on their forty-odd keys was all but worn away, and a learner's memory was therefore put to the test from the start. In the setting down of shorthand symbols, though, far more than memory was called for: swiftness was a requisite, and so was legibility, in order that one might read back writing done at the speed of speech.

Marguerite did not remain a learner long. At typing, she proved to be facile and rapid-fire; more, she had a sure touch, and rarely did she strike a wrong key even while working at a rate of sixty words a minute. As for shorthand, Gregg was the method favored by the school, and she mastered it in a month. For the rest of each course, she merely drilled herself in the skills she already possessed.

Not being gregarious, she took scant notice of her fellow-students, and the extent of her intimacy with them was an occasional lunch-time encounter at a soda-fountain. Notice was taken of her, though, by a classmate named Leonard Roberts. Like her, he was reserved, but where she was distant by nature, he seemed so out of a sense of superiority, and he came and went with scarcely a word for the common company he was compelled to keep.

Reserve did not prevent Marguerite from observing the roundabout world, and her opinion of Roberts was neither high nor low; worse than either, it was in between. She found nothing about him to arouse her interest or detain her eye: he was spare, his looks were unremarkable, and his manner was proper and precise. Aware that he studied her now and again, she did not care enough about his attention to welcome it or warn it away.

One evening near the end of the school term, he spoke to her for the first time. Awaiting her after class, he joined her as she came from the building and headed for home.

"Miss Smith," he said, "I hope you'll permit me to introduce myself. My name is—"
"You don't have to go through all that stuff," she said. "You're Leonard Roberts."
"I wasn't sure you knew."
"I know all the names. I've been hearing them for weeks—and so have you."
"Yours is the only one I seem to recall."
"I don't believe that for a minute."
"It made an impression on me."
"Smith? Smith made an impression?"
"The name's common, but you're not."
"How do you know what I am?"
"I've watched you."
"What if you thought I was like my name?"
"I wouldn't've spoken to you."

He was one prideful little man, she thought; if Pearlie ever met him, she'd call him His Nibs.

"You've been watching me, you say, but you don't see so good. Because I *am* like my name—common as dirt."
"I know better."
At a cross-street corner, Marguerite said, "I turn here."
"I'll turn with you, if I may, I'll walk you home."
"If you like, but stop making more of me than there is."

"Most girls would be pleased. Why not you?"

"To tell the truth," she said, "I don't specially like you."

"Why not?"

"You think you're something on a stick. Look at the way you act in school. Like you were smelling a bad smell."

"You must be stuck-up too, then. I don't see you mixing with any of our future stenographers."

"But not because I think I'm better, and you do."

"I *am* better," he said.

"How?"

"It isn't easy to put into words."

"Try."

"I come from a good family."

She stopped, and in the light of a nearby street-lamp, she sized him up and then sized him down.

"And what do the rest of us come from?" she said. "Trash?"

"All I said, Miss Smith, was that my family is a good one."

"Good. What's good about it?"

"It goes back a long way. They settled in the South in the seventeenth century. In 1685, to be exact."

"Was anybody there when they came?"

"Only the Indians."

"They go back longer, then, so they must be better than you."

"Indians don't count."

"The way you go on, nobody counts but Leonard Roberts."

"You count."

"That's just talk," she said. "I was right to not like you. You're all swole up with yourself."

The sidewalk ended with the last of the lamp standards, and the house she lived in lay beyond. There were no lights now save for the occasional glare in a windowpane.

"Aren't you afraid to walk here at night?" Roberts said.

"Afraid of what?"

"Meeting up with some rough."

"I get along with roughs. They put me in mind of my family." She came to a stop at a gate in a picket fence. "I live here with my father and mother. He's a plasterer, and she sometimes takes in wash—but they're as good as your people any day of the week."

"I didn't say they weren't."

"Sure you did. You've been saying it all along."

"I've enjoyed the walk, Miss Smith. Will you walk with me again?"

"What in the world for? So's you can talk down your nose some more?"

"To others, maybe, but not to you."

"It's like I said: I just don't like your kind."

೮

Two evenings later, he was waiting at the curb again, and when she appeared, he fell in with her.

"Do you realize what you're doing?" she said.

"I'm walking you home."

"But you're a Roberts, and you're walking alongside a Smith. If your people knew, they'd have the flitflats."

"My brother would. He's older and worse than I am. Graves, his name is—Graves Baxter Roberts."

"That's a lot of weight to pack around."

"I'm stuck-up, but he's stuck *way* up. He'd think I was lowering myself to be seen with you."

"You won't be seen long. This is my corner."

"I'll go the rest of the way."

"Not with me, you won't," she said. "Go home to Graves Baxter."

"I don't like for you to walk in the dark alone."

She regarded him for a moment, trying to extract an expression from an inexpressive face. It yielded none, and she turned away from him toward the circles of light that lay in the road.

"Don't you want to know why?" he said to her receding figure.

But she did not stop, and she made no reply.

೮

86

On the following evening, he was awaiting her in the same place, on the sidewalk near the school entrance.

"For an upstuck man," she said, "you don't have much pride."

THE VIEW FROM AFAR OFF

1921: Pottersville, N.Y.

He may be seen working as a waiter at Camp Wakonda, a summer place for boys in the Adirondacks, but not long does he detain the eye, for he's overweight in body, and, wearing a low-watt smile, he seems underweight in mind. To many, he's a lackwit, an opinion that becomes fixed when the waiters go on strike, and he volunteers to present their demands to management. He's fired on the spot and evicted from the camp.

Fall guy for his fellows, he'll be laughed at as soon as he's out of sight, but one day he'll meet someone who'll greet him with praise instead of ridicule, who'll ignore his imprudence and dwell on his good will. You're simple, she'll tell him, but better that than shrewd.

1923

MARGUERITE AND LEONARD

She'd known him now for the better part of a year. He hadn't let himself be put off by her lukewarm response to his fancied merits, and persisting in his attentions, he'd reached a stage with her where the going was somewhat easier. He still thought himself higher-born than most, but his notions no longer stirred her to anger. More prejudicial to his standing, they caused her to appraise him, to measure him against the excellence he claimed for his kind, and he fared poorly. With the loss in rank, however, came a small gain in acceptability, and an arm's-length association was begun.

On Sundays, if the weather was fine, he'd call for her in his little sedan and take her for a drive toward the mountains. Sometimes he'd go through Fort Collins and up along the Cache La Poudre, and sometimes he'd make for the canyon of the Big Thompson, but wherever they went, the Rockies impended, a great wave that seemed about to crest and break over the car, the road, the river, and the rest of the world.

"This family of yours," she said on one such day.

And he said, "What about them?"

"What did they do to get as big as life and twice as natural?"

"Actually, they did nothing. They were landowners."

"Owning land—that's enough to make you grand?"

"Only if you don't work it yourself. Do that, and you're just another farmer."

He parked the sedan on a turnout overlooking a bend in the Big Thompson, and leaving the car, they climbed down to the river, a clear run of melted snow. From the bank, they watched a fly-fisherman whip a riffle.

"So what you're saying," she said, "is that your people got classy on other people's sweat."

"Classy isn't a classy word—but they didn't *get* classy. They *were* classy."

"How did that come about?"

"They were born that way."

She laughed. "What luck!"

"Yes—and you either have it, or you don't."

"Leonard," she said, "I just realized why I spend time with you."

"You're getting to like me."

"I'm getting to feel superior."

The flycaster, having raised nothing in the riffle, was moving further upstream, and she watched him until he disappeared in a stand of aspen.

"You're what Mama calls an educated fool," she said.

"Why? Because I think some people are better than others?"

"No. Some people *are* better. An honest man is better than a thief. A free-handed man is better than a pinchpenny. But *born* better...! That's a joke."

"It wasn't funny where we came from. Roberts was one of the best names in the county."

"Before the Yankees came."

"We didn't lose the name when we lost the war. The land, yes, but the name never."

"If that's so, why didn't your people stick it out in the South?"

"They had too much pride to trade on their prestige."

Prestige, she thought. The word had sent her to the dictionary the first time he'd used it, and she recited its definition in her mind: *Ascendancy derived from general admiration or esteem.* It was a word he'd used once too often.

"Do you know what I think, Leonard?" she said. "I think they quit the South because they were ashamed of the comedown."

"Where's the comedown? My father put himself through Colorado Med."

"Med. He's a druggist."

"Pharmacist. He has a degree in Pharmacy."

She was silent for a moment, and then she said, "My father's a plasterer, and I honor him. Do you honor yours?"

"Of course I do."

"I think you're ashamed of him."

By the time they started back down the canyon, the sun had nearly reached the peaks behind them, and they'd not gone far before the purple shadow of The Needles and Mummy Mountain overcame the road. From the aspens and lodgepole pines that lined it, a cool fragrance was released, and Marguerite sat close by the window to take it in.

"Why did you say that?" Roberts said.

"Because it's true."

1923

THE GREELEY PHARMACY

It was a two-story building at one of the corners along 8th Street, the main thoroughfare of the town, and Marguerite, a now-and-then patron, had come to know the proprietor, Leonard's father. He was a close-mouthed man of fifty or so, smaller than most, but he gave the impression of having been larger once, of having been condensed by some outside force—and the force, she supposed, was the store and all it contained.

"Good evening, Mr. Roberts," she said.
And "Evening," he replied.

He was weighed down by his counters and shelves, she thought, constricted by his jars and tins and tubes, his powders and pellets, his syrups, salves, and expectorants, but most of all was he oppressed by the twin testaments of his profession, the Formulary and the Pharmacopoeia. It was as if he were actually heavy-laden with these things, as if he bore them one and all upon his back, and it came to her that he wasn't simply reticent—he was smothered, buried under his load.

"Leonard and I are going to the movies," she said. "He asked me to meet him here."
"He's upstairs," Roberts said. "I'll call him."

After completing the courses at the business school, Marguerite had found employment in the offices of a lawyer named Paul Meeker. From her salary of $12 a week, she'd insisted that her mother accept nearly all: *No more taking in wash, Mama. Goodbye, Mrs. Gilliard.* The rest, two or three dollars, she retained for the paraphernalia of the purse and the dresser-drawer: barrettes, orangewood sticks, emery boards, and combs. *No more washing for Mrs. Gilliard, Mama,* she sometimes thought while typing a Will or a Whereas, and her mother's face would come before her with a look like a lighted room.

Leonard had studied at Creighton University, where he'd earned a degree in Business Administration, and he'd learned typing and stenography to help him in his career. His office above the drugstore fronted on 8th Street, and from one of its windows, an arc of gold-leaf lettering proclaimed that *L. Roberts* was a *Public Accountant*.

Marguerite, living then in Clarks, was not yet five when she saw her first motion picture, and thereafter, already able to read, she'd sit on the front bench with three or four illiterate urchins, among these Teddy Simmons, and decipher the titles for her gaping company. She'd tell them what John Bunny was saying to Flora Finch, she'd give voice to Bronco Billy's bombast, and she'd spell out placards saying *One minute please* and *Ladies will kindly remove their hats*. There were sights unseen before, there were wonders in the world discovered to her on those voyages in the dark.

❦

Leonard was followed from his office by his older brother, Graves Baxter.

"A real pleasure to see you again, Miss Smith," he said.
And she said, "Likewise, Graves."

It was a pleasure for neither. As she knew, his resentment over the family's descent was a low fire that would never burn out, and one like her seemed to fan it higher. It was her inglorious rank that did the work: he hated the pride she felt in her obscurity; she despised his pride in vanished renown.

"When Leonard told me what was showing," he said, "I had to invite myself along."
"He's seen it three times," Leonard said, "but he never misses *The Birth of a Nation*. He went to Denver for it once."
"The director, this fellow Griffith," Graves said, "he's from the South, you know."
"Yes," Marguerite said, "and that's where he got some of his ideas."
"Such as which, Miss Smith?"
"Oh, about slavery being right. And about the whites being human and the negroes being baboons."
"Anything else, Miss Smith?"
"From what I've read, plenty.. The movie makes the Klan out to be knights of old."

"And what do you think they are?"

"You don't want to hear that, Graves. They burned a cross in front of my sister's house in Kersey."

"If we don't get started," Leonard said, "we'll miss the beginning."

Parting with Graves after the picture-show, Leonard walked home with Marguerite. The warm night was mile-high bright with stars, and seemingly at the end of her street rose the snowy gables of Longs Peak. Though it was still early, her parents had retired, leaving a light in the hallway that made a white gap in the black outer world. Seating herself on the porch swing, Marguerite invited Leonard to join her, and together they listened to small sound coming to them out of the dark—a dog-bark, the whistle of a distant train, the all-but-silent rush of irrigation through a ditch.

"You don't care much for Graves, do you?" he said.

"I think he's a snot."

"What is it you dislike about him?"

"Don't ask. Because I dislike you almost as much for almost the same things."

He laid his arm along the backrest of the swing, but she sat so still that she seemed unaware of what he'd done, nor did she stir when he touched her hair. She heard a moth strum the door-screen.

"How long have I been sparking you?" he said.

"Is that what you've been doing—sparking me?"

"Must be a year now."

"Near about," she said, and then as if the better to appraise his word, she tested it herself. "Sparking," she said.

He moved closer, putting his other hand on her knee, but she was no more responsive than if the hand were her own—less, she thought.

"If you like me so little," he said, "why do you let me kiss you, why do you let me touch you here?" and now he palmed her breast.

"The human brassière," she said.

"I don't think it's right to joke about us."

"I wasn't joking."

"That's all I am to you—a damn brassière?"

A tree frog stuttered, sounding, she thought, like a loose floorboard. "What do you want me to say, Leonard?"

"That I mean something to you."

"Do you know what my sister Bijou calls your brother? Graves Bastard."

"I'm talking about me, and you're talking about Graves."

"He was introduced to her at a dance, and he spoke down to her like he was in a balloon."

"I never spoke that way to you."

"If you ever did, I'd be off you like a dirty shirt."

Under her dress now, his hand had progressed from her knee to her thigh, and though she knew it was time to stop him, she felt that it didn't matter: let him steam himself up, she thought, let him see that she but mildly cared, if indeed she cared at all. But why, then, she wondered, did she accept his company, walk with him, go for jaunts in his car? He had questions too—why had she allowed him to kiss her, to touch her?—and as yet, not even to herself had she replied. He was personable, she thought, he was intelligent, he was decent—but those were adjectives out of slow-running blood, half-hearted ways of saying that he was one of many, all of whom were the same. She didn't know what she was looking for, she didn't even know that she was looking, but whatever she may have blindly sought, she did not find it in Leonard Roberts. He was considerate, she thought, he was attentive, he was temperate and proper, but her blood stayed cool and still ran slowly.

"Take your hands away, Leonard," she said.

And reluctantly he took them away.

THE VIEW FROM THE PLAINS

1922: Niagara Falls, N.Y.

In the photo, he's leaning against a pipe-iron railing, his back to the spill and the spume and the never-ending thunder of the falls. He doesn't know that over the giant lip behind him pour 200,000 cubic feet of water a second, enough to generate the power of four million horses, but even if he knew, it's unlikely that he'd care. He's between semesters at college, and he's gone a little out of his way to take in a wonder of the world, but even more, it seems, to find a place to pose for a picture. Why else would he stand with his back to the flow?

He's on a cross-country hitch-hike, and his route will lie through a town called Clarks, but he'll be no more aware of it than of the telegraph-poles he passes, and later he'll reach a town equally unremarkable, this one Greeley, and there it may be that two roads cross. But he'll not know of the junction till they come together on another day.

1923

TARGET PRACTICE

Leonard was partial to a pump-action Winchester, and it was his pleasure to shoot at paper targets. He kept the rifle under the rear seat of his car, together with a store of .22 longs, and often on his outings with Marguerite, he'd draw up behind an abandoned barn or under the bluffs of the South Platte, and, posting his target, he'd pace off a chosen distance, and fire away at the black heart of the circles. Now and then Marguerite would take a turn, but most of the time she'd watch, wondering what underlay his satisfaction on making a bull's-eye. To her, the sport consisted of shooting for a score, and, high or low, that was the end of it; to Leonard, she felt, it was a great deal more.

Leaning against the car, she was watching now. He'd set up a pair of targets, and having emptied the magazine at one of them, he was reloading it for the other. Running short of cartridges, he called to Marguerite to reach him a fresh box.

"Who are you shooting at, Leonard?" she said.

"You mean *what*, don't you?"

"I mean who—or is it whom? But whichever, you're not shooting at pieces of paper."

"They look like paper to me."

"I don't think they do. I think they look like people."

About to feed a last few shells to the magazine, he paused, saying, "I don't know what you're talking about. I'm a pretty good shot, and I'm only trying to do better."

"Why do I feel it's something else?"

"What, for Pete's sake?"

"You're trying to kill somebody."

Filling the magazine, he shut the slot and jacked a cartridge into the firing chamber. He took aim and held it for several seconds before lowering the rifle without pulling the trigger.

"Everybody wants to kill somebody," he said. "I've been shooting at me."

She knew a stirring, slight only, as of a leaf in a breath of air, and she said, "Why?"

"I don't like myself much. I don't like myself at all."

Where was his magnitude, where was his elevation, where, she may have wondered, was his highgrade blood? Did such things exist now only in his mind? Had glory gone glimmering at Appomattox? The stir she'd felt was pity.

1923

A REAL GENT

Dan said, "You been walking out with that Leonard, they tell me."

"Going about, is all," Marguerite said. "Walking out means more than walking."

"You mind me sticking my bill in?"

"Never you, Dan-boy."

"Then I'm asking if you ever been to his house."

"No."

"How come, baby sister?"

"I've never been invited."

"How does that sit with you?"

"To tell the truth, I don't give a damn."

"Meaning you don't give a damn about *him*?'

95

"He goes around with his nose in the air. Like life was a two-holer."

"If I was you, I'd be off him like a hard collar. You're a sighty little thing, Marg. You could pick and choose."

"He isn't so bad," she said. "He likes me more than I like him."

No liquor was obtainable in Greeley. By law, it could neither be bought nor served, and those who sought it had to cross the city line into Evans, some three miles to the south on the Denver road. There were good restaurants in the little town, and on occasion, as now, Marguerite and Leonard took Sunday dinner at one of them. It was well-filled with emigrants from Greeley, among them Marguerite's employer, Paul Meeker, who sat with a party of four at a nearby table.

"My brother Dan asked me a question the other day, and I couldn't give him much of an answer."

"What was the question?"

"He wanted to know why I'd never been invited to your house."

He shrugged, saying, "It never occurred to me."

"You're foolish if you expect me to believe that."

Their orders were being put before them, a T-bone for Marguerite and a filet mignon for Leonard.

"I'm not looking for an invitation," she said. "I'm just wondering why I haven't had one."

"I told you, Marguerite."

"That's a dodge, and you know it. It *had* to occur to you, and it did."

"Are you saying that I decided *not* to invite you?"

"Yes."

"Why would I do that? Because you hold your fork wrong?"

There was a moment when all around seemed to go unheard, speech, laughter, the knocking of crockery, and then the suspended moment ended, and the hum of voices, the clash of cutlery and china resumed.

"Is there a right way?" she said.

"Yes—like this," he said, and he gave her a demonstration.

"How do you know your way is the right way?"

"Look around you. Do you see anyone else holding a fork as if it were a cello?"

"I don't have to look around—I brought my teacher along."

He was misled by her quiet, and he said, "You take instruction well."

"I'm only too glad to learn, Leonard."

Her anger was still suppressed, and he was still unaware of it. "Try holding the fork the way I do," he said."

"If I do," she said, "will I get that invitation?"

Without a gesture or an expression, with her moderate tone alone, at last he was made to realize what he'd done, and when she saw that he did, she used the same tone to say, "For all your fine manners, Leonard, you're just piss-proud trash."

Rising, she didn't leave him so much as quit him; there was nothing to stay for, her manner of going seemed to say, and she made for the door, a patron who'd dined and was on her way. Outside in the night, she was quite as purposeful, and reaching the road, she was about to start on the long walk home when Leonard overtook her.

"It'll take you an hour to get to Greeley," he said, "and it's another mile to your house."

"And where you come from," she said, "a lady is always seen to her door."

"Where anybody comes from."

"But I'm no lady. I hold a fork wrong."

"I didn't mean to humiliate you."

"You gave me an eating-lesson in front of a roomful of people. What *did* you mean?"

"Can't you forget what I said?"

"No, but I can forget you."

Reaching the road, she removed her shoes and set out over the pavement in her stocking feet.

"You're crazy," Leonard said, and turning away from her, he ran back toward the parking-area of the restaurant. A moment later, he was alongside her in his car. "Get in, for the love of Mike!"

"Go to hell," she said, and she continued walking.

He made a few more attempts to persuade her, but she was resolute, and finally he fell in behind her, and, driving in low gear, he followed her home.

There she paused long enough to say, "Don't ever speak to me again," and then she entered the house and closed the door.

&

But he did speak to her again.

Summer of 1924

WAITING FOR A SIGN

Bijou had brought her infant son John Henry to her mother's house on a Sunday afternoon, and the child lay asleep on a blanket in the shade. Seated nearby, she watched a car cruise past and disappear down the road.

"How often does he do that?" she said.

"Drive by?" Marguerite said. "Two-three times a week that I get to see. Like as not more."

"What's he expect you to do—rush out and lay down in his road?"

"I guess he figures I'll give in some day."

"Will you?"

"He didn't just make small of *me*. We all eat like I do, and he was holding the *family* cheap."

"That ain't what I asked you."

"Will I give in? Oh, I suppose, but not before he crawls."

"He's crawling, all right. If he went any slower, he'd be going backwards."

"I never thought we were better than anybody, Midgie. I only thought we were just as good, but here's Prince Leonard looking down on us. That grinds me."

"I long ago told you they're blowed-up people. There ain't a one of 'em don't think he's something on a stick."

"I agree about Graves. But Leonard, he's sometimes half-human— and sometimes not."

98

Bijou saw him returning now from the road's end, and she said, "Which is he now, I wonder."

༜

It was pleasant on the porch, and in the evening, Marguerite would lie on the glider, and in its to-and-fro, her hand would trail across a sleeping dog's back. As it grew darker, lights would go on and show through the trees, and firefly sparks would make slow arcs above the lawn. Now and again a car would pass, and she'd think of Leonard and of Bijou's question about giving in. What *did* she feel?, she wondered, was she still asmolder with humiliation, resentment, anger?—and it surprised her to find that she felt nothing, nothing at all. The fire had burned without ash.

༜

He came on foot one evening, and he said, "Can we be friends again?"

"We never were," she said, "or you wouldn't've treated me the way you did."

"Can we start to be, then?"

"Why should we?"

"I care for you."

"I didn't like you back at business school, and I didn't even know you. I know you now, and I like you less."

"I'm not the same person."

"Don't fool yourself. You baited the wrong bear, and you got bit. But you're the same Leonard Roberts you always were, and you didn't learn a thing."

"You don't think people can change?"

Her look was contemplative. What prevented him from stirring her deeply, she wondered, what quality did he have, what quality did he lack?

"Some people, maybe, but not you," she said. "You'll still be Leonard Roberts when you die."

"You don't give me much to go on."

"Where would you like to go?"

"Pretty near anywhere, as long as it's with you."

"Doing what?"

"The things we did before."

99

"Driving to Estes Park? Plugging more targets? Sticking your hand further up my skirt?"

"Yes."

"How about dining in public?"

"That too."

"Really? And how about a private place—your home, say?"

"If you wish."

"But think. What would your mother say when I held my fork like a cello?"

"She wouldn't say a word."

"Leonard, I wouldn't go to your house on a bet. Don't ever invite me."

"Does that mean you'll accept other invitations?"

It wasn't that he repelled her, she thought; it was that he was unmagnetic, and, void of attractive force, he left her where she was, quite unmoved.

"What the hell?" she said. "Why not?"

The March on Rome, 1922

THE COLOR OF THE AIR

The King of Castor Oil

> *Keep your heart a desert.*
> —Benito Mussolini

He hardly had to work at it; it was a desert from the start. As a boy, he was a braggart and a bully, and when browbeat failed him, he prevailed with a knife. He wasn't a bright boy, but even a dimmer would've known that while force would work in the schoolyard, he'd need guile as well to rule outside—and Benito had that and much more in his bulging bag of tricks. What did it not contain!

It was full to the drawstring with tall talk and flimflam, with bluff, sham, and much-ado, and along with all that sterling came the baser coin of bluster and vainglory, and mention should be made of the trick he was best at—murder.

Loud and long did he rail at the propertied class, and what it feared most was what it got most of—*Leninismo!* Land to the people! he cried, power to the people!—and they who held both began to dream bad dreams. By then, with his blague about the *proletariato* and the *revoluzione*, he had the lowly behind him...and in a sudden switch, he also caught the ear of the rich with an attack on *Communismo.*

He had them all now, the top, the bottom, and the in-between. With him were forty million from the factory and the soil, and the nobility were with him (Pirelli, Fiat, Olivetti), and of course the makers of castor oil—and thus the March began.

It wasn't really a march; he arrived by train. From afar, all these shenanigans were being observed by a house-painter. His heart too was arid.

1924

LEONARD: A Further Stage

By the time he was set up as an accountant, two others had long been practicing in Greeley, and almost all the local business was in their hands. A clientele of his own was hard to come by, and he took to spending a part of each day on a round of the town, calling at offices and shops in an effort to make himself known. As a newcomer, he found that he could offer little to offset the reputation and experience of his seniors, and he neither filled his ledgers nor swelled his files. Largely idle, he'd sit at his desk and stare at his name on the street-front window—STREBOR. L, he'd read in reverse until it began to spell his direction and compelled him to turn away.

In the afternoons, he usually awaited Marguerite outside her place of work, and when she joined him, he walked her home. She knew that he was ever hopeful of an invitation to enter, but his license expired at the door, and there she left him.

On one such afternoon, Dan was in the house, and he said, "They ought to put him on a train and send hello to Texas."

Marguerite laughed. "He'll be back after supper. Just you wait."

And after supper, Leonard came back. He came in his car, and taking Marguerite for a drive—for a spin, he called it—he went eastward along the Platte, and some way beyond the Kersey beet-fields, he drew up beside the river. It was at low water in that season, and they walked far out across a sand-bar to where a thread of the stream still ran.

"I never seem to get away from this river," she said. "I was born within sight of it, and I've seen it nearly every day of life."

"Are you tired of it?"

"How can you get tired of a river?"

"People, then. Do you get tired of people?"

"Meaning you?"

"Yes."

"Why do you ask?"

"I was wondering how much of me you could stand," he said. "Because I could stand a lifetime of you."

Behind them, their paired footprints were black mars in the sand; ahead lay the trackless bed of the Platte.

"That's a long time and a long way," she said, and in fancy she saw coupled footprints trailing off toward a spun-out unknown end.

"I hope you know what I'm trying to say."

"It's plain enough," she said. "You want me to marry you."

"I do."

"First I'd have to love you."

"And you don't?"

"No."

He stooped for a small water-worn stone and studied it as though he'd come upon something curious, something he'd rarely seen before.

"Is it because of the falling-out in Evans?"

"We had the falling-out because *you* don't love *me*. If you did, you'd not have shamed me out."

"I thought we'd gotten past that."

"We have, or we wouldn't be standing here."

"I made one mistake. Can't you overlook it?"

"If we loved each other, you could make forty, and it wouldn't matter."

"You're on my mind all the time. I live out the day waiting to meet you. I haven't looked at another girl since the first day I saw you. I think I can honestly say I care for you."

She shook her head. "You can't," she said. "It isn't only the Evans thing. That made small of me, and I was angry, but it didn't make me stop loving you. I never started."

"I fail to see why. I'm no lout."

"Sure you're not, but to you, everyone else *is*: we're a bunch of weed-benders in a world you think you own. But it happens we're people, not squatters, and that's something you'll never be able to swallow."

"Not about some people, not about most. But you, you're my equal."

"You really don't think so, Leonard, but even if you did, it wouldn't make you my guy."

"Is anyone else your guy?"

"How could there be? You're always somewhere around."

"I like to be somewhere around," he said, "and I think you like it too. Otherwise, I couldn't touch you here...and here."

"I don't always let you," she said.

"I know."

The small stone made a small splash as he tossed it into the stream.

1924

REFLECTIONS ON A REFLECTION

After sending Leonard away that night, she went upstairs to her room. A low-watt light in the hallway was enough to undress by, and she was about to remove her blouse when she caught sight of herself in the chiffonier mirror. Moving closer, she tilted the glass slightly to make it take in her entire figure, and then she stood before it on the slightly tilted floor. *You're on my mind all the time*, Leonard had said, and this, she thought, was what he saw.

She was a small woman, a half-inch more than five feet tall, and she was small all over. She wore girl-size shoes and girl-size clothes, and her hands were like those of a doll—but she was symmetrical, she fancied, a whole assembled from a set of matching parts. Slowly she turned, and then slowly she turned back, all the while gazing at her image, a separate being in a glass-walled room, and appraising it dispassionately, she found the figure acceptable and the face above it plain. How, then, she wondered, how had she for a year and more held the eye of a disdainful swain?

And now, still looking into the walled-off room, she did remove her blouse, and she studied a likeness that had just done the same. She took stock of that other, she inspected her features, her conformation, her compressed rounds, and in the duplicate room, the duplicate woman undressed some more; she unhooked her skirt and let it fall to the floor, and a petticoat followed, and a brassière, and lastly her thigh-length drawers, and then two bare bodies faced one another through the transparent wall. Is that what he hangs around for?, she wondered, is that what he's after? She surveyed the camber of her mounds, the curve of her concaves, she took in a pair of areolae and a squall of pubic hair, she fingered her navel, she palmed her breasts and belly, thinking as she did so Are these the things he means when he says I'm on his mind...?

1924

SUPPER AT THE SMITHS

The meal was over when Marguerite said, "I won't be going to the office tomorrow. I lost my job."

"That's too bad," her mother said. "I'm sorry for you."

"I knew it was coming. Mr. Meeker was getting ready to retire, and he was only winding up old business. Today he called me in as I was leaving, and he handed me my salary plus a bonus of twenty-five dollars." She produced a check and offered it across the table to her mother. "I want you to have it."

Decky shook her head, saying, "You keep it, child. We're all of us eating regalar."

Marguerite turned to her father and said, "You take it, then, Daddy."

He was touching a match to a pipeful, and he said, "I ain't hurting none. Spend it on yourself."

"I spose you told Leonard," Decky said.

"I haven't seen him to say. But it's really none of his affair."

"I'd've guessed different. You're with him day in, day out."

"That doesn't mean anything, Mama."

"It might—to him."

"He wants me to marry him."

"That's been plain enough."

"But *I* don't want to marry *him*."

Smoke from Henry Albert's pipe flowed into the light below the lampshade, and there it layered itself and surged, but neither he nor Decky spoke.

"You probably want to know why," Marguerite said.

"We don't stick our bills in," her father said. "Our kids live their lives."

"I know that, Daddy, but I'll tell you all the same. Leonard's a decent man, but decency isn't enough. You expect people to be decent, but they ought to be something more, and there's nothing more to Leonard."

"You got to be careful," her father said. "You'd be looking at the same face for maybe sixty years."

"Like me," Decky said.

"You only been looking forty."

"The forty ain't gravelled me. It's the next twenty...." But she laughed.

"So, Daddy, I'll be sticking around for a while."

"You ain't in my road, Dinky."

THE VIEW FROM AFAR OFF

1923: New York, N.Y.

He's standing on the roof of Temple Court a dozen stories above the street. Beyond him rises the Gothic body of the Woolworth Building, where, on the twenty-eighth floor, he's a first-year student at Fordham Law School. With a smile more luminous and behavior less capricious than before, he's reputed to have become responsible at last. Who, then, will credit this, that a few weeks hence he'll cut and run (from what?) and wind up a vagrant in a Florida jail? His father, of course, will bail him out, and as big as life and twice as natural, he'll return to New York—by steamship! The dido is briefly discussed along the Hudson, but not at all along the Platte.

1924

ROUND-TRIP TO DENVER

A summer stock company was presenting *Anna Christie* at the Elich Gardens, and Marguerite had asked Leonard to take her to a performance. The city was a two-hour drive from Greeley on the north-south road that lay across the mile-high piedmont. For part of the distance, they made small talk, and at times they made none at all, and in the silences, Marguerite looked away through her window, noting that nearby things were swiftly left behind while the far-off mountains seemed to pace the car....

"What do you know about O'Neill?" Leonard said.

The words hung as if they were made of smoke, but unlike smoke, they did not ravel and wisp away. *What do you know...?*", she thought, and she weighed the questioner rather than the question. Had he merely been seeking information, the names and numbers and places, the summary of a life, or had she caught an emphasis, just the slightest, on the pronoun *you*? Never far from her mind was the memory of his public eating-lesson, and now, she believed, he was trying to abash her again.

"Turn the car around, Leonard," she said.
"What're you talking about? We're only a couple of miles from Denver."
"I want to go back to Greeley."
"What's gotten into you?"
"The way you put that question."
"What question, for God's sake?"
"The one about O'Neill."
"I only asked what you knew about him."
"I didn't like your tone. As if, what would *I* know."
"Marguerite, your skin is so thin I can see through it. I meant no such thing."
"It sounded small-making to me."
"I don't know beans with the bag open about O'Neill. I'm no reader and never was. Now, what about him?"

106

He didn't want to hear what she had to say: he'd started something without thinking, she thought, and he didn't know how to stop. *What do you know...?*, he'd asked, and whether he cared or not, she'd tell him.

"I came across a play of his in the Greeley library," she said. "*The Straw*, it was called, and I was only riffling the pages when I saw that it had to do with a girl who'd gone to business college. That got me to reading it, and I read right on till I finished it. I was moved so much that I cried."

"Right there in the library?"

"The girl had tb., and she was sent to a sanitarium. She met a man there, another patient and she fell in love with him. He didn't care for her in that way, and when he got better, he said goodbye, and off he went. From then on, it was all downhill for the girl, and finally the doctors gave her up."

"Kind of a gloomy story."

"It didn't end there. The man came back, really only to pay the girl a visit, and he discovered that he did love her after all."

"And she got well, I suppose."

"Not so fast. The question was, could love cure what the doctors couldn't."

"How did O'Neill settle it?"

"He didn't. The play ended with the question."

A highway marker read: DENVER - CITY LIMITS.

"I still want to go back to Greeley," she said.

Leonard returned by a different route, one that ran past Barr Lake and led at length to Kersey. It was zigzag and longer than the other, and the sun had set before he'd gone halfway, but a great fantail of light was still on display above the mountains.

"Marguerite," he said, "I simply don't understand you."

"I'm not very hard to make out."

"This relationship of ours. You've turned it into a see-saw. I never know where I am with you. I'm up, I'm down. I'm down, I'm up."

"You're both."

"How can it be both?"

"Sometimes I like you. Sometimes I don't."

"Is that where I stand, then?"

"Leonard," she said, "what would you like me to tell you?"

"The truth: that you care more for me than you let on."

"You think that's the truth?"

"Why else would you keep on seeing me?"

She laughed. "I told you once. You're the only one who comes around."

"I can't credit that. You're a pretty girl, a bright girl, and I don't just *come* around, I *stay* around."

The county road was little travelled after dark, and stopping the car where it was, on the crown, he pulled Marguerite toward him and took her in his arms. She made no effort to avoid or escape the embrace; the act had been his, not hers, and it was as if she were uninvolved. She gazed past him into the navy-blue night at sparse lights that looked like a fallen constellation.

"Isn't there any love in you at all?" he said.

She drew away to her side of the car, saying, "There's more than you ever dreamed of."

"And none is for me."

"Some is, Leonard, but not enough for me to say what you want to hear."

"What would I have to do to change that?"

"It doesn't depend on what you do, Leonard; you do all right. We've seen a lot of each other, and mostly I've enjoyed myself. There are plenty of blockheads in Greeley, but you're not one of them; you can think, and I admire that. Except for once, you've treated me with respect, and I admire *that*. And you *do* stick around, which is also admirable. But, Leonard, what does it all amount to?"

He toyed with the steering-wheel, and as if he were driving, he turned it a little to the left and then a little to the right, and finally, as if he'd come to a stop, he slapped the rim of wood, saying,

"To more than you seem to know."

"To what, for instance?"

"Encouragement."

SUGAR FROM THE SUGAR BEET

Marguerite lived at the edge of town, where the street petered out and gave way to a beet-field, a vast expanse of furrows that seemed to meet in the distance. Afloat on the green ripples was a squadron of shanties for migrant workers, and far beyond these, as though poised to swamp them, hung the everlasting menace of the mountains. Marguerite and Leonard had gone for a walk, and using an access road, they strolled well out into the field. At either side of them lay an irrigation-ditch, from which at intervals a sluice regulated waterflow into a lateral. Several aisles away stood two field hands, and holding their spades ready, they were observing a channel they'd dug for a set of furrows.

Leonard said, "I wonder what the pay is for watching water run."

"They do a lot more than that," Marguerite said. "My father knows about these people. It's a six-month season, he said, and they only work about two months of it. You know what they make? Something like three hundred dollars a year."

"I haven't done much better."

"You could do worse, and you'd still do better. All this water, and there's none in those shacks."

"Your father tell you that too?"

"That and more."

"What is he—a socialist?"

"Those people work with their hands, and so does he. At heart, he's one of them." And then as they walked on, she said, "Did *you* ever work with your hands?"

"No. None of us did."

"Tell me, did you ever *work*?"

"You know what? I think *you're* the socialist."

"Why? Because I feel for working people and not for the people they work for?"

"Look," he said. "Let's stop talking about work."

"We'd better not. I can't find a job, and you can't find clients."

"You'll land something sooner or later; you're bound to. Me, I've sounded out most of the businessmen in Greeley, and darn few use an accountant. They're secretive."

"What're they scared of?"

"I guess they figure that their business is nobody's business."

"You know what that is? It's crafty."

"I've got a feeling I'll be staring at my window till the lettering peels off."

"Are things really that bad?"

"Bad enough. My father helps out, but I don't like that even a little bit."

The afternoon sun was low now, and its nearly level light glared on the watered rows and made them look like slots in the earth.

He said, "A classmate at Creighton, he's in the same fix, and he wrote to say what he's doing about it. It sounds crazy, but he's on the road selling jewelry."

"It *is* crazy."

"He's got this jobber in Omaha that supplies him with bracelets and rings and watches, cheap stuff, and he peddles it to small-town jewelers. And here's the frosting: he's making scads of money out of it."

"What about his profession?"

"He's thinking of giving it up."

And now the sun was hull-down to the high horizon of the mountains, and it threw a long lavender shadow eastward across the plains.

"It's time we turned," Marguerite said.

1924

INCIDENT BENEATH THE PINES

One late-summer evening, Leonard proposed a fishing-trip for the following day. A friend had told him that some fine trout, Blacks, were still being taken in the canyon of the Cache La Poudre, and he was eager to try his hand before the season came to a close. They'd need little equipment, he said, and waders not at all, for in the narrowed stream, they'd be casting from the banks; he'd furnish the rods, the flies, and a lunch, and if she agreed, they'd get under way at daybreak.

It was a hundred-mile run to the canyon, and first light was showing when they left Greeley. "We'll be late for the best of it," Leonard said. "The sun'll be well up, and feeding'll be over. But maybe we can scare up some late risers."

"Sleeping Beauties," Marguerite said. "Why are they called Blacks?"

"The spots. Their topsides are covered with black spots."

Beyond Fort Collins, they entered the foothills, and there stands of juniper grew among outcrops of red granite—bones, they seemed to be, bones laid bare in some injury to the earth. As the hills became higher they closed in on the road, forming the gorge through which the Poudre poured from pool to pool. In the sunlight, the castled cliffs were the color of blood; in the shade, their color was darker, as if the blood had dried. Climbing a slight grade, the road ran alongside the tracks of an abandoned railway line, and at a turnout between the rails and the river, Leonard brought his car to a stop in a grove of conifers.

A few miles back, they'd passed a small cluster of cabins, all of them boarded up, and no anglers were to be seen along the stream. There were no private fishing-rights in the Poudre, but the place chosen by Leonard that day might well have been his own: no voices were to be heard, and only the pell-mell river broke the stillness of the view. He and Marguerite were alone there with the trees, the spilling waters, and the turreted walls of stone.

He assembled rigs for both of them, and taking stations some way apart, they began to cast their lures at pools and at the rapids that intervened. More often than not, Marguerite's fell too heavily, or her line made a telltale splash, and the fly, ignored, merely drifted away downstream. With nothing to show for an hour's work, she put up her rod and retired to the shade beneath a pine. There, on a spread-out laprobe, she sat watching Leonard display his skill. She admired the way he could cast his line to uncoil above the water, never touching it until the fly had lit, weightless, it seemed, like the insect it was supposed to be.

The tree filigreed the sun, and roundabout her lay a lace of light. Browned needles gave off their thin perfume, a kingfisher plunged, a strident jay beshrewed the world, and from an unknown throat, several silver notes pierced the air. All sound blended into a sedative, and lying back, she gazed at prisms of sunlight, at morsels of sky, at nothing, finally, for her eyes were now closed.

Was she having a dream?

Lying there on her pallet of pine needles (alt. 6,400 ft.), was she dreaming, and if so, of what? Was it of her bygone years, and were they coming to mind as she'd lived them, or had they been changed by time and distance, by the lingering warmth of the season, and even by her resinous bed beneath the trees? And the faces aswirl in her head, were they those of others, or were they all, though seeming strange, merely rearrangements of her own? Was she resurrecting the dead in her aromatic repose, her bull-calf Bolivar, her buckskin pony, was she bringing back Croppy the burro and the Dalmatian Jack? Were there voices in the dingy reaches of the dream, was it Teddy Simmons speaking, was it Vern Cassell, or was it Leonard she heard in the fringes of fancy...?

Was it within the dream that she felt the feel of hands, or were the hands outside the dream, were they real?

Slowly, as though reluctant to leave it, she came from sleep, and with her she brought the sense of having been touched. For a tick of time, she took it that she'd been brushed by a branch above her, by a whiskbroom of yellow-green needles—but it was Leonard that overhung her, his touch that she'd been awakened by, and he was vying with the buttons on the fly of her jeans. *Quit that, Leonard!*, she heard herself say, *I want you to quit!* It was as if she'd commanded the tree (how distinct the furrowed bark, she thought, how clear the scales of the purple-brown cones!). He did not quit, and she knew now that he meant to go still further, whether by her leave or against her will.

She sought to roll free of him, but he was ardent and far stronger than she'd supposed, or so he'd been made by the heat of desire, and the more she strove to avoid him, the greater grew the fire. *I don't want to, Leonard!*, she said, but he violently did, and she could not stay him.

☮

As she kneeled beside the Poudre and bathed her face, again she noted the clarity of details, the grain and shape of stones in the stream, the particularity of shadows, the veins of a sycamore leaf. Why were externals so plain, so vivid, she wondered, why could she count grass-blades at a distance, why could she see textures as though they were under a glass...?

On the way back to Greeley, Leonard said *Please forgive me, Mar-*

guerite, and he said it more than once. But when he left her at her dooryard, though she could recall sights seen on the hundred-mile run—a grove of turning aspen, a roadsign, the lights of Loveland—she could not remember having spoken at all.

1924

THE NEXT DAY

"Do you know what would happen if I told my father?" she said. "He'd take his scatter-gun and scatter your brains."

She'd slept little, and soon after light, she dressed and left the house to wander the few roundabout acres. In the apple orchard, windfalls lay decaying in the grass, and she passed through a zone where bees flew low-speed stunts in the cider air. She heard the small sound of insects and a sudden hubbub in the henyard, and her feet sitrred a sweet smell from a skiff of curing hay. In the shade of a shed, a sawhorse stood against a wall, and sitting on the crossbar, she stared away at nothing until a jay came to blue-and-gray the view. It was there that Leonard found her.

"What're you doing here, anyway?" she said. "I don't want to talk to you. I don't want to see you again ever."

"You've got to, Marguerite. What I did was unpardonable, but—"

"You think I'm going to pardon you. Is that it?"

"I have to put things right."

"Put them right! How, for Christ's sake?"

"By marrying you."

"To hell with you and your chivalry! I didn't care for you *before* you did what you did."

"I cared for you, though. I've always wanted you to be my wife."

"You sure picked a fine way to prove it."

"I lost control of myself. But lying there asleep under that tree, you were so appealing—"

"Not for what I got, you bastard!"

"If that's what I was, I wouldn't be here. I'm here because I did you a

113

wrong, and I admit it, but far more than that, I'm here because you mean a very great deal to me. It's asking a lot that you forgive me yesterday, but please don't say it's too much."

It surprised her to find that it was not too much. She'd spoken to him with more anger than she actually felt, as if it existed for the greater part in the expressing of it. Why, she wondered, was she so little moved? It came to her, as before, that he simply wasn't vital enough to affect her deeply or excite her long. His disdain, the insult of his eating-lesson, and lately his violence, none had really altered her: she held her fork "properly" now, but however he might invade her, he'd never be able to rule.

"You ought not to have done that to me," she said. "It was coarse, it was cowardly, but worst of all, it was false. You got me to trust you, and then—"

"I betrayed you."

"I don't use fancy words. I use plain ones, like, you're a sell when it comes to being noble. You're a damn sight lower than you hold your nose."

"Whatever else I am, I'm not a fool. I know why I look down on the world: it's because I'm afraid to look up."

"Why?"

"I might find it looking down on me."

The disclosure was so unexpected that she scanned him for a sign of deceit. "Coming from you," she said, "that's surprising."

"I'm surprised too—that you never saw it. I put on a show of being one of the best, but if I really were, I wouldn't have to. Baxter's the same. My family's the same. We know we aren't much, and we try to make others think more of us than we think of ourselves."

"It's taken you a long time to get human."

He shook his head. "Only a long time to admit it."

She reached down into the grass for a fallen apple. Its skin had split, and over its browning flesh ran a few red ants.

"Marry me, Marguerite,"

She tossed the apple away and brushed an ant from her hand.

"Do me the honor," he said.

⚜

That afternoon, they drove to Loveland, a town twenty miles to the west of Greeley and across the line in the County of Larimer. There they obtained a marriage license at the City Hall, after which they were married by a Justice of the Peace. They then started on the short drive back into Weld County and the place they'd started from. On the way, it occurred to Marguerite that the word *love* had been absent from their entire year-long relationship. *Loveland*, she thought, and behind a straight face, she smiled.

1924

SISTERS: a dialogue

PEARL: Him living with his folks and you with yours—if not for a license, nobody'd hardly know you was married.

MARGUERITE: I know, and the family knows. I don't care a rap for anyone else.

PEARL: Well, it ain't much of a marriage, being apart like this.

MARGUERITE: It's the best we can do right now. Money's scarce, but I won't live there, and he sure can't live here.

PEARL: How are Mama and Daddy taking it?

MARGUERITE: You know the Old Settlers. They've never been much for sticking their bills in.

PEARL: I'm built different. You're coming up twenty, but you're my baby sister, and I'll say what I think.

MARGUERITE: When did you not, Pearlie?

PEARL: He hadn't ought to got married less he could provide.

MARGUERITE: After what happened, it seemed like the thing to do.

PEARL: A thing like that don't just happen, Marg.

MARGUERITE: Good Lord! I hope you don't think I asked for it.

PEARL: See a man regalar, and he'll take a notion.

MARGUERITE: This one took it without my permission.

PEARL: I only seen him a couple times, but I just don't cotton to him.

MARGUERITE: I've seen him a couple of hundred, and to tell the truth, I don't, either.

PEARL: That's some start you're getting off to.

MARGUERITE: It could be worse. Leonard could be a chaser like your Chester. Or he could be a drunk like John Roach and bust my nose.

PEARL: I didn't know you knew about Chester.

MARGUERITE: He's no secret, Pearlie.

PEARL: You want my opinion, you and me we married low.

MARGUERITE: Leonard's showing signs of growing up. I think he's changing.

PEARL: Pshaw! The man don't live that ever changed. Your nose ain't been broke yet, but it will be, one way or another. When Leonard gets flustrated with setting around that office, he'll show you how much he's changed.

MARGUERITE: He doesn't have to set fire to the Platte for me. I'm not looking for diamonds.

PEARL: Diamonds! You'll be lucky he gives you a roof.

MARGUERITE: You could always put your hand to something and turn a dollar, and I mean to do the same. There's no reason why the man has to do all the work.

PEARL: Just be sure *you* don't.

MARGUERITE: It wouldn't be a scandal if I did. *You* do it. If not for you, Chester would be sleeping in a ditch.

PEARL: And like as not, alongside some spraddle-leg....

1924

CONCERNING PEARLS OF NO GREAT PRICE

"I wanted to go to college," Marguerite said, "and I wanted to go to this one. Don't ask me what I had in mind—a notion to be a teacher, I guess—but whatever it might've been, there was no money for it in the family, and I had to settle for $45 worth of Typing and Shorthand."

On the campus of the one college in Greeley, the Colorado State School of Education, she and Leonard were walking along a tree-shaded path bordering a greensward. Between them and the buildings they passed, there were beds of plantings with markers announcing their common and Latin names. Lupine, she read, *Lupinnus perennis*, and columbine, *Aquilegia coerulea*.

"Even the $45 was hard to come by," she said, "and when I found out what Mama was doing to earn it—taking in wash!—I came near refusing to use it. In the long run, I did use it, but I made up my mind that one day I'd give her a life of ease. A life of ease! Look at me—I'm out of a job, and I haven't got a dime!"

Leonard said, "I have an idea that just might make us a mort of money."

She read Spanish Bayonet and Cat's-claw and Rose Mallow before what Leonard had said overtook and mingled with her mind. Blue Flag, she read, *Iris versicolor*—and then, turning to Leonard, she gave him her attention.

"Remember my telling you about a classmate at Creighton?" he said.

"The one who quit Accounting to peddle jewelry?"

"He sent me the catalogue of the company he works with, and what caught my eye was a line of pearls they put out, artificial pearls. According to the terms, you get them on consignment: you pay the company a couple of bucks a string, and you sell them for five, six, whatever they'll bring, and what you make is yours. My idea is to lay in a supply and unload them all over the state—towns like Grand Junction, Durango, Gunnison, Trinidad, La Junta. And if they pan out, there's Wyoming, there's New Mexico."

"The idea's a good one, but is it wise to give up a profession for it?"

"The profession gave *me* up."

"Even so, it's hard to picture Leonard Roberts as a salesman."

"I wouldn't be selling."

"Who, then?"

"You, *Mrs.* Leonard Roberts."

She stopped short and stared at him. "*Me?*"

"You—you'd be the one who sells the pearls."

"How? From door to door?"

"Nothing like it."

"The only selling I ever did was back of a candy-counter at the Five-and-Dime. But I'm no nay-sayer, so what've you got in mind for me?"

"What we'll do, we'll go to a town like Pueblo, say, or Canon City, and we'll rent us a store-front for the day. You'll stand in the window and model the pearls for the people passing by, people shopping, people going to a movie, people out for a walk, men and women both."

"And where'll you be while I'm showing off?"

"Just inside the door, waiting for the customers you knock dead with your figure and the pearls."

She walked on with him, saying nothing for a way, and at length she laughed. "It's not at you," she said. "It's at me."

"Why?"

"Because all my life, I've kept to myself. I've never tried to get attention—just the opposite, I've always avoided it. Now I'll be on display for all the world to gawk at, find fault with, laugh at."

"Nobody'll laugh," he said. "Not at that trim figure of yours. It's one in a thousand, and what you'll be wearing is a black silk dress, slinky and plain, and we'll put black suede shoes on those tiny feet, and around your neck we'll hang your only ornamentation—a rope of Omaha pearls, courtesy Mecca Gem Company."

"And when I do a sashay in the window, the rubes'll storm the doors, money in hand."

"That's the size of it," he said.

Again she walked on with him, and again she was silent for a while, but in the end she did not laugh. "I've been wondering," she said.

"About what?"

"How Leonard Roberts will feel when his wife displays herself to the public."

"There's nothing wrong with it," he said. "It's like acting."

Shepherd's-purse, she read, *bursa-pastoris*.

And she said, "What do they think of actresses in Carolina...?"

1924

DEPARTMENT STORE

"I've never shopped in Denver," Marguerite said. "In fact, I've never shopped. My Mama makes my clothes."

"I know where to go," Leonard said.

"I asked my sister Pearl, and she says Denver Dry."

"I asked Baxter, and he steered me to Daniels & Fisher."

"I'd be inclined to take a woman's advice."

"No slight to Pearl, but Baxter's up on these things."

They were on their way to the city for the black silk dress and the black suede shoes. Making an early start from Greeley, they had the highway almost to themselves as they passed through La Salle and entered the valley of the South Platte. Driving between irrigated fields of alfalfa and the cottonwoods that lined the stream, they were twice startled when pheasants were flushed from a covert and flashed across their road.

"He must know a lot of girls," Marguerite said.

"He does—and he's watched them buy a lot of dresses."

"The kind you have in mind, I'm afraid it's going to cost."

"We can't skinch on the dress. If we do, we'll be out of business before we're ever in."

"Grand Junction isn't exactly Paris, and neither is Durango."

"True, but if we want to sell pearls in Durango, we've got to look like Paris."

She let a time pass before saying, "I wouldn't've credited you with a head for business."

"What did you take me for—another Baxter?"

"No, but I thought you'd starve before you ever put a hand to making money."

"Everybody's doing it—except Baxter."

They didn't go to Denver Dry; they went to Daniels & Fisher. It was a block-long store on 16th Street at Arapahoe, and its several stories were topped by a tall tower.

119

"You can see all of Denver from up there," Leonard said. "Want to have a look?"

Two hundred feet below them, 16th Street flowed straight away for a mile to the Civic Center and the State Capitol. Far beyond these, the great arrested wave of the mountains was poised, and all unaware, minute people made their insectival way through areas of sun and shade.

☙

"They're small," Marguerite said. "From higher up, we couldn't see them at all."

"Third floor," the elevator operator said. "Ladies' coats, dresses, hats, and accessories. Third floor."

There, when a saleslady gave them her attention, Leonard described to her what they were seeking. "My wife is looking for a black dress, quite plain, but very much in the fashion. In silk, if you have it. If not, in crepe."

"Please be seated," the saleslady said, and she went off to the stock-room.

Marguerite said, "It isn't only Baxter who's up on things."

"Is that a compliment?"

"You gave instructions as though you've given them before."

"Oh, once or twice, maybe."

"More than that. You're—what's the big word?—authoritative."

"I've never been able to command you."

"I'm no saleslady."

Returning with several dresses, the woman hung them on a rack. She took one of them down, exhibited it front and rear, and then put it against herself, gathering it at the waist to suggest the fall of the skirt.

"Like it?" Leonard said.

"No."

"Why not?"

"For one thing, I want a half-sleeve. And for another, the neckline is cut too low."

"I kind of admire the neckline."

"The pearls won't show up against my skin."

"I didn't think of that."

"When it comes to picking a dress, I'll do the thinking."

Three more dresses were shown for Marguerite's approval, and none of them won it. The next one, though, took her eye, and she went away to a changing-room to try it on. Coming out, she stood herself before a two-winged mirror and studied her three reflections.

"Well," Leonard said, "what do you think?"

"It's just the thing."

"I think so too. But if you aren't pleased, we can look at something else."

"No need. This is the one I want."

To the saleslady, Leonard said, "Have it wrapped, please. And when you come back, I'll ask you to direct us to the Shoe Department."

On the way back to Greeley—at Brighton, it might've been—Marguerite said, "Tell me about imitation pearls."

"Let's agree to call them *artificial*. *Imitation* smacks of snake oil."

"Artificial, then."

"I gather they were first made in Europe a couple of hundred years ago. What they are, actually, is little glass balls that they line with a silvery something called Essence of the Orient, which they get from the scales of a certain fish. After that, they simply fill the balls with wax and seal them off."

"A *certain* fish, you say. Which one?"

"The bleak—b-l-e-a-k."

"I'm impressed."

"Don't be. I knew you'd ask some time, and I looked it all up in the Encyclopedia."

"Now I'm even more impressed."

And it might've been at Fort Lupton that Marguerite said, "The skirt's a trifle long, but my Mama will fix that."

MAINLY IN DECKY'S ROOM

Wearing the dress bought for her in Denver, Marguerite was standing on a chair and turning when told to by her mother, who was inserting a row of pins around and above the hemline of the skirt. Nearby, Pearl sat watching.

"Only about an inch shorter, Mama," Marguerite said.

"Make it six," Pearl said. "That way, she can flash her knees."

"Oh, hush up," her mother said.

"Make it twelve. Give 'em a *real* show in Leadville."

Without straightening, Decky said, "Pearl, for a woman that swapped husbands, you hadn't ought to be so starchy about Marg."

"Well, you know me, Mama. I speak my mind."

"Keep on speaking, and you won't have none of it left."

"I'm bound to say this scheme of Leonard Roberts is the giddiest thing I ever heard of. To say nothing of it being a mighty low use to put Marg to. I can't understand why you don't put your foot down."

Now her mother did straighten, and she said, "If I was to do that, I'd first off put it on you. You ain't exactly set the best example for my girls, Mrs. Honnold—or are you fixing to swap a second time?"

Marguerite said, "Stop foaming and faunching, you two. I know you're looking out for me, and I love you for it. But if I'm old enough to be married, I'm old enough to make my own decisions and run my show."

"Turn a little, child," her mother said.

Later in the day, Marguerite visited her sister Bijou and told her of the dispute. "What's your opinion?" she said.

"Go!" Bijou said. "And I only wish I could go along."

THE FLYER

After Marguerite had shown Leonard the alteration, he said. "Your mother did a fine job on that hemline."

"I never heard of anybody so handy," Marguerite said. "She laid hold of some fine material once, and she ran up a blouse for me. I was real vain of it, and I cried when I got an inkspot right in front. Mama went to work with her needle and turned that inkspot into a little black-eyed daisy."

It was a spring evening, and they were sitting on the steps of the porch in the zone of light spreading from the doorway. Out in the road, a cat stopped to beam its brights and then quite suddenly turned them off.

"You admire your mother, don't you?"

"My whole family. And *admire* is a stingy word. I *love* my family."

"You'll miss them, then, when we're on the road."

"It'll be the first time we've ever been apart."

"Will you be lonely?"

"How could I not be?"

"Aside from being your blood, what makes them so dear to you?"

She stared at the night, seeing only what she saw in her mind, a fast run of scenes from earlier times and various places, all of them cast with faces that bespoke an absence of guile, an accessible heart, a tribal welcome.

"Their self-respect," she said.

"The pearls were delivered yesterday," Leonard said. "At two dollars a string, I laid in a thousand."

"Gracious life!" Marguerite said. "Where'd you dig up all that money?"

"Out of my savings. And I still have five hundred to cover our expenses while we're learning the ropes."

"What do you reckon the expenses will come to?"

"Well, there'll be food and lodging and of course gasoline. I figure we'll get by on ten dollars a day, give or take a little."

"We'll have about two months, then, to make a go of it."

"After which, we start eating pearls. Are you worried?"

"Not a bit. My family doesn't worry."

"How is that?"

"They aren't pinchfisted. They don't live by getting and die by spending."

"I like to make plans and see numbers. I was born to be a bookkeeper."

"By the way, what *are* your plans?"

"I expect we'll do best in towns where something's going on—where there's a cannery, a mill, a nearby mine. We'll find out when the payday is and set up shop the day before."

"What do you mean—set up shop?"

"Two things. We have to arrange for a likely place to show the pearls, and then we have to tell people where it is. About the place, I'll make a deal for a store-window on the main street and pay for it with a cut of the sales. And about where, we'll take care of that with the flyer I got up."

"You said you'd bring one around."

"I did," he said. "I'll fetch it from the car."

On his return, he handed her a sheet of paper on which a printed announcement appeared within a decorative border. It read:

ARTIFICIAL ORIENTAL PEARLS
! Can't be told from the genuine !
Price: $5 a string
On sale this day only at

....
Hours ... to ... p.m.

"As soon as we know the location," he said, "we'll fill them in by hand."

"And then what?"

"We'll drive around town and stuff them in every mailbox...every *other* mailbox."

"Why?"

"One housewife will crow, and her neighbor will be jealous—and they'll *both* buy."

Marguerite said nothing.

"Don't you think I'm clever?"

"I'd call it sharp. We'll put the flyer in *all* the boxes."

"As you say," he said.

❦

"When do you look to get going?" she said.

"How soon can you be ready?"

1925

THE LAST SUPPER

On the eve of her departure, Marguerite's family convened at her home. An attractive force, mute and imperceptible, seemed to exist among them, and though none had consulted any other, one by one they'd drifted together as if drawn. For each of them, there was simply no place else to be on such an occasion: their once-and-always baby sister was about to go away. At table, where the meal was just ending, sat the parents, the son, and the four daughters. Leonard had asked to be present, but Marguerite had refused him.

Waving at the board with his cigar, Henry Albert said, "Looks like old times, all you kids around."

"Come morning," Decky said, "there won't be a one of 'em. It'll just be you and I, like in the beginning."

"Alone now is different to alone then. You kind of get used to having a chick or two about, and here's the last of 'em taking off."

"We don't any of us stay away long, Daddy." Marguerite said. "Home is where you and Mama are."

"You'll find that ain't so," her mother said. "You can't go and still be tied. You got to cut the strings."

"I'm thinking of Leonard's strings," Dan said. "They must be tough as whang."

"His folks letting loose of him," Pearl said. "It's a surprise to me."

Dan said, "I wouldn't suppose they'd let him out of sight."

"Time was," Connie said, "when the Smiths would butt out."

"Write to us, Marg," Bijou said.

"I will," Marguerite said. "I hope it won't be to ask for money."

And her mother said, "You can do that too."

THE VIEW FROM AFAR OFF

1925: Long Branch, N.J.

In the hazy snapshot, he's posed on a lawn. Dressed for golf, he'll soon be boarding a trolley for the public links in Asbury Park, and during the six-mile ride, he'll think in fragments only, in color and speed and whirl; he'll think of nothing, really, he'll think of nothing at all. At the golf course, he'll set out alone, but later, while hunting for a ball in the rough, he'll be over-taken by a player whose lurching gait recalls boyhood days in Harlem.

"Hi," he'll say, "aren't you Natchie Weinstein that used to live on Seventh Avenue?"

"It's West now, not Weinstein—and I know you. You're Julie Shapiro, and you were all the time shooting marbles. I guess you gave that up, though."

"I'm on the marble-shooting team at Fordham Law School. What about you?"

"I'm writing a book."

The rest of the round will be played in a daze. There'll be more talk, but none of it will be remembered, nor will the summer. In time, even the law will be forgotten.

Writing a book!

1925

UNDER WAY

It was not yet noon when they passed through Denver and made for Colorado Springs. Overcast at the start, the day had remained so, some-how seeming the longer for the sky's relentless gray. For some distance, nothing had been said of the venture just begun, of the scenery far and near, of the relationship of the pair sitting side by side in the car: for some distance, nothing had been said at all. But above the piston-pound and the sound of rolling rubber, Marguerite caught the unspoken speech of thought, and she had the feeling that she was twain, that she was both the hearing and the heard, and she queried herself in her mind, and in her mind she sought to reply.

With whom, at a speed of forty miles an hour, was she moving into the future? What was this junket they'd embarked on, where would it take them, and where would it end? This partner, this associate, this fellow on the seat beside her, what was he to her and she to him? She wore his name, but what else of his did she own or desire, what quality did he possess, what trait did she admire? This stranger, what was she doing here with this stranger...?

"Pikes Peak," Leonard said, indicating a free-standing rise some miles to the west.

"Ever been to the summit?" Marguerite said.

"Never got around to it. Like people in New York. They live their lives a mile from the Statue of Liberty, and not one in a hundred ever gets nearer."

"There's a place I'd a lot sooner see than a statue or a mountain. It's less to look at, but it means more to me."

"What place is that?"

"A little dump of a town called Blanca."

"Never heard of it."

"Few have. It's on the high flat between Alamosa and Ft. Garland. I lived there when I was five years old...."

In a tar-paper shack, she thought, and she remembered the mines in the nearby hills, and she remembered the burros that were used to haul ore-carts to the surface, and most clearly did she remember that when they aged or sickened or suffered an injury, they were turned loose to shift for themselves in the greasewood and the sage, and that there they usually died. One of them, foraging for food, had strayed to the back door of the shack, and Marguerite had begged for permission to adopt it. When her plea was granted, the ill-used creature underwent an instant transformation: from a galled and dispirited beast, it changed to a steed of noble bearing, afire within and snorting streams of smoke.

"...I called him Croppy," she said.

"Called who Croppy?"

"My burro—Croppy, on account of getting part of his ears blown off in a mine-blast. Dan found me a saddle, and I rode him all over the plains...."

It all seemed so long ago that it might've happened in a prior life. Strangely, though, she could still see the arid alkali flats, the wheel-tracks through the scattered brush, the black sheeting on the shack, even the rows of roofing nails that held the paper in place. They'd been hard times, she remembered. Hunting for work, her father had walked the roads all day, and as often as not, he returned empty-handed to a supper of corn bread and beans. But there was no disorder, no squalor, no ill humor at the board: instead, he sat with his two younger daughters and his wife, and he dined!, he dined!, and in loving company, he lived out another day.

"...Forget about Blanca," she said.
"But I thought you wanted to see it."
"I just saw it," she said.

She knew that her meaning escaped him, but she knew this too, that she didn't much care.

1925

AT THE WATER'S EDGE

Along the highway beyond Colorado Springs, Leonard stopped the car at a picnic-grounds, and there, across one of the tables, he spread a road map of the state.

"We've got to get our feet wet somewhere, and I had Walsenburg in mind. That's here," he said, and using a twig as a pointer, he showed Marguerite a small-print name. "But now that Blanca's out, we don't have to go that far south. We can get going in Pueblo. That's here."
"Pueblo's kind of big, isn't it? We don't need an ocean to wet our feet. A puddle will do."

She didn't think her remark particularly amusing, but she wondered why the extremes she'd suggested hadn't produced a smile. There was no smile; there was only absorption with the details of a map.

"What about Canon City, then?" he said. "Population 5,000."

"The State prison's in Canon City. I don't want to sell pearls in a place like that."

"What do you say to Florence? Population two-three thousand. Fruit-growing country."

"Sounds right. Let's make it Florence."

"We can be there in an hour. That'll give us most of the afternoon to set ourselves up for tomorrow....And if things go well there, we'll take a day off, and I'll show you Royal Gorge."

For some reason (what reason?), she was nettled by the offer, and she chose to take it as a reward for good behavior.

"What if they *don't* go well?" she said. "Do I get stood in a corner?"

"I didn't mean anything like that."

For some reason (the same reason?), she was all the more nettled by his soft reply. She'd've had greater regard for him, she thought, if, however childishly, he'd picked up the glove she'd flung and said if they don't go well, no Royal Gorge.

Strung out along the banks of the Arkansas, the town of Florence lay in the midst of an apple-growing district, and a goodly way before reaching it, the car passed between the vast orchards that lined the road. Gazing into the parallel but staggered rows, Marguerite had the illusion that the trees were wheeling, as if the earth were keeping pace with the car.

"First thing we do," Leonard said, "we find us a place to stay the night. Keep your eye peeled for a Guest Home."

"Why not a hotel?"

"In a small town? My friend from Creighton says the rooms always smell of horses."

"I like the smell of horses. I'd sleep in a barn."

"Then *you'd* smell of horses."

"Many's the time I did. You can't ride them without the smell coming off."

After engaging a room near the business section of Florence, they walked the main street in quest of a suitable location for displaying the pearls. Half a block from the motion-picture house, Leonard found what he was looking for, an ice-cream parlor likely to be frequented throughout the day. Leaving Marguerite outside, he entered the shop to confer with the proprietor.

Rejoining her shortly, he said, "This window here is ours from noon tomorrow till the picture-show lets out at night. We'll have only two showings, of course—a couple of hours for the afternoon shoppers, and another couple for the movie-crowd later on."

"What're we paying for the window?"

"The man tried for a dollar a string, but I jewed him down to six bits....Now we get to work on the flyer."

At the Guest Home, they filled the blanks on a few hundred flyers (*Florence Sweet Shop*), and then they toured the residential section and placed them in mail-boxes at the roadside.

"After supper," Marguerite said, "maybe we can take in the show."

"Buster Keaton?" Leonard said. "You like Buster Keaton?"

"People do. People like me."

Later that night, they lay side by side in the darkness, he asleep and she awake. A light wind made the curtains seem to breathe, and the shadow of their pattern slowly scaled a wall, and then they exhaled, and the shadow returned to the floor. Why did she feel so lonely?, she wondered. Lying there next to her husband, still she was alone in the room, she thought, and alone in the room of the world as well. She'd left a known and cordial round to go wayfaring with this meager presence beside her, a presence she had no other name for but his own—never Len or Lenny or, in some warm and playful moment, Leonardo. With a carload of imitation pearls (imitation, damn it, not artificial!), she was knocking about the country to posture for purchasers at $5 the string.

In all truth, how did she regard the work? By nature and by choice, she'd held herself private always, desiring neither to trespass nor to be trespassed upon, and enjoying only her lenient family and the incurious company of animals—and yet here she was, about to lend her person to public view. What had brought about the change...? Leonard stirred in his sleep, but the reminder of his existence was too slight to be weighed, and she felt quite as solitary as before. For the first time, though, she linked him with her newfound unconcern with the scrutiny of strangers: despite their gaze, she'd still be alone, for they mattered as little as he.

Again and again she watched the slow respiration of the curtains, and then at last she closed her eyes.

1925

THE FLORENCE SWEET SHOP

Afternoon

Part of the customary display had been removed from the window—a few soft-drink emblems, a price-list, a tray of candies—and in the space thus cleared stood Marguerite. Wearing her black dress and her black suede shoes, she was ornamented only by a gleaming catenary of pearls. Propped against the plate-glass front, Leonard's placard made its announcement to passersby—and not all of these passed without pausing.

In choosing the dress, Marguerite had been unerring. It was fine-tailored, but in the simplicity of its design, in its quiet, it offered no affront to provincial taste and fashion; indeed, many may have thought it home-made. Her figure was small and smoothly formed—rhythmical—and the dress merely murmured of the rounds and concaves it so nearly concealed. Making a half-turn now and again and fingering the ellipse of pearls, she at no time sought to be alluring. She could hardly have been unaware of those who stopped to stare through the window, the men and women, the young and old, but it was as if they were on view, not she, as if they were performers she'd paid to see.

Suspended across the roadway, a canvas banner proclaimed APPLE BLOSSOM DAY though the day had long since come and gone. Left aloft, it still backed and filled in all weathers, faded now by the sun and the rain and dingied by smoke from the traffic below. Performers, thought Marguerite, that's what they were, those people in the street—players unknowingly playing themselves, and she beguiled the time by composing words for the words their mouths were making, the speech she could not hear.

Leonard spoke over the partition at the rear of the show-window, saying, "You've been at it for an hour. How about a rest?"

"A rest and a coke," she said, and she stepped around the partition and into the shop.

No sooner were they seated than he said, "Want to guess how we made out?"

"I can't. A lot of people went in, and a lot came out, but I don't know whether they bought pearls or candy."

"They bought twenty strings!"

"That many?"

"We took in a hundred dollars—which means we cleared over forty!"

"Gracious life."

"And we'll do even better tonight!" he said.

Evening

Returning to the Guest Home, Marguerite changed to street-clothes in order to give the black dress an airing, and then she and Leonard set out again to find a likely eating-place. On the main street, only two cafés were serving, and they chose the one that seemed more promising.

At table, Marguerite said, "One thing's clear. I'm going to need another dress—"

"You know what?" Leonard said. "We're going to make money!"

"The Denver dress is a beauty, but if I wear it twice a day, I'll ruin—"

"A hundred a week clear, or I miss my guess!"

"We probably won't get back to Denver for a while, so I'll have to pick something up in one of these small towns—"

"Maybe even better than a hundred!"

"Which won't be so bad, because it'll be in the style they wear out here—"

"Marguerite, are you listening to me?"

"You've been going on about how well we're doing."

"*Well* is simply no word for it!"

"But, Leonard, have *you* been listening to *me?*"

"It won't be long," he said, "before we run out of pearls."

It was dark by the time the evening showing began. Still open were the pharmacy, the two cafés, and the Sweet Shop, but most of what light there was came from the electric-sign in front of the theatre: the *Odeon*. In a column above the entrance, the name was spelled in low-watt bulbs, a few of these flickering and another few burned out. In the street, people appeared now as disembodied faces—masks, thought Marguerite—and with their fixed expressions, they gaped before the glass....

To patrons on their way to and from the *Odeon*, twenty-six strings of pearls were sold that night.

The picture-show had let out, and the Sweet Shop crowd had dispersed, and now, back at the Guest Home, Leonard and Marguerite were in bed, she holding a book and he writing on a loose-leaf tablet.

Without looking up, he said, "What're you reading?"
"A play. Something I found in the bookcase downstairs."
"O'Neill again?"
"Shaw. A man named G.B. Shaw."
Continuing to write, he said, "What's this one about?"
"It's called...I can't pronounce the title—C-a-n-d-i-d-a. It deals with a preacher and his wife and a young man who's in love with her. It's clever, very what-you-call witty, and the people are a lot brighter than you'd ever meet in Greeley, but something's wrong with the way they behave. No one's natural. No one does what people would do in Greeley—or anywhere else. The young man is far too wise for his years, and he carries on in a cheeky way that ought to get him flung out on his ass. But the preacher's a stick, and as far as I've gotten, he seems to be standing for the sass...."

She glanced at Leonard. The loose-leaf notebook was now loosely held, for he'd fallen asleep. She took up the memorandum, and what he'd written were numbers, only numbers.

1925

THE GRAND CANYON OF THE ARKANSAS

At breakfast the next morning, Leonard said, "The Sweet Shop man wanted us to stay another day. I told him I'd see how you felt about it."

Marguerite said nothing.

"How *do* you feel about it?"

"We're peddlers, and peddlers move along."

"You're for moving along, then?"

Shrugging, she said, "It isn't important. We can stay, if you like."

"But you'd sooner not."

"You won't get a demand out of me," she said. "I'm not demanding."

"Which means that you're leaving these things to me."

"Up to a point. I'm not much for following the leader, either."

"I promised you a look at Royal Gorge today. How come you didn't remind me?"

"Reminding is demanding."

"Well, I reminded myself," he said, "and you're going to see the Gorge in about an hour."

The chasm was some twenty miles from Florence, and by mid-morning they were on the north rim. Leaving the car in a parking area, they made their way on foot to the abutment of the suspension bridge. There they paused between the huge concrete blocks that anchored the cables and gazed at the long converge of planking that led to the farther rim. Of the rift it spanned, of the river and railway a thousand feet below, nothing was visible from where they stood.

"It doesn't look like much from here," Marguerite said. "We've got to get closer."

"I've seen photos of it. It's one mighty deep ditch."

"Let's walk across."

They moved on along the dirt approach, but where the floor of the bridge began, Leonard stopped. "This is far enough," he said.

"But we still can't see the bottom."

"I don't have to see it. I know it's a long way down."

Indicating a few cars that were coming and going on the bridge,

134

Marguerite said, "If it holds them, it'll hold us."

"Some day it won't, and this could be the day."

"If it is, you'll know where to find me."

She turned away from him, and staying close to the railing and the stringpiece, she walked out to where the cables dipped to the level of the bridge. There she peered down at the torrent of the Arkansas, which from that height seemed not to flow, and at the giant curves of track that lay beside its course. What if the span did give way, she thought, what if the cables snapped and the roadway broke, what if she tumbled through space followed by four motor cars—how long before they all hit bottom, she perhaps in the stream and they only after bouncing off the walls?

Below, between the tracks and the stream, stood a way station, and alongside it a train had halted to let passengers descend for a view of the Gorge. The sightseers looked like a mere swarm of bees, and the train too was small, vermiform—and at any moment, she thought, all might be buried under a mass of timbers, twisted cable, sedans, and sprawling bodies, hers among these last. The locomotive spoke twice, but its voice ricocheted from the granite palisades, and the sound seemed to have been made in several places.

Returning to Leonard, she said, "You missed a stunning sight."

And he said, "You don't rub it in, do you?"

"Rub what in?"

"You don't razz me for funking at the bridge."

"Why would I do a thing like that?"

"Others would. Why not you?"

"Some people are bold, some are shy. We come in all sizes."

"But is one size as good as another?"

"We're all of us people, which you still don't understand."

He was silent until they were seated in the car, and after working the wheel as if the car were in motion, he said, "You're not bold. You'll never be bold. It was something else that let you go out on the bridge."

"What?"

"You know you're going to die some day, and you never give it a thought."

"And you?"

"I think of it all the time."

135

And then the car was moving.

"Where are we heading?" Marguerite said.

"I'm thinking of Salida. It's a division point on the D. & R. G."

"How big is it?"

"A little bigger than Florence. Three-four thousand."

Salida was fifty miles away.

1925

THE MONTE CRISTO HOTEL

Nearing Salida late in the afternoon, they began to look for a place to stay the night, but they found nothing until they reached the main street, where Leonard drew up before the entrance of a two-story hotel. At sidewalk level, a plateglass front opened a dreary lobby to view, and through the flaking letters of the name, they saw a worn sofa and a few worn chairs, a desk backed by a battery of pigeonholes, and a staircase leading to the upper floor.

"Not very promising," Leonard said.

"I've seen worse."

"*Is* there worse?"

"You've never lived in a tar-paper shack and peed in the tules."

"Have you?"

"In Blanca."

"No wonder you didn't need to go back."

"It was clean inside, though—all spick-and-spandy. Mama saw to that."

"I'd suggest trying our luck further on, but Leadville's seventy miles away, and Gunnison's out of the question this time of day. We'd have to cross Monarch Pass in the dark."

"The *Monte Cristo*," Marguerite said. "One night here won't kill us."

"I guess," he said. "But let's give the pearls a rest and light out for Gunnison in the morning."

Hanging the black dress from a wall fixture, Marguerite went to the window and gazed out across the buildings on the opposite side of the street. Far beyond them rose the foothills of a hundred-mile arc of mountain range.

"The Sangre de Cristos," she said. "They end at Blanca."

"Cristo," Leonard said. "Everything around here is Cristo."

"The blood of Christ. It's kind of beautiful."

"To a Catholic, maybe."

"I never asked, Leonard. What're you?"

"A Baptist."

"Do you go to church?"

"My family does. I used to."

"I've never been to church in my life."

"That's odd."

"So's my reason," she said. "I had a brother name of Harold Anson. He was a fine young fellow, they tell me, and along about the time he was eighteen, he came down with the quinsy. When the doctor gave him up for a goner, Mama sent for the minister to pray over him. He wouldn't come: he was scared of catching the sickness. After that, the family stopped going to church, and I never started."

"Baxter still goes."

"I wasn't even born when Harry died. It's strange, having a brother who's only a name. He was a wonderful shot, Dan says, the best he ever saw."

To the west of the town, another high range was a ragged skirt on the sky, lavender now as the sun set behind it.

"Let's go get us some supper," Leonard said.

"I'm not very hungry."

"Neither am I, but we will be by tomorrow."

A block from the hotel, they found the Railroad Café, a long narrow eating-place with a row of tables at either hand. When they were seated, a waitress brought each of them a bill-of-fare, the print almost illegible through a clouded jacket of isinglass.

"Miss," Marguerite said, "where is the Ladies Room, please?"

The waitress nodded at the rear of the café. "Through the kitchen. Gents too."

"Order me something, Leonard. Something light." Rising, Marguerite made her way along the aisle and entered the kitchen. Very nearly at once, she returned, saying, "Forget it. We're leaving," and she hurried from the café.

Joining her in the street, Leonard said, "What happened back there?"

"The toilet was open."

"So? How else could you get in?"

"I mean it was open to the kitchen—and it had no door!"

☙

Later, when Leonard turned toward her in bed, she said, "I wish you wouldn't."

"The café?"

"That too."

1925

CROSSING MONARCH PASS

In the morning, Marguerite balked at eating anywhere in Salida, and along the way to Gunnison, they halted to breakfast on milk and soda crackers bought at a grocery store. It was a fine day, and standing beside the car as they took turns at the bottle, they deep-breathed the mint air, at seven thousand feet a chill infusion. Ahead lay the jagged line of the Continental divide, looking from there like slates stacked on edge against the sky.

"If I lived in Salida," Marguerite said, "I'd starve to death."

"My people had more advantages than yours," Leonard said, "but I suspect that yours are more choicy."

"We had to be. Things are different when all you have is pride: you take care not to lose it. I'd get plenty dirty when I was a kid, but I never saw the day when I could sit down dirty to eat. Mama would've filled the air with sparks."

"In the South, you get used to dirt."

"Used to it?"

"You don't see it."

"How can you not see dirt?"

"It's always somewhere. You just don't look for it."

The sun was well up by the time they moved off. Snow still frosted some of the peaks of the Divide, and struck by the light, it blazed like glass. Where the foothills ended and the real grade began, the climb was made by switchbacks in the road, a gravel serpentine through stands of spruce and pine. At the crest, Leonard brought the car to a stop near a block of granite that held a metal marker, and he and Marguerite descended to read its legend. *Summit of Monarch Pass,* they were informed, *alt. 11,386 ft.*

"Two miles above sea level," Leonard said. "More than two miles."

The view was four-way and long. Close to the top of the visible world, they could see the great uprising of the Rockies, a vast still photo as of waters in a storm. Range beyond range could be descried, each a further wave paler than the one before it and the furthest a blur in the distance.

Marguerite gazed about at her near and far surroundings, and when she spoke, it was as much to herself as to Leonard. "When it rains here," she said, "some of it runs off to the Atlantic and some to the Pacific."

"What's so wonderful about that?" Leonard said. "It all comes together in the end."

Her wonderment flattened, she said, "Where do we make the next stop?"

"Gunnison. It's small, smaller than Salida, but from what I've heard, it's promising."

"Heard from whom?"

"Baxter."

Gunnison was one mile down and forty miles away.

1925

GUNNISON

Arriving in the little town at noon, Leonard made his way along the main street until he reached an old hotel that proclaimed itself to be the *La Veta*.

"How does it look to you?" Leonard said.
"Run-down and whiffy," Marguerite said. "A four-story *Monte Cristo*."
"Baxter was here once. He said not to be put off by the outside."
"I set no store by Baxter. Being a Southerner, he doesn't see dirt."
"Maybe there's none to see. But I don't insist. Say so, and we'll hunt around for better."
"I was just being shirty," Marguerite said. "Let's give *La Veta* a try."

The room assigned to them was surprisingly large, with figured carpeting and stolid pieces of Victorian furniture. Almost ceiling-high, the headboard of the bed was machine-carved, a florid and massive match for the dresser and the wash-stand. But so orderly was it all, so gleaming and unsoiled, that it seemed never to have been used—and to Marguerite's delight, it came with a private bath.

"Gracious life," she said, "what do they charge for all this?"
"Three dollars a night."
"You're joking. It must be more."
"It isn't, but after the *Monte Cristo*, I'd've paid whatever they asked."
Eyeing the tub, Marguerite said, "Leonard, you'll never guess what I'm about to do."
"And while you're doing it, I'll be out for a look at the town."

Once he'd gone, she drew a bath, and submerging herself to the throat, she felt the sensation of well-being, but she knew that the feeling did not extend to her mind. Would it, she wondered, if she went under head and all—would euphoria then pervade thought, would it tint the colorless and generate joy? To ask was to answer: it would not.
Unaware that she was seeing, she saw the contents of the room, the washbasin, the toilet bowl, the flush-tank on the wall, the two-bulb

chandelier. She dwelt instead on the intangible contents of perception, and what she found there took the edge off her physical pleasure. Before her, on into the far ranges of fancy, lay a future with Leonard, a planetary round repeated until somewhere in the dull distance, death brought it to a halt. Dull, she thought, and it surprised her to learn that the monosyllable contained all that she sensed of the times to come. It was as though they were already in the past, a confusion of sights and sounds and flavors, of places and motion, of grass and streams and trees, of faces seen through glass—a vast accumulation of wasted days. But the worst of it, she thought, was that each was like the last, and that all had been spent with Leonard.

He was there for every start and stop and for the spaces in between, he was beside her on wheels and afoot and for fifty thousand meals, he was with her in all weathers, all moods, all ages, his the countenance she gazed upon, his the voice she ever heard, his the company she kept to the empty end. In that little car of his, they rolled across the earth from here to there and whatever lay beyond, and when the black dress went, its counterpart appeared, and so it was with all places and all things, until the Colorado looked like the Gunnison, and the Rio Grande looked like both. She knew all of it in advance, as though it had already come to pass—Leonard, she thought, Leonard had been there for every rise and fall, every bend in the road. Why, then, she wondered, did she still feel so much alone...?

He returned to their room just as she was stepping from the bath, and he spoke even before he could see her, saying, "Gunnison's a fine little town. This time, you'll be in a drug-store window...," and then, still burdened with words, he was at the door.

He took no notice of the way she tried to hide by shrinking; he saw enough to fill his eye. She was small-scale, scarcely five feet tall, and her figure was so well-turned that it might've been made by hand rather than the accidental action of the years: it was a harmony of hollows and rounds, and, wet and glistening, they were most of them exposed. He did not think her pretty, though. He'd've called her personable, perhaps, or, in a lavish moment, pleasing, but such descriptives were merely masks for the real one, and the real one was *plain*. If indeed she was so, it was much softened by a quality that came from within. Unable to name the quality, he was not aware of its effect: it happened to be fineness, but he hardly knew it was there.

But he did know that her body was very beautiful, and it drew him as on that day along the Poudre. Though he had quite forgotten the rape, she had not, and yet she did not refuse him when he led her, not yet dry, to the bed. Thereafter, she beguiled herself for a while with the notion that she was a spectator as well as a participant, an impersonal witness to an unrelated event, but even as a participant, she was detached in mind, so much so that she was able to observe to herself that no love suffused the act she was performing: none had gone before it, and none would follow.

They made a two-day stay of it in Gunnison, and four showings in the drug-store window resulted in the sale of eighty-some strings of glass beads filled with *essence d'orient*. A most gratifying accomplishment, Leonard called it (*We decked that town in pearls!*), and on the way to Montrose, he declared a holiday in order that they might take in the wonders of the Black Canyon of the Gunnison.

William Jennings Bryan, 1925

THE COLOR OF THE AIR

Species, a New Origin of

Brother, thy tail hangs down behind.
—Rudyard Kipling

Bryan didn't believe that, not for a tom-fool minute, and damn few did where he hailed from, which was along the river Platte. For all such, the Book was the first and final say, and they added no word to it, nor took they a word away. Their truth began in 4004 B.C., and it ended with the Revelation in 96 A.D. There alone did it repose, in those four millennia.

You took the Book, as it stood, said the Commoner, took it bejeweled with the wonders of God—the stars, the sun, the earth, and man, most wonderful of all. You took it whole, because the whole of it was true: the rod did become a snake and then again a rod, and God did move a shadow backward by ten degrees, and Jesus did cure blindness and disease, turn water into wine, and walk upon the seas—and, aye, He did rise up living from the dead.

There came one, a teacher in Tennessee, who taught that God had not so wrought, that man had not been made on the Sixth Day, nor, indeed, on any day, that he had (what term had been used by the blasphemer?) *evolved*, that he was but a higher form of animal life derived from a lower.

A profane assault upon the Book, and the offender was made to stand his trial under the law. With Bryan speaking for the prosecution, there ensued ten days of hullabaloo in the Tennessee heat, and at the end, praise the Lord, a verdict was found in favor of the Book. Fatigued by his labors, Bryan lay down for an hour's rest, but unlike Jesus, he did not rise again and live.

1925

MONTROSE, alt. 5,820 ft.

High though it was, the town lay in a basin far lower than the snowy crest of the Uncompahgre Range, off which ran the many creeks that watered the orchards in the valley below, creeks with such bell-tone names as Roubideau and Kelso, with the tambourine jingle of Little Dominguez. The better of the town's two hotels was the *Belvidere* (rms. $2½), and Leonard chose it over the one near the depot of the D. & R. G.

Finding that no late-hour establishment would be open save the motion-picture theatre, he arranged for the use of its outer lobby. At the afternoon screening, the audience in the main was youthful, and though numbers stopped to stare, no one bought a strand of pearls. At supper, Marguerite proposed that they cancel their plans for the later screening and move on in the morning, but Leonard was disinclined, feeling that their luck would improve with an older audience. It did.

As they left the theatre that evening and walked back toward the *Belvidere,* Leonard said, "Over and above expenses, we made more than fifty dollars tonight."

At the corner of a cross-street, a stranger fell in with them, saying, "Lady, I seen you at the show, and I wonder would you take a drink with me."

"The lady is my wife," Leonard said.

"That don't stop her taking a drink."

"Look," Marguerite said, "My husband and I are tired, and we really don't want a drink."

"Tired, a drink would do you good."

"It wouldn't do *you* any good," Leonard said. "You've had enough already."

"You saying I'm drunk, mister?"

"I'm saying it too," Marguerite said. "Why don't you go home and tell your Mama she wants you?"

"Account of I just been insulted."

"It'll only get worse. If you don't leave us alone, you'll rue the day."

"What's that mean—rue the day?"

"It means you'll be sorry you were born."

As though weighing the danger, the man was silent for a few paces, and then abruptly he turned and walked away.

"I'll be jiggered," Leonard said. "You scared him off."

"I don't think so. Another whim-wham hit him, and he forgot us. Anyway, he didn't mean us any harm."

"I'm not so sure."

"I've seen more drunks than you have."

"You don't scare so easy, do you?"

And she said, "Were you scared?"

1925

IN THE BELVIDERE COFFEE-SHOP

Moving their breakfast dishes aside, Leonard spread a road-map of Colorado across the table, and using a pencil as a pointer, he said, "We're here, in Montrose, and there are three ways out—north, south, and back east to Gunnison."

"What's up north?" Marguerite said.

"Grand Junction. A very good town."

"And south?"

Leonard moved the pencil toward the bottom portion of the map, through the dots signifying Ouray and Silverton and the brackets of Red Mountain Pass. "Durango," he said.

"Durango—that's where the cliff dwellings are!"

"A little beyond, at Mesa Verde. But what's so wonderful about a pueblo?"

"Seems a better way to live than out in the weather under a tent."

"I never knew you cared spit about the Indians."

"I'd care for anybody that bad off. It happens I'm part-Cree through my Daddy. Near where I was born, Clarks, there was a Pawnee village, and sometimes in winter, he'd bring a few home to unfreeze by the fire. They stunk, Mama said, but she put up with it because Daddy loved them."

"There's nothing for us down by Durango. Once we see that Indian stuff, we'll only have to backtrack to Montrose."

"I sure hone to see the Indian stuff."

"If you like," he said.

From the roadway through Mesa Verde, they looked out across a canyon floor of scrub oak and piñon at the face of a cliff. Under its cornice, sheltered from rain, snow, and enemy, stood the remains of the mansions built by the Pueblo Indians. At a distance, they looked like a toppled construction of alphabet blocks, but on climbing to their level, Marguerite no longer regarded them as child's play: here once a long-dead people had lived. Here, a thousand years before her day, a tribe had come and gone, and though but thinly related, she responded to them as to lineal kinsmen. She could not imagine their ways of life, their forms and faces, or the sound of their speech, but some remnant of racial blood told her how the Pawnees had been made to feel by her father: welcome. It was as if she too had been offered a place at the fire.

On the road back to Durango, Leonard said, "Those people believed in hell."

"What makes you think so?"

"Those holes in the floor of the *kivas*—the guide said they were sup-posed to lead to the underworld."

"There's a difference between hell and underworld."

"I don't see any."

"Hell is for punishment. The underworld is where the spirits live."

"Where's the difference?"

At Durango, they put at the *Strater House* (rms. from $2½), and in the evening, they sold pearls at the depot alongside the toy cars of the Narrow Gauge Railroad.

1925

DEAR MIDGIE, she wrote

We've been on the go ever since leaving Greeley, what with finding likely places to sell pearls, also a bit of sightseeing, and this is the first chance I've had to say how we're making out.

Not being much for showing off, I figured I'd have a hard time getting used to modeling. I didn't. After once or twice, I kind of got so I forgot I was being stared at by strangers. It was more like nobody was there except me, and I was modeling the pearls for myself.

Leonard says we're doing better than he expected. All I know is, we stay at the best hotels, and we eat at the best restaurants, and, like I said, we even take days off to see the sights, so I guess Leonard isn't exaggerating.

But I guess what you really want to hear is how things are between him and me. As you know, he's the quiet sort, which is all to the good on account of my tongue isn't slung in the middle, either. But when we do talk, we don't always seem to be talking about the same thing. We have such different slants it's like we're seeing different things.

As to other departments, he's polite and respectful, he doesn't grudge me anything, and his table manners are good (ha ha!), and I guess I'd have to say we get along. Two people being married, of course there's another department, you know the one I mean-- and there it's all right too. Only I feel it ought to be more than just all right, and maybe it would be if there was more in the rest of the day. How can you find love in the dark if you can't find it in the light?

Just tell Mama and Daddy I think they're the best in the world...

1925

A SHORT TALK ON THE ROAD

After spending several hours amid the ruins of another age, they returned to Durango for the night, and in the morning, they set out for Grand Junction, a run of nearly two hundred miles. Is this what they said along the way?

"Why ever did you marry me, Leonard?"
"After what I did, it was the right thing."
"That's all—just to do the right thing?"
"I had to make it up to you."
"Right wiped out wrong—is that what you thought?"
"There was more. I'd gotten to be very fond of you."
"That's kind of a limpsy word. I don't even use it for eggs. I say, I *love* eggs."
"I know, but you don't love me."

From a height in the road, she gazed down at the banks of the Animas and the tracks of the Narrow Gauge as they curved with the stream.

"I never misled you about that, Leonard. Before and after, it was all the same."
"I wish I knew why we're only neighbors. Won't we ever get to be husband and wife?"
"You should've let well enough alone. You shouldn't've married me."
"Do you think we'll stay married?"
"For a while."

"Till when?"

"Till one of us gets tired of being a neighbor and decides to move away."

"Which of us will it be?"

"I think it'll be me, Leonard."

1925

GRAND JUNCTION, alt. 4,587 ft.

Even the approaches to the town told them of its importance, and they said nothing as they took note of the packing plants they passed, the stockyards, the sugar refinery, and the repair shops of the Denver & Rio Grande. When at length Leonard spoke, though, it was of none of these things, nor even, it seemed, of any other thing: his words were a question, and for a moment they hung uncomprehended in the air.

What he said was, "None at all?"

The phrase insisted, repeating itself in Marguerite's mind until it was assigned to its proper place and understood: spanning space, it resumed a conversation that she thought had ended earlier in the day. *None at all?*, he said.

> "I can't honestly say there's *none*," she said. "I'm not a stick or a stone, you know. I have feelings."
>
> "What *would* you say?"
>
> "I'd say there's *some*. After all, we're married, and we do...well, the things that married people do. That has to amount to *some*thing. We're not just strangers in a crowd."
>
> "Sometimes I think we are."

They were on the main street of Grand Junction and heading for a likely hotel, and what she saw along the way were facing rows of modern store-fronts and their merchandise display. Her thoughts were elsewhere, though, and what caught her eye were images only, pictures without captions. She was thinking of the excursion she'd begun, and she knew, despite what she'd said, that it was being made with a stranger.

True, she was his wife, but somehow the tie did not bind her; she was still unattached in her mind.

Earlier, she'd said that he ought not to have married her, but had she not meant the reverse, that *she* ought not to have married *him*? He wanted more of her than he was able to awaken, he wanted her to feel for him what he'd failed to inspire, and she wondered at his belief, his hope, that love came into being on demand. *None at all?*, he'd said, and she'd said *Some*, but she knew it would never flourish in the sand.

The hotel, they found, was the *St. Regis* ($2½-3).

"There's money in this town," Leonard said. "We're going to sell pearls here, lots of pearls."

"First off, though, I buy me another dress."

1925

CONVERSATIONS WITH STRANGERS

In the morning, Leonard left the hotel early to seek a suitable stage for exhibiting the pearls. Thinking the search would be a long one, Marguerite was surprised by his return in less than an hour.

"I got us the *ideal* spot?" he said.

"And where's that?"

"A window in one of the best shops in Grand Junction!"

"What do they sell?"

"Women's wear—nothing but women's wear!"

"That *is* a good spot."

"Here's the other beauty of it: we won't need handbills. Most of the shops in town stay open on Friday evening, and this happens to be Friday. People come in from all around."

"This shop—what's it called?"

"Denver West."

"I wonder if they'd have the dress I need."

"They're expecting you. Ask for a saleslady named Hilda."

Pleased, Marguerite said, "Thoughtful of you, Leonard."

The Denver West, close by the hotel, proved to be much what its name implied—that it was the Big City in the Small Town. Well-appointed and seemingly well-stocked, it held more than a few patrons even at mid-morning. Directed to the saleslady Hilda, Marguerite presented herself.

"Your husband said to be on the lookout for a little woman with a trim figger. He forgot to say you were pretty."

"I'm glad he did, because I'm not."

"I put some dresses aside for you. One of them just might suit."

"Did my husband say what I want it for?"

"He did," Hilda said. "Come along to a dressing room, and I'll show you what I picked out. Remember, though, we've got lots more."

By the time the woman returned with an armload of her selections, Marguerite had taken off her blouse and skirt, and she was standing many ways mirrored in her brassière and petticoat.

While hanging the garments on a rack, Hilda said, "A great idea you folks hit on. Touring the country and getting paid for it, you might say. I wish I could do likewise. My husband would never quit his job, though, and between you and I, I just don't have your figger."

"There's nothing special about it," Marguerite said, and she smiled. "That's what the dress is for—to hide the weak spots."

Pausing, the saleslady said, "Ma'am, you just don't have any."

While being helped into the first of the try-ons, Marguerite said, "My name's Roberts."

"Mine's Nielsen. It's a treat to wait on you, Mrs. Roberts."

"Marguerite."

"Marguerite, then."

By the time the next of Hilda's reserves had been brought to Marguerite, the two might well have been meeting as friends rather than as buyer and seller. Each had found the other open and unaffected; both had sensed a similarity of origin.

"I'll tell you one thing," Hilda said. "I don't guess you're from around here."

"I was born in Nebraska. Town of Clarks, population 500."

"I knew it, the way you pronounce every 'r'. Me, I'm from Salida."

"I've been there, and I left in a hurry. But this looks to me like a crackajack town."

"Some ways, yes; some ways, no."

"How do you mean?"

"Well, we got our rich here, and we got my kind."

"Where is it any different?"

"I wish I knew. I'd go there."

"Me too."

"You got money in Grand Junction, you're in clover. You work for a living, you better keep your face shut."

"Aren't you taking a chance with me?"

Hilda shook her head. "In my line, you get to know people. If they were all like you, I'd want to stay here till I die....I think this is the one you're looking for."

"I like it," Marguerite said. "It isn't too busy, and the neckline's right. I'll take it, Hilda—after my husband pays for it, of course. He'll do that this afternoon. Will you be here?"

"They couldn't drive me away. I want to see the show."

"I only stand there, twiddling the pearls."

"That's all?"

Marguerite laughed. "Oh, once in a while, I twiddle myself."

"That feller of yours, I wonder does he know how lucky he is."

"Well," Leonard said, "did you find yourself a dress?"

"Yes, I did. No work on it was needed, and we can pick it up this afternoon. That woman you sent me to, Hilda. I liked her."

"What's there to like about a saleslady?"

"Nothing much, I guess. After all, that's what *I* am."

They remained in Grand Junction until the middle of the following week. After the Friday opening, they held afternoon sessions only, but even so they fared far better than they ever had before: at each of four showings, they sold some fifty strings of pearls.

"Nearly two hundred and fifty strings!" Leonard said. "I swear, every woman in town bought them."

"Not every," Marguerite said. "On the way out of town, I want to say goodbye to Hilda."

"You take on the oddest people."

"That's the truth, Leonard," she said.

"I couldn't leave without seeing you, Hilda. I enjoyed our talks in the shop and over lunch. I'll miss them—and I'll miss you."

"I'll never forget you."

"This is for you," Marguerite said, and she handed Hilda a small flat box. "It isn't much of a present, but I want you to have a string of pearls."

"Chances are we won't meet again," Hilda said, "but this is what I wish—that you have a good life...."

1925

THE THIRD PASSENGER

Eastward of Grand Junction, the Colorado was a slow flow through mile after mile of peach orchard, and in a riverside grove of willows and cottonwoods, Leonard stopped the car to unfold a road map.

Tracing a route across it, his finger traversed a maze of lines and dots, a profusion of names and numbers, and he said, "There won't be much for us from here on—Rifle, maybe, and Glenwood Springs. After that, we'll be in all this green stuff, a million miles of mountains."

"Colorado's a peculiar state," Marguerite said. "You only realize it when you're looking at a map. It's *two* states, really, separated by the Rockies. In Europe, it'd be two *countries*, like Sweden and Norway....I think *she* was Scandinavian."

"Who was?"

"The woman in the shop. Hilda."

"Forget Hilda."

But Hilda wasn't easy to forget, nor did Marguerite try. In their several conversations, more than once had the woman made mention of her husband, and though never did she phrase her disillusion, it sombered her tone, and yet she spoke without words of hopes relinquished and unattainable fancies. In the woman's mood, Marguerite wondered, did she sense her own a dozen years hence?

"When we get back to Greeley," Leonard said, "I'll order another batch of pearls."

"Forget her? Why should I forget her?"

"Hilda again?"

"I liked her," Marguerite said. "I felt sorry for her."

"Why?"

"I just did."

1925

A MILE-HIGH DIALOGUE

Rifle, a town of a thousand, seemed to be a mere supply depot for the cattle ranches roundabout, and believing that it promised little, Leonard hardly paused as he passed through its single street. Beyond the outskirts, the range began, an expanse much of which was cactus and sage.

Marguerite was examining the map now, and she said, "The name of the next town is Silt."

"Ought to be the name of the county. Look at that desert out there."

"Back in Greeley, you'd've thought it a good place for shooting."

"The place for shooting was Rifle," he said, and hearing no laugh, he said, "I made a joke."

"You make a lot of jokes. I have no kick about *that*."

"What *do* you have a kick about?"

"We don't say anything to each other."

"Seems like we're doing that right now."

"We aren't. This is only talk about why we don't talk."

"What's there to talk about?"

She glanced at him before speaking. "Are you serious?"

"People talk too much."

"You mean, people *jaw* too much. Talk's different." Her gaze went past him to a mesa miles away and a mile higher than the road. "If we have so little to say now, how will it be in a year, in five years, in ten?"

"Talk isn't the answer to everything."

"Maybe not, but it's the answer to why we say more to waitresses than we do to each other."

"All right, what do you want to talk about?"

"You and me."

"Us?" he said. "There's a subject we can cover in no time: we're husband and wife."

"And that explains all?"

"We're together, day in and day out."

"Why do I feel so lonely, then?"

"That's unkind, Marguerite."

"I didn't mean it to be. It was a way of saying there's got to be more to marriage than eating together, sleeping together, walking side-by-side down the street."

"More? *What* more?"

"Something in common," she said. "Sometimes I sort of stand outside myself, and I watch us, listen to us, and it isn't like we were married at all. There's a space between us."

"Not at certain times, there isn't."

"Even then, because the 'more' I'm talking about is love, and you never use the word."

Holding the wheel fixed, as if he were aiming the car at an object, he said, "And if I did use it, what would you feel?"

Nothing, she thought, and she said, "Silt. Why do they call it Silt?"

1925

GLENWOOD SPRINGS, alt. 5,756 ft.

Some distance in advance of the town, a series of billboards began to proclaim the virtues of its waters. They were both thermal and mineral, the traveler was told, and with temperatures ranging between 120-140° Fahr., they were extolled as well-nigh sovereign in the treatment of rheumatism, gout, and diseases of the blood. Here and there among these, other signs advised of the lodgings afforded by the town.

"I didn't know the place was a resort," Leonard said. "We ought to do well here."

"Selling pearls to invalids?" Marguerite said, and then she read from one of the signs: "*Kendrick's Cottages, 75 cents per night.*"

"Invalids make the best customers."

"Why so?"

"They feel better when they put on the dog."

"They can do that at home. Why come here?"

"For the baths, the minerals. The minerals are in the water, and they soak in through the skin."

"*Hotel Glenwood, $2¹/₂-3¹/₂,*" Marguerite read. "Do you really believe that?"

"Sure I do."

"But if something can get in that way, whatever's in can get out."

"*The Colorado, $4-5,*" Leonard read. "Why didn't I think of that?"

"You went to Creighton. I worked at Woolworth's."

Pine forest and rimrock had given way to fencing, to workshops, to a lumberyard and a fire company, and finally to the business blocks of the town.

"You don't get fooled much, do you?" Leonard said.

"Some, but never by myself."

"You're what's called a realist."

"I got that way when my Mama took in washing."

They were at the main corner now. Clustered there were the town's best shops, among them two that dealt in hunting and fishing gear.

"It's more than a health resort," Leonard said. "It's a jump-off point for sportsmen."

Marguerite laughed. "They need more than a rod and a rifle out there. They need a rope of pearls."

"I think *Kendrick's Cottages* are up that street. You want to give them a look?"

"75¢ a night is a little too real even for me."

"That leaves the *Glenwood* and the *Colorado.*"

"Make it the *Colorado*. I feel wasteful."

155

Neither sportsman nor invalid came, and no pearls were sold in Glenwood Springs, not a single string.

1925

LEADVILLE, alt. 10,152 ft.

The town was animate, but among its three thousand living walked the ghosts of other days. There were no gunfights now, no whores bared their wares in windows, nor did the doors of ninety-six saloons spill tinkle-tankle tunes into the streets. The tarts were in the grave, and the crap-shooters had left for distant parts, along with the thimbleriggers, the grubstakers, and the actual diggers of the yellow dust. Leadville was dead—and yet alive.

Its latter-day drunks were tourists in shorts and sneakers and flow-ered shirts, and tanked on Moxie and orangeade, they posed beside relic bars and cribs, the sites of sudden death, the stopped-up mouths of played-out mines. They were many, those prospectors of a newer time, and, oddly, they brought gold along and left the earth as they found it. Some of that gold they spent on pearls, which, on being taken home to Wichita and Baton Rouge, became gems of the first water, free from flaw, translucent, and of muted iridescence—who can say what tales were told in San Antone and Syracuse...?

They were in the breakfast-room of the *Vendome* one morning when Leonard said, "We've been here a week, but even so I hate to leave."

"Are we leaving?" Marguerite said.

"We've got to. We're down to our last carton of pearls."

"I had no idea we were doing that well."

"Nowhere better. Other places, it was the people that played out. Here, new ones come every day. If we had enough pearls, we could stay in Leadville forever."

"Get some more, then."

"I can't. I've been sending most of our money back to Greeley. To order more pearls, that's where we have to go."

"Maybe we can come here again. I like the place."

"Except for the tourists, what's to like about an old mining-camp?"

"The *old* part."

"That's just what I *don't* like."

"This hotel. In a folder I got at the desk, I read that it was built fifty years ago."

"You wouldn't've wanted to stay here then. You'd've had to go out in the cold to pee."

"I feel sorry for old things. For old people. old animals."

"You do?" he said. "Why?"

1925

NOW AND THEN

For the return to Greeley, Leonard chose a route out of Leadville that ran down the valley of the Arkansas to Buena Vista before bearing eastward toward Colorado Springs. Much of the roundabout way lay through long-abandoned diggings past rusted hoists, sealed shafts, and towns of caved-in houses, many of these still brave with a lace of weathered fretwork.

"There's one with windowpanes and no roof," Marguerite said.

"Old things," Leonard said. "You say you like old things."

"Wild days, those must've been."

"You think you missed something?"

"We always miss something."

"We miss less now than we did in 1880."

"It was *now* in 1880. It's always *now*."

"We're getting in deep."

"What's deep about it? All I'm saying is, every time in the world had a *now*. I happen to like the one they had around here in 1880. What about you?"

"I like the one in 1860."

"Why?"

"That's when Carolina seceded."

It was miles later before Marguerite said, "You never forget that, do you?"

And he said, "I can't."

❦

157

Beyond Wilkerson Pass, they reached a small group of buildings named Florissant. Amid these at a fork in the road, a sign read: *Petrified Forest: 2.5 mi.*

"Talk about old things," Leonard said.

"Sometimes I think you're one of them."

&

Once they'd passed Divide, the summit of Pikes Peak could be seen.

"I've never been up there," Marguerite said.

"You won't be able to say that tomorrow."

1925

THE MANITOU & PIKES PEAK RAILWAY

More familiarly known as the Cog Road, the line from Manitou Springs travels a distance of nearly nine miles in its rise of 7,500 feet to the summit. The ascent is made at an average rate of some 850 feet per mile, the steepest gradient being 1 foot in 4....

–passenger brochure

The pusher locomotive was low in front and high behind, looking rather like a kneeling elephant, its rounds somehow ground down to planes and angles. The single car was underslung, a thing of windows with slender frames that scarcely marred the panorama. Arriving early at the starting-point, Leonard and Marguerite were able to secure two of the four front seats, and with nothing before them but the rails and the rack for the cog-wheels of the engine, they knew some of the feeling of being the train's engineer.

"That folder," Leonard said. "How high does it say we go?"

"14,110 feet."

"Close to three miles. That's higher than I've ever been."

"I didn't know that."

"I'll manage."

"How high have you gone?"

"Nothing much in Carolina; it's sea-level, mostly. Out here, maybe nine-ten thousand, but only for a few minutes going through a pass."

"Some people can handle altitude; others can't. Don't be so sure you can manage."

"Stop worrying."

"Up ahead, there's a place called Halfway. We could get off and catch the down-train."

"Forget it. I'm doing fine."

And because he was expending no energy, fine he did for upwards of an hour. But at the summit, when he rose to leave the car, he found that in the rarefied air, he was light in the head and overweighted in the leg, and he could barely perform the suddenly singular feat of walking. Even speech was now too much for his powers, and it came from him as if freighted with sleep.

"Legs feel like full with sand." he managed to say, and leaning heavily on Marguerite, he made his way to the Inn.

She seated him at a table, brought him a few postcards and a pencil, and went outside to climb the steps of the observation tower, a steel skeleton resembling a power-line support. At the time, she was alone on the platform several stories above the roof of the Inn, and she let her gaze wander away into the mist of distance. Eastward, beyond the blur of Colorado Springs, lay the long slow fall of the Piedmont and the plains; everywhere else were the spellbound stock-still mountains. A posted chart showed that one of the heights far to the south was Blanca Peak, and Marguerite thought herself back to a burro named Croppy, a tar-paper shack, and the far-gone year of 1910. What more did she think of seventy-five feet above the man whose ring she wore? Looking at the band, the bond, did she wonder how long it would be before she cast it off and became unbound? Where would that happen, and would she be able to explain the disjunction when she couldn't explain the union?

She found him almost as she'd left him, pale, short of breath, and staring at vacancy. The only change she noted was the effort he'd made to address a postcard; he'd scrawled part of an illegible name when the pencil escaped his grasp. With the help of a fellow-passenger, she put him aboard the train, and not until they reached the timberline did he begin to recover.

They were at Halfway before he was able to speak. "I thought I was going to die," he said.

"You could have, Leonard, and I feel terrible about it. I should've thought about altitude sickness. It *is* a sickness."

"I'll know better next time.... There won't *be* a next time."

1925

HOMEWARD BOUND

They spent the night at a guest-cottage near Colorado Springs, and the following day saw them on their way north toward Greeley.

"As soon as we get there," Leonard said, "I'll put in an order for another shipment of pearls."

"How long before they arrive?"

"Four weeks, usually. Six, outside."

"And till then, where will we stay?"

"With my family. Where else?"

Silent for an interval—a mile, was it, or more than a mile?—Marguerite said, "I've never even sat at their table."

"You were asked."

"Not as their daughter-in-law. Only as your wife."

"That's simply what you felt."

"It's what they *made* me feel, taking so long to invite me. I will not go where I'm not wanted."

"If it comes to that, I've never sat at the Smith table. Where does that leave us?"

"It leaves me at home."

"My notion is, your home is with me. Unless you're only at home with your people."

"Where else would I be—with yours?"

"You don't know them. It isn't their way to be discourteous."

"Courtesy!" she said. "You're talking about manners; I'm talking about warmth. They have none for me, not even as your wife. I don't mind—that's their lookout. But I'm not the kind to take condescension—is that the right word, college-boy?—from anybody, least of all from brother Baxter."

"We should've spoken of this before."

"Yes—before we got married."

The interval now was made by Leonard. "What does that mean, Marguerite?"

"We should've taken our differences into account. If we had, we wouldn't be in this fix."

"You call marriage a fix?"

"What do you call it?"

"Anything but a fix. These differences you talk about—they weren't worth a mention."

"That's just stuff, Leonard, and you know it. We're so different, we don't belong on the same planet. You'll never get used to my notion that people are pretty much alike, and I'll never get used to yours, that you're better than everyone you meet."

"I don't feel superior to you."

"So you once said, but either it wore off, or you didn't mean it."

"As to you, I *did* mean it. As to others, let them look out for themselves. What're you—the Great Leveler?"

She let the question float, and finally it floated away. "I will not live with your family," she said.

"How about me renting a flat? Just till the pearls arrive."

"I want to be with my own people."

"*I'm* supposed to be your people."

She did not say *Come with me, then*. She said, "It won't hurt us to be apart for a while."

"I guess not. But will it do us any good?"

She did not say *Nothing will*. She said, "The sooner you get the pearls...."

QUESTIONS AND ANSWERS

One day soon after her return to Greeley, Marguerite took the stage to Kersey in order to visit her sister Connie, the mother now of five. At the hour of her arrival, the younger among these were napping in an upstairs room, and the elder were still at school.

Over coffee-cups at the kitchen table, Marguerite said, "I have to say it, Con, but you look wore to a nubbin."

"Don't I know it?" Connie said. "I'm thirty years old, but what I see in the glass is fifty. Five kids in a row will do that."

"I hope to God you don't make it six."

"Never fear. I'm past caring what the priest says."

"How about Tom?"

"What he don't know won't hurt him....How about you, baby sister? What's doing with you?"

"Not a thing."

"You making sure?"

"No, but nothing happens anyway."

"That might change one of these days, and then where'll you be?"

"Remember that mare of Dan's—Laura K.? He bred her and bred her, but he never could get her in foal."

"At least, he took her out of the barn. You, you're staying at home."

"Oh, when he takes a notion, we manage."

"Where?"

"In his car."

"You ask me, that's a hell of a marriage you got."

Marguerite said nothing.

"How does he treat you?"

"We get along."

"That's not saying much."

"There isn't much to say."

"That's saying a *lot*."

"You met him. You had a chance to size him up."

"So did you, but you went and married him."

"After all, he's not exactly a ridge-runner. He's a college man."

"You defending him now?"

Marguerite laughed. "Well, he needs defending."

"If you had it to do over, would you do it again?"

"Turn it around. Would *you*?"

"Yes," Connie said. "Account of, kids and all, I love Tom. But, baby sister, I never heard about you loving Leonard."

Marguerite said nothing.

"You don't, do you?"

"I'm not blazing, if that's what you mean."

"You're not even lit—and you never will be as long as he's in one house, and you're in another."

"I can't dump him and his ways on Mama and Daddy. And I sure God won't let myself in for any snot from Baxter."

"I guess that only leaves Leonard's sedan," Connie said. "Lucky thing you're little. Your feet won't stick out."

Marguerite had risen and gone to a window, where she stood looking out at a tree, a lawnmower, a one-car garage, a cat curled in the sunlight—objects that merely registered on her sight, producing no thought beyond identification.

"We'll be getting more pearls soon," she said, "and off we'll go on another tour."

"Yes, and back you'll come to where you are now. What then?"

"More pearls, I guess, and still another tour."

"My God, Marg! What're you in for?"

She was still gazing at the yard when she spoke. "I got friendly with a saleslady in Grand Junction. When I was leaving, she said, `I wish you a good life....'"

SUPPER AT HOME

When the meal was over, Marguerite reached into the pocket of her blouse and drew forth a check, which she offered to her father.

"Money?" he said. "Money goes to your Mama. She has the say around here."

The check was handed to Decky, who said, "You don't have to pay your way in this house, child. And sure not a hundred dollars."

"If I'd've knowed it was a hundred, I'd've kep it," Henry Albert said.

"Get something nice for the house," Marguerite said. "Or for you and Daddy. Or for Dan-boy."

"You're a good one, Marg." her mother said.

"No better than your other kids. We all think you two are the best Mama and Daddy in the world."

"*I'm* the best, I'll allow," Henry Albert said. "I ain't so sure about your Mama."

As always, Decky's laugh was ventricular and silent, its only sign being a heaving belly. "Hush up, you old addlewit, and let's hear about Marg's travels."

"Nothing much to report, Mama. I saw a slew of Colorado, is all."

"Did you get to see Blanca?"

"To tell the truth, I didn't want to. Times were bad when we lived there, and I didn't care to bring it all back."

"Pshaw! When've times been good?"

"We always had a roof," Henry Albert said, "and ain't none of us ever been hungry. That ain't particalar bad."

"I was talking cash-money times, but I wasn't complaining, and I don't know why I spoke so."

"Maybe it's account of Marg being here and Leonard some place else."

"Henry," his wife said, "it ain't every day you outthink me."

"Ma'am, it ain't every day you admit it."

"We don't ask questions, Marg," her mother said. "We don't run nobody's marriage for them."

"I'll tell you anything you want to know."

"Not enough to ask after. But I'll tell *you* something: you always got a home here and a welcome." She fluttered the check, saying, "And you don't need these to get in."

"I wonder what's going on over at Leonard's."

"Same as here, I guess," Henry Albert said.

"Oh, no," Marguerite said. "If it was the same as here, I'd be *there*."

1925

THE MOTHER WIT OF SISTER PEARL

"He came to the house this morning," Marguerite said. "With an invitation to have supper with his family."

"Go," Pearl said.

"I'd sooner not."

"Go, I tell you."

"Leonard and I have known each other it must be all of two years, and all of a sudden, his people invite me to their house. Why now?"

"Go, and maybe you'll find out."

"Yes, and maybe I'll get a look up their nose."

"I say go. It won't hurt you—and it just might hurt *them*."

"I'm not out to hurt them. But why give them a chance to hurt me?"

"How could they do that?"

"By being snooty."

"Snoot 'em back."

"That's just what I want to avoid—a go-around with them. The way things are, we never meet. That's not the best way, I guess, but it's better than a shindy."

"It'd be of their making, not yours."

"It's pretty plain I'm not wanted in the Roberts family: I'm the daughter of a plasterer. Happens he's the best damn plasterer in the world— and the best damn man—but that cuts no ice with those people, and they can go to hell, for all I care. They're nothing to me."

"Nobody's saying hug 'em and kiss 'em. Just go and set with 'em, and be free and easy, like you belong there—which you do. They might think they're God's gift to Greeley—which they ain't—but you got more in your pinky than their Leonard has in his head. In my opinion, baby sister, *you'd* be honoring *them*, not the other way around."

After a moment, Marguerite said, "All right you old crow, I'll go."

"Don't give offence," Pearl said. "But don't take none, either."

"Thanks for all the good advice."

"Don't mention it."

"And thanks for the rotten supper I'm in for."

"Ain't nothing wrong with chitlins, child," Pearl said, and she laughed.

1925

A SUPPER CALLED DINNER

The Daniels & Fisher dress had been cleaned, and Marguerite wore it, along with the black suede shoes. Circling her throat was a string of gold beads, on loan from her sister Pearl, and these were her sole decoration.

"You look mighty good, Marg," her mother said.

And her father said, "Pretty as a little red pair of shoes."

Marguerite smoothed his hair, saying, "I don't know about the pretty, Daddy."

"You're a pretty girl, and don't ever think you ain't."

"All my girls is pretty," Decky said.

Marguerite laughed. "We'll never take any prizes, Mama."

"Maybe so," her mother said. "But that Leonard of yours, *he* sure got one."

"Me? You think *I'm* a prize?"

"Don't ever think you ain't," her father said.

❦

The Smiths had finished their evening meal by the time Leonard called for her, and in the oncoming darkness, he drove her to his home in a distant part of town. Its all-around verandah embraced a spacious house bright with light from within, and as she mounted the steps, a moth wound up and pitched itself against a screen. She watched it rebound into the night, and then through the door held open for her by Leonard, she entered his home for the first time.

Shown into the living room, she was greeted by his father. "It's good to have you here, Marguerite," he said.

"Thank you, Mr. Roberts," she said.

"Leonard's mother will be down directly. Won't you kindly take a chair?"

Leonard moved to a side-table on which a row of decanters stood, and as he poured from one of these, Marguerite took in his segment of the room, sensing from it that it was not as spacious as it had seemed outside—that, or its furnishings had once graced a more capacious room. The several pieces were fine, she thought, finer than any she'd ever seen, but there were too many for the area, and they appeared to hold themselves clear, as though they resented the nearness of their neighbors.

Leonard was offering a stemmed glass, saying, "Dry Sack."

Accepting it, she said, "I don't know what Dry Sack is."

"Sherry."

"I don't know what that is, either."

"A fortified wine."

"I'm still in the dark, Leonard."

"It's wine strengthened with alcohol. Try it."

She turned the glass a little as if to study its yellow-brown glow in the lamplight, wondering the while why she was pretending ignorance. At Pearl's house, many a time had she taken sherry, both the sweet kind and the dry, and very well did she know the character of the wine. Here she was, though, putting on a show of being simple, her intention being...what? Was she testing the family attitude toward the artless, the uninitiated, and if so, what if they were contemptuous, what if they made no attempt to hide disdain...?

It was then that Mrs. Roberts entered the room, and when Marguerite rose for Leonard's presentation, the woman offered her hand, saying, "My son's descriptive powers are very poor. He gave me no idea of what you were like."

Marguerite smiled and said, "I don't know how to take that, Mrs. Roberts. Was I built up or torn down?"

"He said you were small and shapely, but he made no mention of your charm and your sparkle."

"That would've been laying it on thick, Mrs. Roberts."

Coming in at just that moment was Baxter, who said, "Laying what on thick?"

Leonard said, "Mother thinks my description of Marguerite was inadequate."

They were making too much of it, Marguerite thought, and she said, "He described what he saw, and there wasn't much to see."

In the doorway now stood a maid in a dark dress and a starched apron. "Dinner is served, ma'am," she said.

The Roberts' table was a long one, created to grace a larger space than their present dining room provided. Here too there was a sense of over-crowding, to Marguerite's fancy much like that of furniture in a store. In its descent, the family had been crammed into smaller quarters, and refusing to part with its possessions, it seemed now to be hemmed in by them, turning them into customers threading narrowed aisles.

The dinnerware was china, delicate and fine, and for the coin silver cutlery, it gave forth chimes. The cuisine was one that Marguerite had never before sampled, but she found it to her liking, and especially did she admire the dexterity of the carver and the quiet efficiency of the maid.

The talk meanwhile was of matters on which opinions might differ without disaster—the new state highway that would bypass Greeley; the character of the man for whom the town had been named; the difficul-ties in the construction of the Moffatt tunnel—and at last it turned to the next expedition contemplated by Leonard, into southern Wyoming.

"This late in the year," his mother said. "Aren't you likely to run into snow?"

"We'll only be gone a month," Leonard said. "There isn't much in the lower part of the state, and we'll stick to the U.P. tracks from Cheyenne to the Utah line. Then we'll double back and lay up till spring."

"Where will you stay?" she said.

"Marguerite," Mr. Roberts said, "let me refill your glass."

They were his first words, Marguerite realized, since he'd greeted her. "If you please," she said. "But only halfway."

"Isn't it to your taste?" Baxter said.

"I'm not used to wine. We don't have it at home."

He raised his own glass. "It's a rather nice claret."

"Is that what it's called?"

"In this country, it's usually called Bordeaux."

"Where is it called claret?"

"In England."

"I didn't know that."

"Not many do."

"There doesn't seem to be much drinking in your family," Mrs. Roberts said.

"Oh, I don't know. Daddy manages to find his face now and again. Never with wine, though. His particular kind of stingo is straight rye whisky. Mama, now, she hates the sight of the stuff. Won't allow it in the house, in fact. Says it's pure blue ruin."

Mr. Roberts erased a smile as he said, "Marguerite, we have a few Caruso records. Would you care to hear them?"

"I'd love to, Mr. Roberts," she said.

While driving her home, Leonard said, "My father likes you."

"He's quiet, and he's gentle," she said, "and I like him."

"Do you know why he's that way?"

"He's sad."

"And do you know why he's sad?"

Two street-lamps were passed before Marguerite said, "Does she?"

He was silent then until her door was reached. From the hallway, a light spread a wide white welcome before the world. "There's no sadness in this house," he said.

"They don't live backwards. In there, it's always today."

"I wish I belonged."

And she said, "So do I."

1925

EXPEDITION INTO WYOMING

Cheyenne: Inter-Ocean Hotel
3 days at $3
91 strings. Net $225
Laramie: Pacific Hotel
2 days at $4
45 strings. Net $105....

—from Leonard's account-book

At far-west Evanston, after one-day stops in Rawlins, Rock Springs, and Green River, he said, "Do you know what we're averaging?"

"You're the bookkeeper."

"Better than fifty dollars a day."

"Really? That much?"

"Board, room, and gas come off that, of course, but even so, we're doing better than forty. "We're clearing three hundred a week."

"Seems like we ought to knock off for a while and take in the sights."

"Like which?"

"Yellowstone and Jackson Hole. We may never again be nearer."

"You're on," Leonard said.

Late that afternoon, they passed through the village of Jackson and began to rim the eastern shore of the lake. From the water's edge on the opposite shore, the Teton Range rose, its snowy summits kindled by the setting sun behind them.

"That supper the other night," Marguerite said. "Or dinner, as you call it."

"What about it?"

"Your mother asked a question that wasn't answered."

"I don't recall the question."

"Sure you do. She wanted to know where we were going to live when we got back from this trip."

"Well, now that you've been there, why not at my house?"

They'd moved beyond the lake now, and they were nearing Yellowstone along a paved aisle through a forest of pine. No other car was in sight, and they had the road to themselves save for a pair of bear cubs wrestling on the crown of the blacktop. Clumsy at the game of catch-as-catch-can, they fumbled in vain for a hold and finally bowled each other over.

As Leonard stopped the car, Marguerite said, "If we lived there, you and I, our marriage wouldn't last a week."

"I don't agree. Everything seemed to go right the night of the dinner."

"Seemed, Leonard. Seemed."

"My father took to you. That didn't just *seem*."

"And your mother?"

"She doesn't warm up quite as fast."

"Meaning she's colder."

A large bear came from a thicket of blueberry bushes and, attracting her cubs, disappeared with them into the underbrush at the far side of the road.

"You must be like your mother," she said. "You took a while to warm up too."

"Why don't we give it a try? If it doesn't work, we can move out." He laughed. "To *your* house."

"I'm not dumping a husband onto my folks. Anyway, there's a family saying: *As out of place as a pewter dollar in a mudhole.* Which is what you'd be amongst the Smiths."

"Why pewter, I wonder?"

Husband, she'd called him, but more did he seem a fellow-passenger. "I think we ought to have a place of our own."

"If that's your wish, it's mine. I want to please you."

What he'd said was true; he did want to please her. He opposed her in nothing, he denied her nothing, and so far as his nature permitted, he was a compliant man, often an anticipatory man. Why, then, was she so unresponsive? Why, even to herself, did she seem ungracious? Why could she not repay in kind? Again the word *husband* rose through her mind—carbonation, she thought—and she wondered whether she'd be more receptive if the relation were less near. Was it the attachment that separated them?

They were within the park boundary now, and off across a flat, they saw what seemed to be a cannonade: white against a line of low-lying hills hung the vapor from a battery of fumaroles. As Leonard slowed for a better view, they passed a roadside marker reading: *To the Shoshoni, this is The Valley of Ten Thousand Smokes.*

"What a lovely name for the place!" Marguerite said.
"A hundred would be more like it," Leonard said.

🐂

Taking a different route for the return-trip, they followed the course of the Bighorn through the central part of the state. On reaching Greeley, they rented a small furnished flat near the Teachers College, and there they would spend the winter.

1925-1926

A SMALL FLAT ON 12TH STREET

It was one of those usually rented to students at Colorado State Teachers. Within a few blocks of the college campus, it consisted of a living room, a bedroom, a kitchen, and a bath, and it was fitted up with pieces that were merely furniture, all of it nondescript and hard-used. But the quarters, taken for a season only, mattered little to Marguerite and less to Leonard: the place, however unappealing, was their own, and it gave them the freedom to come and go as they pleased.

Much of Leonard's time was spent assisting his father at the pharmacy and visiting with his family at home. On several occasions, he returned with invitations for Marguerite, but she refused to accept them at secondhand, and eventually they ceased. Often, though, he'd accompany Marguerite to the Smith home, and there, in Decky and Henry Albert, he found beings the like of whom he'd never before encountered. Within their walls, he felt a vast spaciousness, as if they'd brought all outdoors inside—a sense, it seemed, of boundless room and unbreathed air. He sensed even more, the pride of the pair, their quiet bearing, their equality despite their unequal share of the world. There a couple calmly dwelt, envious of no one, resenting nothing, and pleasuring in each other the livelong day. In time, he took to calling on the Smiths even when Marguerite was elsewhere: he felt at ease in their company. As for them, they were at ease with any and all.

After many weeks on the move, rarely if ever left to herself, Marguerite enjoyed these solitary hours. At first, she passed them in walks along the streets and the outlying roads, the less frequented the better, but in no long time she was drawn to the paths and lawns of the nearby campus, and there she went among the throngs that crisscrossed the grounds. She spoke to no one, nor was she spoken to, but though isolated and ignored, she felt that at last she was in the place where she belonged.

College!, she thought, *college!* Ever since her grade-school days, she'd yearned for the learning that was obtainable only here, yearned as peoples did for their promised land. But sad to say, it had not been promised to her, for it had never been within the gift of a broken-knuckled plasterer, and she'd had to be content with what her mother earned by taking in washing—a three-month course at a business college. *Business college*— what a misnomer the name! At no time, though, did she fault her parents for being unable to provide what she so deeply desired. Far from it—so far that she felt them to be the deserving, and she looked ahead to the day when *she* could provide for *them*.

Daily now she strolled the quads, her slow pace exposing her the more, as she fancied, to the influential air, and being in it, she let herself imagine that she was of it, that she, like those in the halls, was absorbing lore. How she longed for what the fortunate teemed with, even for what they forgot! *Marguerite Roberts, Class of '25*, she'd dream...and then, her power of levitation waning, she'd find that she was on the ground again, walking through the flower-beds and around the specimen trees.

A day came when, as she passed one of the college buildings, she read *Crabbe Hall*, read it for some reason aloud, and then she read *Cranford Hall*, and she was moving away when she recalled an anonymous structure that lay between the two. Wondering what it might house, she crossed its sward to stare back at its staring windows. What was revealed to her were the stacks and shelves of a library larger than any she'd ever seen: it was like looking into a brain, she thought. Books by the thousand lined it, tight little containers of knowledge that came in many colors and various sizes, each with a different name.

Entering its two-story main room, she approached the young woman in charge of the desk, and said, "I wonder if you'd tell me the library rules about borrowing books."

"Well, the first one is, you have to be a student or a member of the faculty."

"I guess we can forget the second, then."

"Why don't you use the Greeley library? The town's supposed to have a pretty good one."

"Pretty good isn't good enough."

"Look," the young woman said. "I'm a student here, and I work part-time to pay my tuition. I oughtn't to be telling you this, but if you happen to know somebody who knows somebody—one of the Trustees, say...."

"It happens I do," Marguerite said.

"Get him to write a letter, and the place is yours, rules or no rules. Only don't let on I said so."

"You're a good one, and I'm obliged."

Returning to the doorway, she passed through an aisle of reading-desks lighted by green-shaded lamps. At several of them, student-teachers sat before open books, and Marguerite had the sudden notion that they were eating with their eyes. They were filling their heads with what the books contained, she thought, but how wonderful that the books were inexhaustible! What was in them remained even after being taken away!

The "somebody" relied on by Marguerite was Lawyer Meeker, her former employer. It was he who furnished her with the letter that gained her the privilege of using the college library—and use it she did. She had much spare time that fall and winter, and few were the days when she was not gazing upon the displays that covered the walls—tapestries, she thought them, vivid and varied hangings that she fingered with caution, as if her touch might ruin their design. At the outset, she took books down at random, for a magnetic title, for an unheard-of subject, and even for a binding or the lettering on a spine. What she sought was print only, pages filled with words, food of any kind, for she was hungry. But presently she began to compare one kind with another, to form a preference, and to understand why—and with such evaluations, she became a reader for fair.

The name of the student-librarian was Cleo Daly, and she hailed from Pueblo, which she pronounced Pyeblo.

"Will you be teaching in Pueblo when you finish college?" Marguerite said.

"Not if I can help it. I hate the place."

"I come from Nebraska, place called Clarks. There wasn't much to hate in a town of five hundred. In fact, I kind of liked it."

"I don't usually pay any mind to the books people take out, but with you it's different."

"It is? Why?"

"*You're* different."

"That's nice to hear, but I'm not such a much."

"First off, you were taking whatever you got your hands on. All sorts of stuff, like it came out of a grab-bag. That's changed. You're—what's the word?—specializing. It's plays now, one after another."

"I like to read them. I don't know why, really. Maybe it's because I think I can hear the characters. In a novel, the author seems to drown them out."

In a few weeks' time, the two of them were friendly enough to join in walks over the college grounds or along one of the dwindling roads at the edge of the town. It was cold now even when the sun was high, and soon snow would fall.

On one such day, the librarian said, "It isn't very often that you speak of your husband."

"Husband?" Marguerite said.

"You wear a ring."

Marguerite spread her hand before her as if to verify the observation. "So I do," she said. "Sometime I forget it's there."

Her companion seemed to be changing course when she said, "You know why I hate Pueblo? A fellow there wants to marry me."

"That's not much of a reason."

"For me, it is."

175

"What's the objection? What's wrong with him?"

It was a day of low-lying clouds, like furled suits of sail, and the snowy peaks were hidden, as if piled upon them were all the canvas in the world.

"It isn't him," Cleo said. "It's me."

Marguerite started to speak, but after a glance at the other, she remained silent.

"I tried to tell him a couple of times," the young woman said, "but he'd only have thought I was crazy."

"Worse than that, probably."

"Will it stop you being my friend?"

"Of course not."

"It'd put others off. Why not you?"

"Look. My family long ago found out that people come in all sizes, none of 'em better than any other. We're not much for laying down the law."

Out of the stubble along a fence-line, a pheasant flew and fled, an iridescent missile that swiftly disappeared.

"I knew I could talk to you," Cleo said.

"No, you didn't; you just took a chance. My advice is, don't take too many. People like to say *Live and let live*, but don't ever believe it. They'll kill you."

"You, though—you'll keep coming to the library, won't you?"

"Sure I will," Marguerite said, and she laughed. "I haven't read all the plays."

"Would you think I was fresh if I recommended one?"

"Not at all."

"It's called *A Doll's House*," Cleo said. "I must've read it four-five times."

"Is it that good?"

"The woman, the main character—Nora, her name is—in the end, she walks out on her husband."

"That happens all the time."

"I know, but I have the feeling she's going to wind up like me."

On their return to the library, Marguerite borrowed the play and took it home. She read it in something less than an hour—and then she read it again.

When she saw Cleo a few days later, she said, "What makes you think you and Nora are alike?"

"I left Pueblo to get away from a man. Nora leaves home to get away from Helmer."

"Is that all you've got to go on?"

"I think we both left for the same reason."

"The reason being...?"

"We were through with men."

"I believe that about you, but I don't about Nora. You're as different as a crow and a crane. You're intelligent; she's silly. You're open; she's sly. For two acts, she's simply a dizzy skirt stuffing herself with macaroons. She's such a ninny that she committed a crime in order to borrow money. Then all of a sudden in Act Three, she turns into the Woman Who Knows All. You got taken in, Cleo. You overrate the play, and you underrate yourself."

"Careful when you knock Ibsen. Shaw thinks he's a giant."

"He's no giant in *A Doll's House*. In fact, I think he's as big a fool as Nora."

"I don't agree with you about Nora. I think that when she leaves Helmer, she's really leaving men."

Marguerite laughed. "You know what would've happened if Ibsen had written Act Four? Nora would've taken up with another man before she'd gone a block."

"You don't think much of women, do you?"

"No, and Nora's kind are the worst. They give all of us a black eye."

The play lay between them on the librarian's desk. Turning back the cover, she stamped the date of return on the flyleaf slip, and then for a moment she gazed at Marguerite.

"When do I get to meet *your* Helmer?" she finally said.

"Come by this evening, if you like."

Leonard's greeting of Cleo was cordial, and after showing her to a chair, he poured sherry for all and gave her a glass.

"Marguerite tells me you're from Pueblo," he said. "We were thereabouts this summer—over in Florence. Too bad we didn't know you at the time."

"You'd not have found me. I steer clear of the place."

"But your people—surely you visit them."

"I've seen the last of them," Cleo said, "and they of me."

Leonard glanced at Marguerite, perhaps in the hope that she'd mend the broken conversation, supply the missing step in the stair, but she said nothing.

It was Cleo who supplied it, saying, "You look as if you'd like to hear the reason."

"And you look as if you'd like to tell it," he said.

"My parents want me to marry a certain man, and I don't want to get married at all."

Watching him, Marguerite sensed that ideation had begun to stir him, and to still it, she said, "I think this is getting too personal, Leonard. If it goes any further, you'll be prying."

But she was too late: the inkling had turned to knowledge, and with its growth, he seemed to congeal. After some moments of frozen warmth, he rose, and with a mumbled something about helping his father at the pharmacy, he left the flat.

"Coming here was a mistake," Cleo said.

"*You're* the mistake," Marguerite said. "You're bound and determined to advertise."

"I'm not ashamed of what I am."

"You don't have to be. But you're also plain reckless, and that *is* shameful."

"It wasn't reckless to tell *you*."

"That's because I happen to come from the kind of people who let other people alone. But Leonard's kind—good Lord, you give them fits."

"I was right about him," Cleo said. "He *is* a Helmer."

"Keep on like you do, and you'll find that pretty near everybody's a Helmer. You're going to get into trouble, Cleo—or deep down, is that what you want?"

But Cleo had only half-heard, and she said, "He's Helmer, and some day you'll leave him."

"Maybe so," Marguerite said, "but it won't be for a woman."

༃

Leonard returned so soon after Cleo's departure that Marguerite was certain he'd waited outside and watched her go.

"A person like that!" he said. "What was she doing in our home?"

"I invited her," Marguerite said.

"Why?"

"She's a friend of mine."

"Friend! That kind of woman!"

"That kind of woman can be a friend."

"People'll think you're the same."

"If you know that, you must be one of them."

"They make the rules. Fly in their face, and you'll get what your friend is begging for."

"She's in for a terrible life, and either she doesn't know it, or else she doesn't care. I'm sorry for her, and I wish I could save her from grief."

"You can't. You'll only get what she does."

"It doesn't seem right to shun her. What harm has she done?"

"What would your folks say if you brought her to their house?"

"Not a thing. They've seen all kinds in their time—Indians, tramps, wrestlers, horse-traders, even flippin'-jinnies off the high road."

"What're you out to do—provoke me?"

"I'm trying to reason with you."

"This is no debate," he said. "I want your word that you'll stop seeing that Cleo."

"Are you serious, Leonard?"

"Never more so."

"In other words, you're to pick my friends."

"Put it any way you like."

"Think for a minute," she said. "I know I can't change what she is, but being friends with her, maybe I can tone her down. I swear, one of these days, she'll wear a sign."

"So will you if you don't steer clear of her. I say you've got to put an end to this friendship, or whatever it is you have going."

She studied him for a moment before letting herself speak. "I've kept my temper so far," she said, "but say one more word, and you'll be the sorriest man that ever lived." She started for the bedroom, but at the doorway, she paused to speak back over her shoulder. "Nobody," she said, "nobody picks my friends," and she closed the door behind her.

1926

A TALK WITH BROTHER DAN

On her way to call on him, Marguerite scuffed through a new skiff of snow, leaving a trail of scars behind her on the road. White streaks lay in the stubblefields she passed, and the fences around them wore a piping of lace. Dan's place, a spread of half a dozen acres divided into paddocks, lined a lane that ended at his gate. She found him in a box stall, where he was trying to fit a halter to a restive foal. The dam, a blaze-faced bay, stood dozing in a corner.

"He sure is on the muscle," she said.

"He wants out of here," Dan said, "but it's too chancy in the snow. He might bust hisself up."

"Too bad he doesn't take after his mama. She'd snooze while the roof fell in."

"What brings you, baby sister?"

"Nothing particular. Just I haven't seen much of you lately."

"Don't say I said so, but I'm gladder to see you than the others."

"You don't mean that, Dan-boy. They've all got me beat."

"Not with me, they ain't."

"That Connie, she's got more brains than the rest of us put together."

"Five kids, and her a scant thirty?" Dan said. "If that's brains, she's got 'em well hid."

Marguerite laughed. "She should've hid something else."

"Speaking of which," Dan said, "how's that husband of *yours*?"

She put her hand palm up against the foal's muzzle, a texture that felt like cold china. "He's all right," she said.

Having adjusted the halter, Dan produced a curry-comb. "Hold still, you little feist," he said. "This is for your mingy mane, and it ain't going to hurt you none....Only all right?"

Marguerite fingered the foal's ears, stiff little shells that flicked at her touch. "All right isn't so bad, is it?" she said.

"Baby sister, you got more due you than *all right.*"

Joining her now in the aisle, he walked with her through the doorway and down the ramp. There he lit a cigarette, and its smoke, mingling with Marguerite's breath, ravelled away into the open air.

"I'm no great shakes, Dan."

"You come along late," he said, "but it was like Mama and Daddy was saving best for last."

"There's no best in our family."

"I got a picture of you I wouldn't part with for riches. You're I guess about a year old, and ever once in a while I take it out just for the look on your face. Those gooseberry eyes of yours are staring wide, like you was gacking at all creation."

"I must've been seeking my future."

"Don't tell me it was Leonard Roberts."

"It was someone else, but you can't always have what you dream of."

"Does he treat you bad?"

"No. Why?"

"I'd cut him loose of his prides."

And laughing again, she said, "Don't! Think of me!....But seriously, there's no evil in him, and many a girl would be glad to have his name. I just don't happen to be one of them, but I've got it, and it's my fault. I knew I didn't love him, and I never should've married him."

"A lawyer can fix that in no time."

"I'm not suffering," she said. "I'm just not doing a lot of living."

1925-1926

CHANGES OF SEASON

More snow would fall that winter, at times heavily enough to be drifted by the wind, but as often as not, only a flurry would fur the earth. To the west of the town, as in a photo, always the avalanche of the mountains would loom. but with spring, it would waste away to water, and then leafless trees would bud and bloom, lifeless no more.

LEONARD: The shipment from Mecca Gem came in yesterday. It's at the U.P. freight office.

MARGUERITE: How many strings did you order this time?

LEONARD: Three thousand.

MARGUERITE: Good Lord, that's a year's supply.

LEONARD: If things go well, who knows? Maybe we'll be a year on the road.

MARGUERITE: I've never been away that long.

LEONARD: From what? From whom?

MARGUERITE: From home. From my people.

LEONARD: Your home is supposed to be with me now, and I'm supposed to be your people.

MARGUERITE: I'm sorry. I hate nay-sayers, and I must've sounded like one.

LEONARD: Well, you *do* have your opinions.

MARGUERITE: I don't think you'd want a wife you could lead by the nose.

LEONARD: A wife who listens to her husband isn't exactly being led by the nose.

MARGUERITE: We're talking about Cleo Daly now, aren't we?

LEONARD: You still see her, I take it.

MARGUERITE: Now and then, yes....But let's get back to selling pearls. Where do you propose to go?

LEONARD: I've been asking around, and from what I hear, New Mexico's up-and-coming.

MARGUERITE: The nearest I ever got to it was Blanca.

LEONARD: Albuquerque's about the size of Greeley, fifteen thousand or so, just the kind we handle best. Santa Fe's smaller, but it's the capital and historic. Tourists all over the place.

MARGUERITE: When do you figure on starting?

LEONARD: In a month or so. How about clothes? You need another dress?

MARGUERITE: Mama fixed me a couple of changes. What I have will do me. If we're away a year, though....

❧

182

The days had grown longer, and now when she walked the campus or a tree-lined street, it was beneath a haze of new leaf, a pale green veil that laid a thin shadow at her feet. On the lawns, dew glimmered in the sunlight, and fragrance rose from the flower-beds, from the occasional blossoms, and always from the earth.

CONNIE: Dan came over to see the kids last Sunday. He said you and Leonard would be taking off for New Mexico any day now. Why New Mexico?

MARGUERITE: New Mexico—the Land of Enchantment. I guess he's enchanted.

CONNIE: Are you?

MARGUERITE: It'd take more than New Mexico.

CONNIE: You don't sound very happy, little sister.

MARGUERITE: The only happy people I ever saw are Mama and Daddy. They *like* each other.

CONNIE: You're kind of young to be so down in the mouth. It's bad, to expect nothing.

MARGUERITE: Expect something, and you'll be disappointed. Expect nothing, and you won't be—because nothing is what you'll get.

CONNIE: I hate to hear you talk like that.

MARGUERITE: What can Dan expect, married to that slob of his? What can Pearl expect from skirt-chaser Chester? What about you, with five kids to look after? And me—I can expect a long ride through New Mexico. All I see ahead is more of the same.

CONNIE: I can say that, but not you. You can pick up and walk away; I can't.

MARGUERITE: I've had the notion.

CONNIE: Act on it. Maybe you'll start expecting again.

℘

When Leonard announced that they'd be setting out from Greeley on the morrow, Marguerite paid a final visit to the college campus. It was a bright day, and the trees were in full leaf, stencilling the pathway with light and shade. At the hour chosen, the library was quiet, only a few readers being at the tables and none within earshot of the desk.

MARGUERITE: We leave in the morning. I couldn't go without telling
you goodbye.

CLEO: I'll miss you. You've been a friend. A better friend than
my—friend.

MARGUERITE: I wish you'd let us meet. Why did you keep her
hidden away?

CLEO: She hid *herself*. She's ashamed of what she is.

MARGUERITE: She might just as well be ashamed of having two feet.

CLEO: How is it you've never tried to give me advice?

MARGUERITE: You're what you are, and you're living your life. You don't
need advice—and if you did, I couldn't give it.

CLEO: That wouldn't stop most people. They'd say go see a
doctor, take cold showers, eat a lot of fruit.

MARGUERITE: Well, Cleo, thanks for the walks and the talks—
and even for Ibsen.

CLEO: Write to me, won't you...?

All day they drove southward across the instep of the Rockies: to
their left, the long slow downfall of the plains; to their right, range after
range, ridges that backed each other like spare sets of scenery stored
against a wall. All day they drove past the mile-high wall of the Ram-
parts and the San Juans, their coping of snow aglare in the sun. Creeks
flowed from every crevice in the slopes, some narrow and some broad,
but all only melt, an intermittent flow that would soon run dry.

MARGUERITE: These creeks we're crossing—have you noticed
their names?

LEONARD: No. Why?

MARGUERITE: They're odd, but they're beautiful too. The Huerfano,
the Apishapa.

LEONARD: They're odd, all right, but what's beautiful about them?

MARGUERITE: It's hard to rightly say, but they seem some better than
Middle Fork.

LEONARD: A name's a name.

MARGUERITE: It doesn't matter, I guess....How far do you plan on
going today?

LEONARD: Trinidad. It's on the banks of a creek—the Purgatoire.
Now, there's a name for you.

MARGUERITE: A *hell* of a name.

LEONARD: I had no idea you were a joker.

MARGUERITE: That wasn't a joke.

LEONARD: I read somewhere that the old Santa Fe trail ran through Trinidad. That *may* have been a joke.

MARGUERITE: Why are we baiting each other?

LEONARD: Don't you know?

Gazing at the pavement ahead, at the roadside rocks, at the grease-wood and the sand and the sagebrush, she said nothing for some way, and only then did she speak, as though all the while she'd been weighing her reply.

MARGUERITE: I guess I do.

LEONARD: Do what?

MARGUERITE: Know the reason.

1926-1927

WHERE THE GODS STILL DWELL

They entered New Mexico through Raton Pass, and at once its watercolor hues lay outspread beneath them. The earth seemed to billow, a main of wildflowers impelled by the same wind that enwound the aquarelle clouds. In the coves and creases of the hills, rills ran, and there grasses grew and small stands of maize, and here and there smoke rose and strolled away on the air. Far off, there were bright slants of sunlight and a darker slant of rain, and across the middle distance raced a squall of rolling dust. Eroded cliffs reared from the roadside, some of them streaked with red and yellow like semi-precious stones, walls for artless pictographs—running deer, suns and sunrays, symbols—and for crafty proclamations that only *Jesus Saves*.

☙

Dear Midgie:

We made our first showing in New Mexico at Las Vegas, a town of maybe four-five thousand, and not expecting much of it, we figured on a one-day stay. Were we ever wrong! Here it is a week

185

later, and still there's no let-up in the pearl business. We've sold more than two hundred strings so far—but only to the whites! The natives (and natives is what I mean—Indians and Mexicans), they just come and look and walk away. They have their own kind of jewelry, handsome stuff of silver and turquoise, but with their dark skin, you'd think they'd go for pearls—and yet as I say, they just look and walk away. I couldn't wear the screaming colors that they do, I'd turn freaky, but somehow they go well with their black eyes and beautiful black hair. And speaking of beautiful, it's their children that take your breath away. They're little dark-faced dolls....

❧

Always there were long views, always a deckle-edge of mountains at the bottom of the sky, and sometimes there'd be a far-off fall of rain, and then they'd see a seven-colored band appear, a vivid arc above the cloud-dark land. They saw churches awash in seas of clover, they saw pueblos and the ruins of pueblos, they saw forsaken towns dead of exposure to the sun and wind, they saw black eyes trained on something beyond sight, something that only other such eyes were able to see. What had they found there?, Marguerite would wonder, what had she missed?

"I can't figure them out," Leonard said. "Here they've been living among the whites for centuries, and we don't seem to have changed them at all."

"Would you change if you were a Navajo?" Marguerite said. "Would you change if you were a Mexican?"

"Well, my surroundings would have *some* effect on me."

"These are *their* surroundings. Why haven't they affected us?"

"What—and dance for rain?"

Marguerite laughed. "Maybe we ought to. We might get it when we need it."

"Take off their fireman shirts, and they're just what they were before we came."

"And they'll be that way after we go. My guess is, they don't buy pearls because they don't want to look like whites. What's so wonderful about us, anyway?"

"That's your Indian blood talking."

"You're wrong: it's my white. I know what we are, and I'm not so swole up about it."

❧

Dear Connie:

You'd love Santa Fe. It's just the right size, about seventy-five hundred, and its location—well, you'd have to see that for yourself. My descriptive powers wouldn't do it justice. It's the state capital, as you know, but nothing at all like Denver. Its streets twist and turn, and the saying is, it was laid out by a drunken Mexican on a blind mule. But it's seven thousand feet up in the clearest air ever breathed, and the place simply sparkles; you feel better just by being here....The pearls are going as fast as we can hand them out. Looks like we'll be sticking around here till everybody's wearing a string. Even the Governor....

For all she could've said, the people outside the window might well have been the ones she'd seen before, people with penny-colored faces and ripe-olive eyes, and at the things that were there for them alone, they gazed past her through the glass. She was unaware of the dim shapes and flimsy substance of what they saw, for they were shades merely, the souls of their undying dead, but she sensed that though all had been lost by them, they were still undefeated, and she understood without thought why they had no need of pearls.

"Do you ever get the feeling that we're trespassers?" Marguerite said.

"No," Leonard said.

"You think we have a right to be here?"

"Every right: we own it."

"We didn't use to."

"That was then. This is now."

Their stay in Santa Fe, as in Las Vegas, proved to be week-long, and being equally successful, it prompted Leonard to propose a semi-holiday in Taos. Some seventy miles to the north, it lay along the Rio Grande, there an inconsequential stream close to its rise in Colorado. They were still some way short of the town when they saw that it was quite likely to be far more than a white church in a pueblo of adobes; from the traffic going and coming, it was clear that they were nearing one of the ornaments of the road.

"Baxter used to talk of this place," Leonard said, "but I must not have been listening. Look at those license-plates. They're from all over—Tennessee, Alberta, Michigan. We'll send 'em all back with pearls."

"Virginia," Marguerite said, "Rhode Island," but her mind was elsewhere. "The way you spoke the other day, I gather you don't like the Indians."

"I like *you*."

"I'm only part-Indian. What if I were all Indian?"

"How can I answer a question like that?"

Alabama, she read, *South Dakota*. "You just did," she said. "Let's find us a place to stay."

౿

Dear Pearl:

I didn't just barge in here to use the stationery. Leonard splurged, and we're actually guests of the Taos Inn (best place in town). Parts of the building are as old as the hills, but we were put in one of the newer wings. Some class to little Marg, what?

We got to Taos early in the day, and while Leonard was scouting for a likely spot to show the pearls, I wandered around looking at the shops and the people. They're out-of-staters, the biggest part of them—I even saw a license that said *Quebec*.

The streets are chock-full of tourists snapping pictures, chasing children, lugging souvenirs—and eating! I never so many gully-jumpers eating on the hoof. I watched them for a spell, but it was more interesting to watch the *natives* watch them. They put me in mind of lions watching the crowds at a zoo. Somehow they see them without looking at them, and you'd swear they were thinking *This wouldn't be a half-bad place if they'd all go away*.

I feel the same about Taos. If outsiders stayed where they belong, you'd see it for what it is, a beautiful reminder of where a wonderful people once lived, a little Indian town baking in the sun, and as if the year were still 1500, you'd see their women filling jars at the Plaza well....

Leonard? Leonard is Leonard. And having written that, I wonder what I mean. If you know, big sister, tell me.

౿

The route south from Taos followed the Rio Grande as far as Espanola, and somewhere along the way, Leonard spoke as if to the road ahead, the canyon, the sky, the stream. "I'm still in a daze," he said. "I can't believe we put in two whole weeks back there."

"I ran out of poses," Marguerite said. "I used every one I could think of, and finally I stood there and stared out at the people staring in."

"You could've sat down and read the paper. They'd've kept on buying if you'd fallen asleep."

"Their taste was in their mouth. Otherwise they'd've walked away."

"What makes you say that?"

"I'm standing in the window of a shop that deals in the handiwork of Indians—weaving, pottery, jewelry, lovely things of beads. And what am *I* dealing in? Little glass balls filled with wax!"

"Why not call them pearls?"

"Because they *aren't* pearls. But that cuts no ice with the rubes from Milwaukee and Chattanooga. They don't know the difference between trash and art—they buy both!"

"Do you know the difference?"

Though the labor of the motor and the gnash of grinding gravel, she thought she heard an emphasis on the word *you*—slight enough, true, but almost surely there.

"I do," she said, "but I'm beginning to think you don't."

"We've been selling these pearls for a year now. All of a sudden, you drag in art."

"I've been thinking about it ever since I noticed that our only customers are white. The Indians, the Mexicans—they can tell good from bad."

"So can you, it seems."

Again she heard the emphasis, this time a little more distinctly than before, but they were some way down the road, past Espanola and distant from the stream, when she spoke the words for a thought she'd brought along.

"Don't ever do that again, Leonard," she said.

"Do what?"

"Make small of me."

"When did I ever?"

"Going to Denver one day."

"You got sore then over nothing. You dream things up."

189

"This was no dream just now."

"Marguerite, you're too sensitive."

If so, to what? to his implication that she knew less than he?

She was his equal in every way, she felt, and in many a way his superior. His pretensions to bluer blood struck her as a confession of his debt to others for any quality he might possess, an unwitting admission that he had little or none of his own. Her regard for Decky and Henry Albert ("the best Mama and Daddy in the world") was of the highest, but she'd've been diminished by the notion that she owed her worth to them.

More ignorant than Leonard?, she thought. Not even if his best day and her worst had been the same!

Attending college, as he had done, was her unfulfilled desire. All that her family had been able to provide was a three-month course in Typing and Shorthand, but wherein had Leonard, with his greater advantages, excelled her? For all his exposure to knowledge, he knew nothing of people, nothing of sympathy, nothing more of history than the past. His reading had ended with his days on the campus, and so, it seemed, had the ranging of his mind. What might she have done, she wondered, if she'd been free to dwell in the halls within the walls of ivy?

"Sensitive?" she said. "Yes, I am, and you'd best remember it."

℧

Albuquerque, alt. 4,930 ft., pop. 15,000 (1925)

All through their ten-day stay, they put up at the *Alvarado*, a mission-style hotel close by the mission-style depot, each made part of the other by a connecting arcade. From their windows, Marguerite could see the come-and-go of trains, freight-cars with their heralds and Pullmans with their high-flown names. At night, flyers would pass, their trucks pounding over the track-joints on the way to an unknown somewhere else, and if wakened by the sound and the shaking, Marguerite would lie until the room was still again, but all the while she'd wonder to what end she herself was running—and sometimes she'd wonder with whom.

They'd never shown the pearls in a town as large as Albuquerque, but the demand for them seemed to have no relation to the size of the place, the smaller at times proving to be the better. Here, after several full-swing days, Leonard spent a morning at his account-book in order to report on their progress.

At length he turned to Marguerite, who was looking down at the Santa Fe yards, and he said, "We've been on the road for about two months now. You care to guess how we've done so far?"

A short-stacked Pacific had just steamed to a stop at the depot, a gauze of smoke trailing back over the varnished cars and vanishing in the air. The locomotive seemed to be breathing hard, as if the run had tired it.

"How can I guess?" she said. "I haven't been keeping count."
"Since leaving Greeley, we've sold—*you've* sold—over a thousand strings."
"I don't believe it!"
"A thousand—you and that cute little figure of yours. It sells pearls everywhere—cities, tank-towns, whistle-stops."

Smoke climbed straight up now from the engine stack, and in the stillness, it lasted long before thinning out and shredding away.

"My figure's good enough, I guess, but it'd never sell a thousand of anything."
"Well, *something's* selling the pearls, and it surely isn't me."
"All I do is show them. I thought they kind of sold themselves."
He laughed. "If they did," he said, "I could've left you in Greeley."
She turned away from the window to study him. "You mean I'm just bait in a black silk dress?"
"Without you, we couldn't *give* the pearls away."
"What we're really doing, then, is selling me."
"It's done all the time. Look at the magazine ads, look at the billboards. They're not selling goods. They're selling faces and figures."
"*Unknown* faces and figures. But you're selling your wife's!"
"I thought you knew that."
"And I thought you knew *me*. Far from it, you don't know me at all.

I've never flashed myself in my life. It took a lot of doing to get me to pose with the pearls, but it was always the pearls I was showing, not myself."

"And yet it was you they were buying, not the pearls."

"This is no better than a peep-show, and I'm ashamed."

"Of what? Of having a trim figure?"

"No, of using it like this. We're not selling pearls for five dollars a string. We're selling me for five dollars a feel."

"That's ridiculous. Nobody's touching you."

"They'll be touching me from now on."

"With their eyes. Their eyes have been on you all along."

"But now that I know it, they'll seem to be hands."

"I never expected you to take a stand like this, Marguerite."

"Did you think I'd like it when I saw what you had in mind?"

"What did *you* have in mind—standing in a window wearing a string of pearls?"

"Up to now, I was also wearing a dress."

"And from now on...?"

"It'll be like I was only wearing the pearls."

"Where's this leading us?"

She turned back to the window and the railroad yards. The locomotive whistled twice, two shorts, and as a jet of vapor shot from its steamchest, the train began to move.

"I don't know," she said, "but how can it be anywhere good?"

Dear Marg

Like you asked Im sending this General Delivery Albuquerque and it's a good thing you spelt it because I never could of. Why didnt you make it Gallup? I could of spelt that myself.

You wrote Lenard is Lenard and if I knew what you meant I should tell you. Well you asked the right person.

Us Smith sisters didnt have much luck with our men me least of all, being married first to a violet drunk and then to a do nothing, nothing that is exept run after anything with titties.

You been married a year now and what youve got you cant even discribe. Thats bad Marg. A wife is either satisfied with her husband or she aint, but she ought to be able to say which. Seems to me like youre hooked up to nothing. Oh I know hes respectible and he dont cuff you around and hes edjucated till hell wont have it but whats it add up to? To Lenard is Lenard. If thats all you want that all youll get.

Me I'm thinking real serious about picking up sticks and going to Los Angelus Calafornia and for all I care Mr Chester can go along or stay here.

Mama and Daddy send love. Me too.

Pearl H the section boss

After reading Pearl's letter, she destroyed it, but when their stay in Albuquerque ended, Leonard headed for Gallup almost as though the name had survived and suggested itself as a destination.

"What did she say?" he said as the road entered the Laguna Reservation.
"What did who say?"
"Your sister Pearl."
"Are you asking what one sister wrote to another?"
"Yes, because she wrote about me."
"How do you know that?"
"Why else would you tear up the letter?"
"Some people keep everything—letters, programs, recipes, all kinds of stuff. I don't."
"You could've kept it, you know. I wouldn't've snooped."
"What's got into you, anyway?"
"That letter."
"All right, it *was* about you."
"And not very favorable, I take it."
"Pearl's hard to please. Don't worry your head about it."
"What is it that she doesn't like?"
"Leonard, here we are riding through country we've never seen before and might never see again—Indian reservations, pueblos, lava beds, mountains coming up like clouds—"
"Clouds coming up like mountains."
"—and all the while, what's addling your mind? Something you think my sister might've said about you."
"Something she *did* say."

193

"What she wrote was between her and me. If she'd meant it for you, she'd've sent it to you."

"Well, I can't force you to tell me."

"That's very true."

"At least, tell me *why* you can't."

"You might be hurt. I don't go around hurting people."

"I'm *asking* you to hurt me."

"For Pete's sake, Leonard! Look at the scenery. Look at the rocks, the colors. Look at that road-runner. It's going faster than we are...." *Look at the streaks in the earth, at the snowbank of sheep, the sand dunes, the plains, anything. Look at the hogans in those hollows, look at the surf of hills in the distance, look at the Navajo women at the roadside and the chips of turquoise sky in their jewelry.* "Why are we going to Gallup? What's in Gallup?"

"I'm hoping to run into one of those Indian ceremonials. People come from all over to watch them dance. They've got a dance for everything— for buffalo, bear, deer, turtles. They've got a dance for snakes, corn, rain, they've even got one called a Sundown dance."

"It isn't a bad way to get God's attention."

"You think they really believe in all that hopping around?"

"You know of anything better?"

"Christianity."

"I'd just as soon dance."

They were nearing Gallup, a division-point of the Santa Fe, and they passed the shops and side-track of the line.

"What did Pearl say in that letter?" Leonard said.

"I'll tell you one of the things. She said she was thinking of leaving her husband."

❧

Leonard and Marguerite were long in Gallup, longer there than any-where else so far, and they'd've stayed even longer had they not had their fill of caravans arriving on Route 66. The throngs were constant, their behavior slapdash, their voices shrill and wearing. They'd come from afar to pause here, but all through the pause, they seemed to remain in motion. Their darting, their lunges, their changes of speed and direction, all had no aim, and with scarcely a glance, they'd pass dazzling arrays of Indian art—the plane geometry of Navajo weaving the painted symbols on their pottery, the things of bead and buckskin, of beaten silver containing shards of skyblue sky.

"I kind of hate to leave," Leonard said. "Those dirt-farmers were buying pearls till hell wouldn't have it."

"Where are we off to now?" Marguerite said.

"Nowhere in particular. We've got a pot of money, and we'll take in the sights."

"We just crossed over into Arizona—that was the state line back there....And speaking of sights, how about the one on that sign? *Petrified Forest—4 mi.*"

Paying the entrance fee, Leonard drove some way through the Reserve before drawing into a turnout. There they left the car and followed a posted footpath that led to the sprawled remains of a prehistoric grove. The trees, like toppled columns, lay in great disjointed blocks—crystals tinted by the mineral deposits of the earliest ages. All about them lay prisms of heartwood and wafers of bark, some of these containing intaglios of sea shells and the leaf-prints of fern.

"Christ!" Leonard said. "Don't tell me there was water here once!"

"There was. All this around us used to be the bottom of the ocean."

"I won't ask how you know. You'll only get sore."

"Not this time. I read it on the signboard at the gate."

He fingered the impression of a shell, saying, "I wonder if this one held a pearl."

On their return to the highway, he said, "You know what we'll run into in Flagstaff? The yearly powwow—three days of Indian dances and Indian bronco-busting. They gather from all over the southwest for that shivaree."

"I never saw an Indian rodeo."

"The whites pour in to watch. We'll make another killing."

When the powwow came to a close, the several tribes dispersed to their reservations, and with them went much of the flair and flash of Flagstaff. But with the Grand Canyon only ninety miles away, it was still astir with pilgrims bound for a sight of the great wonder—and they made an endless stream before which the pearls were displayed. At breakfast one morning in a diner along the highway, Marguerite sat gazing through a window while Leonard built a maze of arithmetic on a paper napkin.

Traffic passed, and faintly she heard motors and ripping rubber. Little worlds on wheels were going by, she thought, each with its own numbers and its own tongue, and for all she knew, they'd be on the go forever. Emerging out of the vanishing point of the past, they'd vanish in the converge of the future, but more would ever appear, she thought, little separate self-sufficient worlds, and they too would soon disappear.

"We sure *God* made a killing" Leonard said. "Give or take, we only have eight hundred strings left."

On the far side of the pavement, a car came to a stop, and Marguerite watched the driver lift a small boy from the rear seat and place him at the road-edge. Urgently the boy thrust a hand through his fly and drew forth his spigot, pink and puny, and no sooner did it show than it began to flow, a yellow arc pouring over the asphalt.

"Another week in Flagstaff," Leonard said, "and all we'd have to sell is boxes."

The spill ended in a series of spurts, whereupon the boy looked up at the man, his mouth forming a great *Ooh!* of relief, and then he smiled the smile of pride.

"What're you looking at, Marguerite?"

The man picked the boy up, hugged him, and placed him back in the car. Starting to climb behind the wheel, he paused long enough to rough the boy's hair.

"Marguerite!"
"Yes?"
"Were you listening?"
"I was watching a little boy take a pee."

"Did you hear what I said about sales?"

"Every word, Leonard: we're running low on pearls."

"What I'm wondering is, do we order more now or join the crowd and see the sights?"

"From what you say, I take it we're flush."

"Couple of thousand to the good—more, even."

"How far away is Grand Canyon?"

"Sixty miles above Williams, which is thirty miles from here."

"I say, let's rubberneck and see the Canyon."

"When we get back to our room, pack."

It was early afternoon when, east of Williams, they took the fork leading to the Canyon. From there, the road crossed country covered by a counterpane of junipers, dwarfs the size of seedling pines—the offspring, they seemed to be, of the ponderosas lying beyond them. As yet, the Canyon was screened by these stands, and so it stayed until the road rounded a bend near the rim, and, astounded by the sight, Leonard stopped the car and stared.

Unable to see the far side of the fissure, he said, "This is like the place they used to be scared of—where you fell off the earth."

"Let's go closer," Marguerite said.

Once the car was clear of the curve, the other facade of the Canyon came into view. Twenty miles away, its rounds were found by the going-down sun, and its bays and buttresses were grazed by the slanting light. The sheer was scored, as if the pit had been dug and deepened by some titanic machine and showing now as a mile-high wall of russet rock. There were folds in it, like those in a drapery, and glancing off these coves, the sun left them in shadows made of many shades of blue, from rare above to dense and dark below. Atop a far-off butte, a spindle of stone caught a splay of rays and glowed as though from within.

Leaving the car and moving as near to the cliff as the pathway allowed, Marguerite gazed into the chasm at its cause, the Colorado, which from where she stood was only a rill held still by distance. She called to Leonard, who'd stopped at a display-case holding a topographical map of the area.

"Come see this, Leonard!" she said. "There's nothing like it in all the world!"

"Come see *this*," he said. "The names they've pinned on those formations."

She cared nothing for the names. Whatever they might be, she thought, they could never describe the indescribable, and she wished he'd let them be.

He did not. "*Osiris Temple!*" he said. "*Tower of Ra*! What and where is Ra? *Siegfried's Pyre*! Who thinks these things up?"

"The colors!" she said. "I've never *seen* such colors?"

"*Freya's Castle!*" he said. "*The Tabernacle!*"

"Come here, Leonard. Please!"

"You know me and heights."

They put up at *El Tovar*, a hotel built close to the Canyon rim, and during the night, sensing that Leonard had left the bed, Marguerite spoke his name into the darkness of the room.

"I'm over here," he said. "Sitting by the window."

"What's the matter? Can't you sleep?"

"The Canyon gives me the willies."

"Even when you can't see it?"

"All the more when I can't see it. It *really* gets to be the edge of the world."

"What is it that troubles you about heights?"

"They're attractive."

"Attractive?"

"Magnetic is what I should've said. They make me think of falling—or jumping."

Not knowing what to say, she said nothing, and after a moment, she rose and joined him at the window.

"What time is it?, I wonder," she said.

"Must be close to dawn."

"It was wrong to bring you here. I should've remembered Royal Gorge."

"I'd've brought *you*. How could I have made you miss the Canyon?"

He was well-meant, she thought. To gratify her, he'd kept his dread to himself and endured it—which she admired as an act of courage. He was a well-meant man, she thought...but what, she wondered, did well-meant mean? what words came to mind that defined it? Would *benign* do, would *kindly*? If not, what of *warmth of heart, the Christian spirit, indulgence*? If none of these alone, what if one and all? What if the meaning she sought combined every degree of goodness? What then? What would she feel for him then?

"I think it's getting light," he said.

The windows gave on blackness that would've been total save for the faintest dye of dawn, and as light grew, the square of night acquired a frame, and a pane of glass became visible.

"Why don't we talk about important things?" she said.

"Such as...?"

"Us."

"You think we're important?"

"More so than where to eat, where to sleep, where to show the pearls. That isn't talk. It's asking for directions."

"Did it ever cross your mind that you and I don't add up to *us*?"

She glanced at him, saying, "You feel that too, then."

"I'm not filled with sawdust. Sure I feel it—and something ought to be done about it."

"I'd do it, but I don't know whether the fault, the failure, is yours or mine."

Spokes of sunlight were raying through the Canyon and setting fire to all they touched, the dome, the mesa, the spire of stone, the faraway rim.

"That day along the Poudre," he said. "Is it still between us?"

She shook her head. "We're long past that, Leonard."

"What is it, then? What *is* between us?"

199

"I'm afraid there's *nothing* between us. I've never understood what I do for you, what I mean to you. It can't be much, because I can't recall hearing about it."

"What would you want me to say?"

Again she shook her head, this time at his wrong reading of her mind. "It has to be what *you* want to say," she said.

Would he ever stop being so *contained?*, she wondered, would he ever break free of his restraints, his repression, would he shake himself loose from the customary Leonard, would he just once, once!, use the word *love?* To ask, she knew, was to answer: he would not.

Later, on the way down to the coffee-shop, he paused to say, "Well, we sure talked important *that* time."

She did not pause. Speaking back over her shoulder, she said, "More than you seem to know."

They left the Canyon that morning and drove south on Route 66. A two-day stop was made at Williams and another at Ash Fork, and in each of those small towns, the pearls caught the smalltown fancy, and they sold in goodly numbers. Moving on now, first to Prescott and then to Wickenburg, Leonard found that he was nearing Phoenix, the state capital, with the last of his merchandise. From there, he telegraphed to Omaha, ordering two thousand strings for delivery at Yuma. When they left Phoenix and headed west for Gila Bend, the rear of Leonard's car was barren of boxes bearing the Mecca Gem label.

"We're temporarily out of business" he said. "We're tourists."

"Then let's tour," Marguerite said.

With several days to squander before the arrival of the pearls, they idled across the desert, riding the ups and downs, the undulations of the roller-coaster road. Wherever a way opened, they swerved into a landscape of sage and mesquite to take in a lava bed, a reservation, a painted rock, all the while marvelling at the plant life able to sustain itself through nearly rainless years—the sprays of buggy-whip cactus, the ironwood thickets, the thousand-spiked yucca—and even more did they marvel at the bright-winged traffic among the thorns.

At length, after more than a week of roaming, they set out for Yuma. On reaching the town, Leonard drew up at the freight office of the Southern Pacific depot. He entered briskly; he came out dazed, walking toward the car in slow motion. In his hand, he held a letter that seemed to weigh far more than a sheet of paper, and the weight, Marguerite fancied, was great enough to make him sluggish.

"What's the matter?" she said. "What does it say?"

"It says I was wrong: we're *permanently* out of business."

"I don't understand."

"We get no more pearls from Mecca Gem at two dollars a string."

"Why not? What did we do?"

"Do? We did too well, that's what! We made it look so easy that they raised the price to five."

"That's a *normous*-big jump."

"We'd have to ask ten, and that's out of the question. Who's got that kind of money for frippery?"

"Look, Leonard," Marguerite said. "At ten dollars a string, we'd only have to sell half as many as before. Why don't we give it a try—not with two thousand strings, though. We could order, say, five hundred—"

"I can't *pay* for five hundred."

"I thought you said—"

"We *did* do well, but we've been living high, and...well, Baxter touched me for a thousand."

Touched *him*? Baxter had touched *her*, she thought. She'd been swinging and swaying all over the southwest for Graves Baxter! But all she said was, "I see."

"So we're out of pearls," he said, "and we're near about out of money and a long way from home."

She gazed past him at the depot, the tracks, and the slow brown flow of the Colorado just beyond the yards. "Funny," she said. "I sent pearls to Mama and all my sisters, but I never kept a string for myself."

"When we get back, maybe they'll lend you one."

"We're not going back."

"What do you mean—not going back?"

She indicated the bridge across the river. "We're going that way," she said.

"What for? That's California over there."

"California's where I'm going, and if you like, you can come along...."

201

VIEW FROM AFAR OFF

1927: At sea, aboard the "France"

He's coming home from another of his frivolous excursions out of the three-dimensional world: he'd flitted to Oxford under the gauzy urge to study International Law—he who was still ill-acquainted with the Ten Commandments. In the precincts along the Isis, he'd lasted no longer than a single interview, after which he'd pondered how he might explain his folly on returning to the States. But what explanation could he give save this, that he was Julian, and like Julian he'd behaved?

There he is, then, dressed to the nines and smiling at a lens from the steps of a companionway. He seems troubled by nothing; his costly junket is behind him, and in his guard's coat and green velour hat, he appears to be quite serene. He's largely forgotten the two wops who were lately in the news, and of course he's unaware of a young woman working as a studio secretary five thousand miles away.

May 1926

CAUTION: THIS IS A ONE-WAY ROAD

The same bridge carried the railway and Route 80 across the Colorado and into California. The two continued together as far as Pilot Knob Siding, where the tracks veered toward the Salton Sink, and the highway, paved no more, became a corduroy of planks laid down over the swales and swells of what once was an ocean floor. From it, nothing could be seen but sand lying in the graceful heaps made by the wind, a wind so whimsical that it was ever at the work of undoing what it had done, and devils of sand were ever on the move from dune to dune.

When they were some distance into the sand hills, Marguerite spoke, saying, "What happens if we meet another car?"

"The sign said to pull into a turnout."

"Suppose there isn't any."

"Then one of us has to back up."

"How do you decide?"

"By whoever's closer to a turnout."

"Suppose the other driver is closer, and he won't back up."

"Then I kill him and push his car out of the way."

She laughed, and then she said, "I don't know why I'm laughing. People kill all the time, and for less than that."

Turning away, she gazed out at the contours of the swept sand, aglare in the sunlight and blue in the shade.

"This place is fascinating," she said, "and it must be even more so at night. It's like the Sahara."

"And just as hot," Leonard said.

"I've never seen a desert at night, but my sister Pearl says the sky looks near enough to write your name on."

"Sand holds the heat."

"If we lived around here, I'd come and see if it's true that the nights are so clear."

"What's magical about a desert?"

"It's clean, and it's quiet."

"It's dead."

"Oh, no. There's lots of life in a desert. You have to know where to look for it."

"I'd sooner look where water runs over rocks."

It was clean and quiet, she thought, because no one was here. There were no footprints, no tin-can traces of man; there were only the wind and the sweeps of sand.

"On what we have left," she said, "how long can we go?"

"Another month, maybe."

"I think it'd be foolish to keep on going till we're broke. I think we ought to stop and look for jobs."

"We'll do that—at the next oasis."

"We'll do it at the first thing that looks like a town."

As the car chattered over the planking, Leonard glanced at her, saying, "You're sore about the loan to Baxter."

"I never said so."

"But you are, aren't you?"

"Yes, but not on account of the money. I'm sore because you let me show myself off for someone I don't like."

"He'll pay the money back."

"You miss the point. You could've made the loan to anybody else, and I wouldn't've said a word. After all, it's your money. But I helped to earn it, and it grinds me that your pissant brother gets the benefit."

"Why do you call him a pissant?"

"A car's coming," she said.

It was Leonard who signalled that he'd clear the way. The other driver was grateful, and he stopped alongside the turnout.

"Colorado," the man said. "That's a place I never been to."

"Are you from around here?" Leonard said.

"El Centro, back of me about thirty miles."

"Is it much of a town?"

"Five-six thousand, but it's up-and-coming. Why—you figure to stay?"

"We might, if I can find a job."

The man produced a box of soda crackers and offered it to Leonard. "Saltines," he said. "We eat 'em all day in this country."

"Why?"

"The heat sweats out your salt."

"How hot does it get?"

The man laughed. "Mister, we go to hell to cool off. You talking job? It's coming up the Hundred Days, and you can just about take your pick."

"What're the Hundred Days?" Marguerite said.

"What you'd call summer, ma'am. We're below sea-level here in the Sink, and it hots up to 120 pretty regular."

"You don't make it sound very inviting."

"It ain't. People got money, they clear out for San Diego."

"What about the ones who don't?"

"Stick around, ma'am, and you'll find out....Well, I got to be going. Nice to met you folks."

After the man had gone, Leonard returned to the main line of planks and continued toward El Centro. Dunes blocked every view save that of higher dunes, and in places segments of the way were dredged in wind-borne sand and buried except for the stringpiece.

"120!" Leonard said.

"Does that feaze you?"

"It'd feaze an Arab! Don't tell me you're thinking of El Centro."

"I'm thinking of a job—and not just for you."

"You're not going to work."

"Why not? That's what I was doing up to last week."

"You weren't working. You were helping me."

"I didn't know."

"What else did you think you were doing?"

Shaking her head slightly, she let the question pass. "Those pearls," she said, "they gave us a mighty good time—a long vacation with pay. But that time is over, Leonard, and we can't live like it's coming back."

"I maybe could find something in my line—numbers. But what in the world would you do?"

"Anything I had to mind to."

Glancing about at reaches of pristine sand, she found herself reminded of other days, of the graceless places in which her family had lived and of her family's graceful ways. Spic-and-spandy, she thought, no slough, no rinsings, no rodents of dust and hair, no flyblown woodwork, no fingerprints on the mind. Rude, all those boxes of tar-paper, cinder block, and frame, but there as here the unclean was unknown.

"Leonard," she said, "pull over into that turnout, won't you?"

It was at the top of a rise, and when he stopped the car, she climbed down, removed her shoes and stockings, and then paused in the act of stepping onto the immaculate sand.

"I hate to do it," she said.

"Do what?"

"Track it up."

"You're not the first," he said, "and you won't be the last," and he watched her question the untrodden expanse. "The wind," he said. "It's been washed by the wind."

Of course, she thought. Others had been here, others had made their mars only to have them vanish in an hour or two, a day, and the same would happen to hers and to those that came after. The wind, she thought, would wash them away, and she moved out along the blade of a shadow made by a dune.

"Wait," Leonard said. "I'll join you."

Some way from the planking, she stooped for a grasp of sand. Escaping her fist, it poured and formed a minute mound at her feet. Near it lay a shard of shell, and she took it up to finger its smoothness.

"That was a lovely thing to say," she said. "Washed by the wind."
"Poetic, don't you think?"
"You ought to do that more often—let your fancy fly."
He laughed. "I'm afraid of heights."
"There's more to be afraid of in a ditch." Again she took in her surroundings, a dried-up sea with its sediment of the past, its remains. "Where did that man say he came from?"
"Man? Oh, El Centro."
"Why don't we give the place a try?"
"Alongside all this sand! You must be joking."
"I could get to like it here."
"There's sand where I come from, but in Carolina, it's on a beach."
Some grains remained in the crevices of her palm, and studying them, she said, "Did you ever notice how many colors there are? They're like little precious stones."
"Semi-precious," he said. "The man warned us, remember: people run away from here in the summertime."
"Good. That means they leave jobs for us."
"They leave the heat too. What's this craze of yours to get cooked for a hundred days?"

Washed by the wind, she thought. How many times, if ever before, had he let himself go long enough to say that kind of thing—and when, if ever, would he say the like again?

"Speaking of the man," he said. "He forgot his box of crackers."

It seemed to her that she'd spoken, saying *I thought maybe we could get off to a fresh start in a place like this,* but what she'd heard had been said in her mind.

"And then again, maybe not."
"Maybe not what?"
"Nothing, Leonard." she said.

1926

IMPERIAL VALLEY

The plank road gave way to pavement at Gray's Well, a ramshackle depot of corrugated iron. Beneath its dented overhang stood a glass-jar gas-pump, and above it a sign announced that supplies were also for sale, among them ice-cold soft drinks.

"Ice cold," Leonard said. "Out here, not even ice is ice-cold."
"I'm ready for whatever's wet," Marguerite said.
Leonard disappeared through a dim doorway under the shed, and when he returned, he was carrying two bottles of soda pop. He gave one of them to her, saying, "The man said it's another thirty miles to El Centro."
"Where'd you get the pamphlet?"
"He gave it to me. It's about this valley."
"Let's have a look."

No long way beyond the rusting station, great spreads of cultivation could be seen at either hand. Running off into the distance were wind-rows of alfalfa, vast fields of melons, and berry-hill regiments that seemed to wheel as they were passed.

Folding the pamphlet, Marguerite said, "The Indian name for this place was The Hollow of God's Hand."

"That should've kept the whites away."

"Nothing keeps whites away." She took a swig from the pop-bottle and said, "This stuff—when I was a kid, I called it Cokey-Coley."

"Where I come from, we call it dope."

Far out on a mirage floated a fleet of shanties. Blistered by the heat, their paint had flaked, and some were listing as if their seams had been sprung by the sun.

"Well, if all else fails us," Leonard said, "we can join the harvest-stiffs—the rag-heads and the spics. Plenty of running water...in the ditches."

Eucalyptus trees, forever shedding buds and strips of bark, made an aromatic tunnel for the road. A metal marker read *El Centro—24 mi.*

"If you really don't want to stay there, Leonard, I'm willing to go on."

"What the heck, one place is as good as another."

"I don't insist on El Centro."

"Come to think, you don't insist on much of anything."

"Not much is worth insisting on. As you say, one place is as good as another."

"People ought to have opinions."

"About important things, yes. If they have an opinion about *every-*thing, they're a pain in the ass....Well, do we go or stay?"

"You decide."

"I'm for staying, but I'd be just as happy anywhere else."

"Have you been happy so far?"

"The Hollow of God's Hand," she said almost to herself as she gazed at a grid of ditches on a great green sweep of land. And then she said, "Some of the time."

Her answer to his question had been so long on the way that he said, "Some of the...?", and then he said, "Oh," after which he said no more.

EL CENTRO, pop. 3,550

The Center itself had a center: the point where Route 80, running east and west, intersected Route 99, northbound from the Mexican border. At that crossing and for a short distance in all four directions, the main come-and-go of the town was to be found. There, from under their arcades, business-fronts stared at traffic passing through the outside glare. These shaded blocks were few, though, and they soon gave way to a mesh of lesser streets, some of them merely lanes paved only with the offcast of the blue-gum trees. Blown in from the Sink, silt lay everywhere, a powder so fine that it stirred for the slightest air.

Along one such byway stood a row of bungalows. None was old, but, withered by the sun and weathered by the wind, all had aged beyond their age; built with oversize eaves to shield their walls, they looked rather like birds with wings fanned to fend off the heat. Emerging from a doorway, Leonard and Marguerite paused on the porch to take in the prospect—the mottled gum trees, the dead-and-gone lawns, the jellied air above their sun-baked car.

"Well," he said, "what do you think?"

"I've seen worse," she said. "I've *lived* in worse."

"You don't mean that."

"Don't I, though. Sometimes Daddy had to go 'way off looking for work, and when he found it, he sent for Mama and us kids. Gracious life, the dumps he brought us to!"

"What did your mother say?"

"Nothing. Her skirt was off in a whipstitch, and she set the dump to rights."

"*Us kids*, you said. Didn't you pitch in?"

"I was little, and I did what I could, but mostly I got in the way. It was Mama and Midgie did the donkey-work."

"Not your father?"

"Never. Mama wouldn't allow it."

"Why not?"

"After he'd put in a ten-hour day slapping up plaster? She sat him down to read the papers while I drew a beard on him with a burnt stick."

Leonard nodded back over his shoulder, saying, "This dump'd take some of that donkey-work."

"Nothing the like of what Mama did."

"I'll help."

"No need. Just keep out of the way."

1926

AN EXCHANGE OF LETTERS

Dear Midgie:

Well, we're all done with the pearl business. When we got to Yuma, instead of the new shipment we ordered, what we found was a notice from Mecca Gem hiking the price up out of sight, and that put the kibosh on a pretty good thing.

Being we were so close, we figured we'd look for jobs in Californ-i-ay, and here we are, doing just that. Meanwhile, we rented a little house (three rooms $30 per mo.). It's run-down like those cha-teaus Daddy was famous for, but I'm getting it in shape. Puts me in mind of how you and Mama neatened up those places in Beatrice and Genoa and Fullerton.

I was talking about jobs. We hear they're not too hard to come by, and right now Leonard is out having a look-see for something in his line. Me, soon as #12 Holt Ave. is livable, I'll try for what I studied for, secretarial, but believe me I'll take what I can get. If the two of us hit pay-dirt, we'll make ends meet.

That sounds like I'm feeling you out for a loan, but get this straight, you little squirt—any money from home goes right back where it came from! Mama and Daddy are all done looking out for me. I swore I was going to look out for *them*, and I'll do it yet.

Leonard? There's nothing wrong with Leonard. It's just that I can't decide if there's anything right.

How's Ed, and how's that little squarehead kid of yours? Love to all three of you. Address above if you want to write.

Dear Marg:

I sure was sorry to hear about you losing out on the pearl thing. Thats life I guess up today and down tomorrow and all you can do is take it on the chin. Which the Smith family is pretty good at having a lot of expirience doing same. Well your a Smith and I say they cant keep you down long.

First off about money. You maybe dont want any now but if you ever do just holler. Me and Ed will scrap up enough to keep the wolf from the door.

The big news around here is Pearlie Arizona has took out for Los Angeles. Her and Chester just loaded up their Dodge and high tailed it for where the streets is paved with gold. When they get there they aim to set up a hair dressing parlor.

They. I dont know why I say they. Its Pearlie does it all and Chester just sets around goggling at the girls. At his age youd think his mind would be above the waste.

Baby sister, theres another thing Im sorry about and thats you and Leonard. The way you write I can tell there isnt much spark to him. But think. If he had more he might be another Chester.

Ill send you Pearlies address soon as I know it. Meantime keep your chin up. I know thats how it got hit but keep it up anyway.

Love to both of you.

1926

ALL AROUND THE TOWN

The bungalow, with some six hundred of feet of floor space, was divided into three rooms, a bath, and a kitchen. Its furnishing were sparse and plain, evidently chosen with the torrid climate in mind: the livingroom suite was made of bamboo, so too were the roll-down blinds, and the floors were covered with mats of straw. There were two bedchambers, each of these with a single bed.

I gave that scant thought at first, she wrote to Midge, *but then it came to me: in this neck of the woods, people don't want to sleep with themselves, let alone with somebody else.*

On the porch, there were a pair of woven-wicker rockers and a wicker swing to match, and in the rear yard, a few smoke trees grayed the view of the yard next door. Along the fence-line, one agave had become many, a hen hovering over its brood of agave chicks, all, large and small, armed with backswept spikes to snag the careless, and nearby grew a second trap, a thicket of aloes. Across the open space, a hose scribbled its way from a standpipe to a sprinkler.

> *There's nary a blade of grass out back, so I guess the whirler's used to wet the ground and cool the air. It isn't hot enough for that just yet, but we've been warned, and maybe it'll come in handy.*

The porch and the grounds were of small concern to her; what mattered most was the interior of the bungalow, and it was there that she spent her labors. Early had all four daughters heard their mother say, "Clean is decent; dirty is trash," and they'd heard this too, "Let things slide, and you slide with 'em." So taught, all four were fastidious, none more so than Marguerite. The first area to receive her attention was the bathroom. To it, she gave the better part of a day, much of that on her knees with a bucket of suds, a scrub-brush, and disinfectant, and by the time she looked back through the doorway, the walls, the tub, and the shower-stall shone.

> *Tell Mama that only then would I sit down to pee. She'll say, "Well, leastways I learned the child good."*

She was far longer at the work of restoring the kitchen. Abused by former tenants, it had suffered their successive neglect, so that what Marguerite faced were layers of impairment—grease encrusting grease, stains stained by later stains. Below the faucets of the sink, rust bled toward the drain, and on the counter, grime gummed the grouting of the tile. The walls and woodwork were painted over with points of spatter, and the icebox gave off the bad breath of food gone bad, an indissoluble blend of decay.

> *The place put me in mind of that slob Jos that Mama used to redd up after. I was three days scraping and scouring before I could make myself take a drink of water from the tap. Last night, though, we had our first*

*supper in, and it sure tasted good. Anyway, it was better than eating out,
which in El Centro is tempting fate.*

Calling out as he entered the bungalow one evening, Leonard said,
"Well, I got the job at Haas, Baruch!"

"Really?" Marguerite said. "That's just wonderful!"

"They're taking me on as a bookkeeper, but I'm laying odds I soon get
to be their accountant."

"I don't see why not. You're a wiz with numbers."

"Speaking of numbers," he said, "aren't you going to ask what they're
paying me?"

"That's kind of personal, isn't it?"

"A wife has a right to know a thing like that."

"I don't make a big thing about rights."

"Fifty dollars a week!"

"Fifty? That much?"

"I asked around, and there's no better packing-plant in the valley. In
the state, even."

"I'm happy for you, Leonard. Seems like a fine opportunity."

"The job means more than the fifty a week. It means there's no reason
for *you* to work."

In the silence they imposed, she seemed to hear the words again.
"Oh, but there is," she said.

"I don't see the need at all. I'll be making enough money."

"I wouldn't be out for the money. I'd be out for the job."

"But why?"

"Because in my family, no one sits around on his ass."

"You wouldn't be doing that. There's the house to look after."

"Housework was never my lick."

"You did just fine with this place."

"I know what's gravelling you, Leonard. You think I'd be lowering you
if I took a job."

He ran a finger along the strakes of a blind, and then he said, "Maybe
I do."

"I hope we're not getting into a go-around about this."

"Me too. I'm not looking for a quarrel."

"That's the last thing I want, but you'd better pay attention: I'm no
dirt-chasing homebody."

"What would they think at Haas, Baruch? What would I say when they asked me why my wife was working?"

"Say you beat the whey out of me, but you couldn't make me stay at home! If anybody sticks his bill in, say take it out! Say anything! It's our affair."

"You're going to go against me in this, aren't you? Just like you did about that woman in Greeley."

"I won't be told what I can do."

"Not even by your husband?"

"Especially by my husband. You ought to trust me to know what's right and what's wrong."

After saying nothing for a moment, he left the room and went to the rear yard. She followed and found him watching the somnolent revolutions of the sprinkler.

"I hurt your feelings," she said, "and I'm sorry."

"In my family, it's unheard of—a wife going to work."

"That's their way, and I respect it. But what about my way?"

"Your way reflects on me."

"A while back, you allowed that I had a right to ask about your salary. Why won't you allow me other rights?"

"You have no right to hold me up to contempt."

"That's just fiddle-faddle, Leonard. In this day and age, and in a whistle-stop like El Centro, who's going to jeer because your wife holds a job?"

"'What's the matter with the guy?' they'll think. 'Can't he support his wife?'"

"To hell with what people think! Fret about that, and you'll be scared to get out of bed."

"What people think is important."

She shook her head, saying, "I hoped I was making myself clear, Leonard, but it looks like you need more....If I can find a job, I'm going to take it."

"It's clear now."

"I wish you hadn't made me say it like that."

"I wish you hadn't said it at all."

✲

214

During the next few days, Marguerite studied the Want-ad columns of the *Imperial Valley Press*, but she found nothing in any way like what she was qualified for. One morning, though, she came upon a call for a typist, but on applying, she learned that employment would be temporary only, and she refused it. Being in the business quarter of the town, she made unsolicited inquiries at a bank, a dry-goods store, and the gas company, all to no avail. On the point of returning home, she saw, half a block away, the building occupied by the newspaper she held in her hand. Why not?, she thought, and she moved toward the entrance.

Asking for the editor, she was directed to a glassed-in room commanding the rest of the floor. There a gray-haired man looked up across a row of reference books and said, "Well, state your business, young lady."

"I'm looking for a job," she said.

"Are you good at anything?"

"I can type."

"Everybody types around here. What reporter can't type?"

"I don't want to be a reporter."

The man raised himself a little for a better view of her. "Nobody ever said that to me before. I can't believe my ears."

"I went to business college in Greeley, Colorado. I don't know beans with the bag open about reporting."

"And you don't want to learn?"

"Not particularly. I'm a typist."

"I've got a friend works for the *San Diego Union*. When I tell him about you, he'll call me a liar."

"All I want is a desk and a typewriter—and a small salary."

"How small?"

"Just enough to call it a salary."

"What name do you go by, miss?"

"Marguerite Roberts. Mrs."

"What's your husband do?"

"He's a bookkeeper over at Haas, Baruch."

"Did he tell you to get a job?"

"He told me not to."

The man rose and rounded his desk. "My name is James Erskine. Jimmy to all. Would you work for twenty dollars a week?"

"I sure would, Mr. Erskine."

"Jimmy. I mean as a reporter."

❧

At the supper-table that night, Leonard had little to say. He replied to Marguerite's questions about his work at Haas, Baruch, and he supplied a few details on his own, but that was all. After washing the dishes, she joined him on the porch, where he was sitting on the steps and staring into the night at lights near and far, colors, motion, shadows, or only at something he was seeing within.

She took a seat on the swing, and letting it sway until it fell still, she said, "I got a job today."

He responded after a moment, saying, "I hate the idea."

"I showed myself off in a hundred windows. You didn't hate that."

"That again!"

"The job's with the *Imperial Valley Press*."

"Doing what?"

"Reporting."

He turned to her slowly and said, "Did I hear you right?"

"If not, I can say it again."

"Don't tell me they were advertising for a reporter, and they picked you."

"I just walked in cold and asked for work as a typist."

"And they said, 'You're no typist, ma'am. You're a reporter.' Just like that."

"That's how it *did* happen."

"Well, I'm dead against it."

"You'll have to come back from the dead, then. Because I'm keeping the job."

"In other words, I have no say about your doings."

"You have a say, and you're saying it. But you're my husband, not my boss. You can't just hand down orders."

"Is that how it works in the Smith family?"

"You can bet big on it. My Mama and Daddy are equals, and neither one runs the other, like you're trying to do."

"*Somebody's* got to be the head of a family."

She laughed. "Well, I come from a two-headed family."

"It's no joke, Marguerite. If a man isn't the head of a family, he gets no respect."

"Mister, you never in your born days saw more respect than Mama has for Daddy—or more love!"

Rising, he walked out over the parched earth, and through the darkness, she could hear him cracking blue-gum bark underfoot, and then she heard him coming back.

He stopped below the bottom step, and he spoke up to the shadowed swing, saying, "We don't agree on much, do we?"

And she spoke down into the dimness to say, "We never did."

"Why?, I wonder. We're decent people, we're intelligent, we're serious-minded. Why don't we ever see eye-to-eye? Will we always be strangers?"

The question, she thought, required no answer: it contained its own. Strangers, he'd said, meaning that he knew at last what she'd known from the start. He said no more now, and mounting the steps, he crossed the porch and entered the house. She sat where she was, listening to a passing car, to a distant train, to the small sound of the lives all around her. As if powered by her pulse, the swing swung a little, and now and then its chains spoke their single syllable.

On her arrival for work in the morning, she was sent to the office of the editor.

"Sit down," he said. "I want to talk to you."

"Did you change your mind?"

"I never change my mind. I'd only wind up with worse."

"I'm relieved."

"I saw you drive up in a car."

"My husband thought I might need it."

"A thoughtful man. What did you do—drop him off at Haas, Baruch?"

"He said it was out of my way. He offered to walk."

"A *very* thoughtful man....What does he call you?"

"Marguerite."

"Every time"

"So far."

"It's a mouthful."

"My family called me Marg."

"I like that better. I can holler it."

217

"What did you want to talk to be about, Mr. Erskine? Jimmy."

"First off," he said. "I told my wife about you, and she liked what she heard. I'm ordered to ask you and your husband over for breakfast next Sunday."

"We'll be glad to come."

"Next, I want you to know why I hired you."

"It's a mystery to me."

"Right off the reel, I liked your manner. You're quiet and direct, and my guess is you come from the best kind of people—poor but open-handed."

"I'm getting all swole up."

"Most of all, I liked the way you spoke—to the point. When you answered a question, you didn't speak like a character in Henry James. Which indicated you might write the way you talk."

"I'll sure as life try."

"And finally, I want to warn you about the climate. You come from—where did you say—Nebraska? It gets plenty hot there, I hear, but hot in El Centro is another kind of hot, and if you forget it, it can kill you. Here, during the Hundred Days, it sometimes gets to be 120, 125, and by God, that's too damn hot even for a snake!"

"I'm in for it, then."

"But it isn't enough to stand the heat. You've got to stand the heated-up people. Mild ones, soft-spoken and steady ones, all of a sudden they reach their limit and explode. Afterwards, they don't remember what they did—the nose they broke with a beer-bottle, the store-front they drove through in their car. We had a woman once, she walked stark naked into an ice cream parlor and ordered a soda."

Marguerite laughed. "What flavor?"

Erskine laughed too and said, "One last thing. When it starts hotting up, women start shedding, and in the end, they're down to a limpsy cotton dress. Don't ever get between a man and the sun."

"Why don't you tell me how to be a reporter?"

"I can't. You have it, or you don't."

"It must be like honor," she said.

He nodded, slowly, and then he said, "After a while, I'll take you over to the County Courthouse and show you around," and when she was at the door, he stopped her, saying, "That was a reporter's question."

"Which one?"
"What flavor?""

⸱

"...I'd just as soon not hear about your job," Leonard said.

Sitting across the table from him, she stirred the ice in a glass of tea. It was important, she thought, to stir it slowly, as if by so doing, she'd impede her anger and slacken the speed of a reply. The spoon barely moved, and the ice made muted music against the glass.

"It's wrong to spoil my pleasure," she said.

"We're even, then. You spoil mine."

"Leonard," she said. "Are we keeping score? Are we playing a game?"

"Maybe we are. Maybe that's all this marriage ever was—one side against the other."

"I don't look at it like that. We're a couple of far-apart people trying to come together. It isn't easy. It doesn't happen overnight."

"How can it happen at all if you wear the pants?"

The ice had melted, and the spoon made no music in the glass. "Are you serious, Leonard? Do you really think I want to rule you?"

"What else? You walk all over my wishes."

"That simply isn't so. I come from a family where everybody's on a long tether. Nobody runs the show. Nobody lays down the law. Why would I be different?"

"I don't know, but you are—and my mother thinks so too."

She rose and went to the ice-box, where, using a pick, she chipped a small chunk from the block. She returned to the table with it and dropped it into her glass.

"Does she?" she said.

"She says you're strong-minded."

"She ought to know. She sure runs *your* family. I like your father, but he's a beaten-down man, and it's your mother's doing."

"How can you say a thing like that? They're devoted to each other!"

"Devoted!" she said. "What a word! My Mama and Daddy *love* each other, but yours don't, and it's plain to see. There's no love in their house...and sad to say, there's mighty little in this one!"

219

Again she rose, and throwing down the spoon, she left the room. In the rear yard, she walked on the glade of light laid down by the doorway until it dwindled to a glow. Underfoot there, as everywhere, lay the slough of the blue-gum trees, the shreds of bark, the buttons, the slender red-brown leaves, and trodden on, they gave a coughdrop flavor to the air. *Mighty little*, she'd said, but was there any, she wondered, was there any at all?

Leonard made his way toward her through the yard, and when he reached her, he said, "We got pretty tight-wound in there."

"Yes," she said. "We did."

"I really don't grudge you your pleasure. I'm sorry for what I said."

"I got kind of hot myself."

"Tell me about the job...."

"I can't imagine why they invited me," Leonard said.

"I wouldn't've gone if they hadn't."

"I don't see why not. You're the one works for the *Press*."

"If Haas, Baruch invited you, would you go if they left me out?"

"Suppose it had to do with business."

"On a Sunday morning?" she said.

༃

It was a ten-mile drive to the Erskine ranch, a citrus grove on a side road west of Brawley. The house, a cube of logs and adobe, was partly shielded by a grape arbor, and nearby stood a three-stall stable built to match. Beyond both rose the rolling rounds of the Superstition Hills. Erskine awaited the car in the driveway.

"Jimmy," Marguerite said, "this is Leonard, my husband. Leonard, my boss, Jimmy Erskine."

His wife was now with them, and her guests were presented, after which Erskine led Leonard away toward the stable, and Marguerite was shown into the house.

"I want to thank you for having us out, Mrs. Erskine."

"Clara," the woman said. "Jimmy had good things to say about you, but I like to see for myself."

"There isn't much to see, I'm afraid."

"If you don't mind, we'll feed ourselves out under the arbor. Everything's ready but the biscuits. Meanwhile, tell me about Jimmy's new reporter."

"I honestly don't know why he took me on. I went in looking for work as a typist."

"He said he didn't think typing was your lick."

"It's all I know."

"How do you know that's all you know?"

"I never got further than high school. Three months of business college was all my folks could afford. Daddy's a plasterer."

Mrs. Erskine opened the oven door slightly and closed it again. "I notice you don't say *only* a plasterer."

"Only!" Marguerite said. "Plastering fed Mama and him and a slew of kids!"

"I take it you care for the man."

"There's no one better in the world."

"Something tells me you're not *only* a typist."

"I can go like sixty on the keys, but that doesn't make me a reporter."

"I like you," the woman said.

"I'm glad. I was worried you wouldn't."

"Why?"

"I don't impress people."

From the oven, the woman removed a pan of baking-powder biscuits, a brown-topped crowd. "You impressed Jimmy. When he came home the other day, he said, 'Guess what, Clara? A good one walked in off the street.'" Then, placing the pan on a tray of food, she started for the doorway, saying as she went, "I hold a degree from Arizona U., and you're impressing *me*...."

On the way back to El Centro, Marguerite said, "What did you think of the Erskines?"

"Decent enough people, I guess."

She repeated his comment to the road ahead. "Decent enough," she said."

"All I meant was—well, I mean decent."

"Won't you allow they're better than that?"

"After one breakfast?....The biscuits were good, by the way."

221

"I've seen Erskine more than you have, but this meeting with his wife was my first as well as yours—and I think she's a dandy."

"I couldn't figure her, but I don't think he likes me."

"What do you base that on?"

"I'm not his kind."

"No? What kind are you?"

"You know, college and all."

"Maybe he sensed your attitude."

"He'd've had to be pretty sharp. I didn't exactly sneer at him."

"Leonard, my dear fellow, you sneer in your sleep."

He drove for a way before saying, "Not at you."

"If you felt dislike, it didn't come from Erskine."

"From his wife?"

"She has a degree from Arizona U."

Her first piece for the *Press* was roughed out in longhand and then transferred to type. It read:

> In the Southern Pacific yards today, a brakeman threw a switch too early, and a string of freight-cars went one way and the caboose another. Only slight damage was caused when a buffer was hit by the caboose. Which, your reporter learned, is never so called by a railroader. In his parlance, it is either a crummy or a clown-wagon.

She laid the single sheet on Erskine's desk and left the room. Within a few moments, she heard his signet-ring tapping on the glass partition, and looking up, she saw him beckoning her.

"Not too bad," he said. "Not too bad at all."

"Really? I didn't think you'd like it."

"Why not?"

"It doesn't say anything important."

"Guess again. It tells people they're people, and anybody can make a mistake—butcher, baker, brakeman. It also tells them something they never knew. Where'd you get that bit about crummy and clown-wagon?"

"From the brakeman."

"I'm going to run the piece—"

"Oh, that's wonderful!" she said.

"—after you rewrite the last sentence."

This time, she merely said, "Oh."

"Get rid of *parlance*. That's a Boston word."

"Mr. Erskine," she said. "Jimmy, I mean. When I was down at the S.P. yards the other day, I got an idea for another story."

"Shoot," he said.

"It's about the Plank Road."

"A dead issue—or should I say dead *wood*? They'll be opening the paved road any day now, and everybody'll be happy."

"My story would have to do with a man who won't be."

"Are you saying you dug up somebody who longs for the good old days? Busted springs, flats, breakdowns, abandoned baggage?"

"Yes," she said.

"Write it."

On the following day, she turned in her new story:

> A few weeks from now, on August 12th, a paved highway will connect El Centro with Yuma and points east, and the era of the Plank Road will end. There are some, though, who will not rejoice, and one such is Carlos Fonseca.
>
> Carlos owns a salvage shop on Commercial Avenue close by the railroad yards. Every item in his huge stock is a throwaway that he picked up along the route of the Plank Road. Included are fenders, mufflers, springs, motor parts, car seats, nuts, bolts, lugs, tools, and even a steering-wheel. In addition, there is an assortment of clothing, books, luggage, dolls, phonograph records, and, oddest of all, a toy sailboat.
>
> Asked about his collection, Carlos said, "When I see all these stuff in the sand, I say there is a good business you go in. You will not pay for *mercandias*. You will pick it up *gratuito*....But now they go close that road, and no more is these stuff throw away. Soon I will have to go in a different business, so is very bad for me, this *camino pavimento*."
>
> For Carlos Fonseca, it would seem that progress is anything but progressive.

When Erskine finished reading the piece, he came to his doorway and stood there for a moment, gazing without expression at Marguerite. At length, he nodded her to his room.

"At the ranch the other day," he said, "you told Clara that all you know is typing. Why?"

"Because it is."

Taking up the Fonseca piece, he shook it before her. "This is not typing!"

"You mean you actually like it?"

"It won't win you a Pulitzer, but it suits me fine."

"Well, I'll be darned."

"The smart alecks say that writing is simply putting one word down after another. True, but you've got to know what words to put down. Where did *you* learn? Being only a typist!"

She shrugged. "Around home," she said, "there was mighty little jibber-jabber. We said what we thought, straight out and plain. When we wanted to say the car got stuck in the mud, we said the car got stuck in the mud."

"In a newspaper, that's all you ever say. You can be talking about the *Titanic* or a ball game, but what it comes to is the car got stuck in the mud. You seem to know that. You write as you speak...except for *parlance*, of course."

"That won't happen again."

"If it does, it won't be in these tidbits you pick up around town. From now on, you go out on assignment."

"Jimmy, that's just wonderful. I never expected—"

"Beat it," he said, and he let her reach the doorway before saying, "How come you don't ask what I think of Leonard?"

She turned, and for a moment she studied him. "That's the first time you've said something wrong."

"I wanted to see what you'd say."

"About my husband?"

"No. About my question."

"I think it was crude," she said, and she left the room.

౿

Dear Marg

    Well I made the move and here I am in Los Angelus and wouldnt you know it Chester tagged along. All I can say is he better tow the line or out he goes no more of him fooling around.

We rented a little turkeytail bungalow 1452 West 39 St off of some people name of Ives really Ivello. Its near Western Ave where I took over a beauty parlor that the owner wanted out of. Its got four sinks and four dryers pretty well equipped with sheets curlers scissors and the like and we ought to do pretty good it being in a home part of town.

Of course it was a rench parting with the Old Settlers not knowing when Id see them again but theres satisfaction knowing Midge and Connie are close by. Well you got my address now oh I almost forgot. Theres a small extra room in the house so any time you want you can come and stay. Chester says regards. Love from

Pearl the pill

P S Im sending this through Midge. You write and say where I can reach you direct.

Erskine came to her desk and said, "Drive out along Route 80. Someone called to report a car on fire between Seeley and Edgar Siding. It might be worth a hundred words."

The car, she found, was just off the highway in a field of alfalfa. The fire was out by the time she arrived, and she was alone with the charred skeleton of what had been a high-slung touring car. Gone were the seats save for their spiral bones, gone too the tires and the wheel-spokes, and thus lowered, the machine gave the impression of having been brought to its knees. Walking around the remains, she felt strangely moved (why?, she wondered) when she read the blackened license-plate: 27206 Tennessee. It became the lead of the piece she wrote for the *Press*:

> The first paragraph of a newspaper item is supposed to tell who? what? where? when? and why? This paragraph cannot do that.
>
> A Ford touring car burned to its axles in a field near Seeley today. Its license-number was 27206 Tennessee. Beyond that, nothing is certain.
>
> The frame for its canvas top was bare, and strewn about were

parts of the car and its cargo—a headlight, a water bucket, bits of rope, an oil can, a washboard, a child's bonnet.

The scene brought to mind scenes of bygone days—covered wagons covered no more, pillaged by the Indians, burned and left to weather on the Plains and turn to dust. Had the same happened here? Could such a thing still be? Pikes Peak or Bust, those wagons once said, this one only 27206 Tennessee.

"It's more than a hundred," Erskine said, "but it runs just as it is..."

THE VIEW FROM AFAR OFF

1930: The Wandering Jew

Where is he not seen that year?

He can be found among the snows and pines of Jersey, and later, when the ground is clear, he turns up at Long Lake in the Adirondacks, there to fish a little and fiddle with a novel.* Now, with summer at hand, the shore calls him for sunning and swimming till late in the fall, whereafter, to avoid the chill, he takes himself once more to Europe, and there he's spotted in Paris and Pisa, in Venice and Rome and Madrid, before running out of money and taking ship for home.

The young woman he'll one day meet is no longer a studio secretary, nor is she any longer a studio reader of other people's writing. She's a writer now herself, and in a photo she's shown entering the Writers Building at Fox Western. She's looking back at the camera—or possibly at a cloud of dust coming toward her from the distance.

1926

THE HUNDRED DAYS

In the rear yard, the sprinkler spun languidly and sprayed a circle of barren ground. It seemed to have been drained of power and slowed by the heat, and it sowed only a small area of wet around its feet. On a pair

*The Water Wheel, 1933

of straw mats nearby, Marguerite and Leonard lay naked in the navy-blue night.

"That whirler," he said. "You think it's doing any good?"
"No," she said, "but it makes me feel that something's trying."

A hot wind made the satin-sound of a passing skirt as it stirred the blue-gum leaves. It came with a charge of silt so fine that it could be felt only after it had settled on the skin.

"At the *Press* today, I was talking to the typesetter. He said to wink at the numbers we give out. If we say it was 90°, it was 90° in the cellar, not in the street."
"Talk about the heat, and it only gets hotter."
"It'll get hotter, talk or no talk. This is just the beginning, they say."

Somewhere in the distance, a dog barked twice, and a car-horn cursed, and as through a door briefly opened, she heard a few bars of music. A drop of sweat crawled down her side, leaving behind it the feel of where it had been, the memory of its tingling trail—and then another drop formed and began to flow. Reaching across the space between them, Leonard put his hand on her thigh.

"If you don't mind," she said, "no."
"You don't usually say that."
"I'm wet all over. You'd slide off."
"It isn't far to fall."
"I said no, Leonard."
He removed his hand.

She stared at the stars, reminded of the cut-outs she'd pasted on her grade-school drawings—paper stars, she thought, stars made of col-ored paper.

"These days," Leonard said, "I don't hear much about Erskine."

The shift was so sharp that for a moment she felt that she'd missed a step in the stair of thought. Lying quite still, she sought the sky for the connection, but finding none, she raised herself on an elbow and looked down at Leonard.

"Erskine?" she said. "Where does *he* fit in?"

"You used to run on about him. What made you stop?"

"Your mind was on something just now. All of a sudden, it jumped to something else."

"It wasn't much of a jump."

A wind shook the blue-gum leaves, and they whispered in the darkness overhead. She listened until the wind fell, and the leaves were silent.

And then she said, "Don't tell me you're jealous."

"I wouldn't exactly say that."

"No, not exactly. But you do think I'm keeping something from you."

"Yes."

"Well, I am," she said. "I didn't want you to know I'd had a run-in with Erskine."

"What about?"

"You. He said something that gravelled me."

"About me?"

"The day after we were out at his place, we spoke about this and that—the ranch, the horses, the *Press*—and finally he said how come I didn't ask what he thought of you."

"What's so bad about that?"

"Asking a stranger what he thought of my husband? You're joking."

"Not at all."

"Would you ask somebody what he thought of *me*?"

He said nothing, and she lay back, the damp mat feeling slightly cooler beneath her than before. She thought of the word *evaporation*.

"Why *didn't* you ask him?" Leonard said.

"Because his opinion of you doesn't count for beans with me."

"Were you afraid of what he'd answer?"

Now she sat full up, saying, "What in the world are you getting at, Leonard?"

"Your reason for not asking. Your *real* reason."

"Real! The heat must've addled your brains!"

"Where was the harm in asking?"

She contemplated him, and then she said, "You're an odd one. One minute you're sensitive, and the next you're dead as a stump. You want to know what Erskine thinks of you? Go ask him. Don't send me."

She rose, her small figure glistening slightly in the starlight, and she stood fingering the wet on her belly and breasts; she knew even without looking that the silt had grayed it and made it streak. After a moment, she turned away and entered the house.

❦

"I've been bringing lunch from home every day," Marguerite said. "Why didn't somebody tell me about this place?"

With Clara Erskine, she was seated at one of the tables in Clements Drug Store, a tunnel-like shop running in from an arcade near the offices of the *Press*. The older woman had driven in from the ranch that morning and invited Marguerite to join her. Their orders had been taken by a waitress, and Marguerite was surveying her surroundings—the stamped tin that covered the high ceiling, the five overhead fans, the drug counter, the patrons at the soda fountain.

After they'd been served, Clara said, "I came to town today for two reasons. One of them is to make peace between you and Jimmy. I love the guy, and we both admire you. It's a shame that a remark of his put you off. He meant no harm, Marguerite."

At the soda fountain, patrons sat on stools with their backs to the drug-counter wall, a coatless row of male customers, white-shirted all.

"To think that I'd ask him—ask anybody—what he thought of my husband! That's holding me pretty cheap, Clara. That's harm."

"If you *had* asked, he'd've told you that he liked Leonard."

"Then he should've said so—or said nothing."

"Jimmy's dead honest, and he'd've told you more—that he envied Leonard his college degree. Like you, he went no further than high school. Unlike you, it bothers him."

Patrons left the soda fountain, and other patrons came, but for all the change they made, they might've been the same twelve white shirts all the time.

"You're wrong, Clara. It bothers me too."

She heard the hiss of carbonation from the fountain, the clash of crockery, the grinding of the milk-shake mixer, and under all hummed the fans.

"You're getting experience at the *Press* that you probably couldn't get anywhere else. Stay there, Marguerite—but don't stay too long. For you, it isn't the end of the line. You're better than the *Press*."

"I never thought of a job that way. At Woolworth's in Greeley, I was back of the candy counter. It was dreadful stuff, but it made me a dollar a day."

"You're a long way past Woolworth's—"

Suspended in a row over the center line of the store, the five fans slowly turned, their blades churning the warm air below them and the warmer above, somehow making the blend seem cooler.

"—and you still have a long way to go."

"To go where, Clara?"

"I don't know. But one thing's sure—you won't get there writing nice little pieces for the *Press*."

"I never expected a lot from life. I love my family, and I love dogs and horses, and not much else. My Mama and Daddy are the best people in the world, and all I want is enough to take care of them."

"I don't suppose I'm likely to meet them, but I don't have to. Knowing you, I know what they're like."

"The Old Settlers, I call them," Marguerite said, "No schooling, no headstart, no anything but work. And I never saw the day when they didn't have me beat."

"Reporting fires and fist-fights—you were meant for more than that."

"Who can say what people are meant for? Most of us get knocked about like a pin-ball."

"You're not one of those."

"I don't think I'm a nonesuch."

"A sure sign that you are."

"You know me better than I know myself, then. You must've gotten your degree in Psychology."

Clara laughed and said, "Agriculture. But I've given you some thought, and I have you down as a natural."

"Which is...?"

"Someone who isn't sly, who isn't crafty. You're direct. You say your mind, and you say it quietly. There's no cunning in you, no backbite. In short, you're a lot of things I wish I could say of myself."

"Don't wish too hard. Sounded to me like you were describing a rube."

"I'm twice your age," the woman said, "and if I could go back, I'd want to be like you. My people had money, lots of it, and it got me travel, clothes, college, whatnot, and a quarter-section of the best grapefruit ever grown. You got nothing from your people except class—and I'd swap you for it, mine for yours."

Marguerite shook her head, saying, "I'm not that good, Clara, not nearly."

"You don't *know* how good you are."

"Back in grade school, I made some drawings that my teacher liked. She sent them to the Chicago Art Institute, I think it was, and the verdict was: Shows the talent of the average schoolgirl. I'm average, Clara."

The waitress came to the table, saying "Will there be anything else, ladies?"

"Thanks, no," Clara said, and the waitress went away. "Are you wearing a slip under that dress?"

"Yes, I am," Marguerite said. "Why?"

"I'm wearing one too. I always do when I come to town. You'll find out why as we walk toward the door."

A dozen men still sat facing the soda fountain, an always changing dozen that always seemed the same, white-shirted, sweat-stained, and wearing cheap straw hats.

"Watch that bunch," Clara said as they rose from the table.

The store-front, deep in under the arcade, blazed with the sunlight burning in the arches, and as the two women moved toward the glare, heads one by one turned to follow them—and then one by one they turned back.

At the doorway, Clara said, "If we hadn't been wearing slips, they'd be staring yet."

"Does it ever get past the staring stage?"

"Once in a while. Some redneck'll get red all over and start acting proud."

"What happens then?"

"The better element takes care of him," Clara said, and she laughed.

"The better element!"

"Thanks for the lunch," Marguerite said. "And for a right-down idea!"

On parting with Clara, Marguerite went to Erskine's office, and being nodded in, she said, "I got all pursy over nothing the other day, and I'm sorry."

"Noted," he said.

"Also, I have an idea worth a hundred words."

"Write it."

She composed her article in less than an hour, and when she handed it to Erskine, she was told to wait while he read it:

The Hundred Days are upon us again, and the Peeping Toms of El Centro are up to their old "transparent" tricks.

Here in the Valley, it's a fact of life that as the temperature rises, fewer and fewer clothes can be borne, especially by women. Ultimately, they can bear nothing more than a dress of flimsy material.

For the Peeping Toms, the flimsier the better. They know that sunlight, acting like an x-ray, will reveal what's underneath. They manage, therefore, to place themselves where they can see what the dress was intended to deny them.

Doubtless they gained their knowledge on the prowl, peering through lighted windows from the dark. But during the Hundred Days, they grow bolder, and as though they didn't care, they let themselves be caught in the act.

What act?, they seem to be saying: we're only taking a free look.

Nothing is free, gentlemen. You're paying for the look with what's left of your self-respect—if you ever had any.

"I guess it's more of an editorial," Marguerite said.

"And it's a stinger," Erskine said. "Look for it tomorrow...."

"Jimmy's on his way to Yuma," Clara said. "Ever since they opened that paved road, he's been crazy to try it."

"I haven't been out there yet," Marguerite said. "Holtville's as far as I've gotten."

At the Erskine ranch, they were readying horses for a Sunday morning ride. One of the mounts was a rangy bay mare with a black mane and tail; the other, on which Marguerite was cinching a Western saddle, was a palomino gelding.

"Have you ever ridden English?" Clara said.

"Where I come from? They'd shoot off guns."

"You ought to try it some time. You have to do more to stay on."

"I've had plenty falls riding Western. I even fell off a dog, the Dalmatian that taught me to walk."

They were making their way now into one of the aisles of the citrus grove. Here, where the plantings were immature, the foliage had not yet become widespread, and they were able to ride side by side.

"Back in eastern Colorado, they grow a lot of sugar beets," Marguerite said. "You irrigate like they do—through the lanes."

"Citrus wants water," Clara said, "but it doesn't want to drown. You can flood alfalfa and a few other crops, but not this one."

"Flooding—I read an article about that in a back-issue of the *Press*. It said that when a field is flooded, there's hell to pay with whatever lives there. Pack rats, mice, ground squirrels, all those things race for their little lives. I could see it happening."

"You must be—mourning for vermin."

"When I was three-four, my sister used to read to me about a goat named Billy Whiskers. He got into all kinds of trouble, but I loved him, and I'd cry my eyes out."

"You're a softy about animals."

"They touch me. Like old people. And another thing—they aren't crafty."

"You like them, then, because they're a lot like you."

"I never thought of myself as being—"

"You never thought of *yourself*."

The soil was still slightly damp from a recent irrigation, and it gave off a savor that mingled with the one extracted by the sun from the trees, the bitters of leaves and rind.

"I was in the town of Gunnison a while back," Marguerite said. "I stayed for only a week or so, but I got friendly with a saleslady in a dress-shop, and we talked. When the time came to say goodbye, she said something I still think about: 'I hope you have a good life.'"

"What's remarkable about that?"

"Nothing. Everybody says it....But nobody ever tells you what it is or where to find it."

Nearing the main ditch of the ranch, they were among full-grown plantings heavy-laden with clusters of fruit, and there they had to ride in tandem, for the aisles were narrowed by the outreaching trees. The ditch, some six feet wide, ran along an access road between two ruffs of reeds. On the embankment stood a bench, and tethering their horses, they sat watching the slow-flowing water and birds seesawing on the reeds.

After a while, Clara spoke, saying, "The other day you said your aim was to look after your folks. How do you expect to do that on what you make at the *Press*?"

"I don't."

"You must be thinking ahead, then. To what?"

"To whatever's out there."

"That's not much of a plan."

"The future's a fog. What good is a plan?"

A bird took off from a swaying reed, skimmed the water for an insect, and flew away into the grove.

"What you're saying is, you'll take what comes. *Nothing* may come."

"Nothing *big*, maybe, but there'll be something. There always is."

Tied to a rack, the horses dozed in the shade, their tails now and then making an indolent sweep.

"Marguerite," Clara said, "I value your friendship, prize it, but I'm going to take a chance on losing it."

"How?"

"By asking a question very much like Jimmy's." (She's about to say *Why don't you ever talk about Leonard?*) "Ask," she said.

"Is your marriage a happy one?"

—No, It isn't.

—I gathered as much.

—I've never told anyone but my sisters.

—Not your father and mother?

—Oddly enough, they like Leonard.

—Why not you?

—That's what I ask myself time after time. All I can say is, he isn't what I want.

—What do you want?

—Somebody to turn on the light! Somebody to light the room!

—Why don't you leave him?

—For somebody else, maybe he *would* light the room. He isn't hard to look at, he speaks well, he's courteous and quiet, and he comes from a good family. A gentleman, somebody else would call him, and that's what he is, I guess. But if I loved him, I wouldn't care a nickel's worth if he was loud and stupid and dressed like a clown.

—Why don't you leave him?

—It wouldn't matter what he looked like, it wouldn't matter whether he ate with his fingers or his feet, and it wouldn't matter if he didn't come from a long line of gents, because go back far enough, and something's covered with hair. If I loved him, he wouldn't even have to love me back.

—Why don't you leave him?

—He'd only have to light the room. Leonard doesn't. He can't.

—Why don't you leave him?

—Don't ever think I won't...!

Is your marriage a happy one?, she said. "Why, yes, Clara. What makes you ask?"

Near a sluice-gate, a flagpole was set in the embankment. Its halyards were tied to a cleat, but no colors flew.

"What's the pole for?" Marguerite said.
"Whenever I take a dip in the ditch, I run up a flag to warn visitors off."
"Why?"
"Because I'm bare-ass naked," Clara said, "and I'm just as private as you."

It was quiet in the grove. Birds quibbled among the reeds, and sometimes a horse stomped the ground, but for the most part, the heat seemed to beat sound down, and what made itself heard was subdued, as though it came through a wall.

"How much hotter does it get in the Valley?" Marguerite said.
"One of these days, your lipstick will flow like chili sauce. I keep mine in the ice-box."
"I hear about women clearing out for Coronado—those that can."
"Some of us can and don't. We stay, living on iced tea and lettuce till we're skinny as a skillet."
"Only a fool would ask you why."
"I love him," Clara said.

🐦

"You've gotten to be pretty friendly with her," Leonard said.
And Marguerite said, "I like her."

They were on the Dunes. Late in the afternoon, when the sun was nearing the Superstition Hills, they'd driven out along the Plank Road and parked the car. Each of them carrying a straw mat, they'd walked across the sand to where only sand could be seen—no cars on the new highway nor even their own on the old—and there they'd stripped and lain down to stare at a sky that looked like bluing.

"What do you like about her?"

236

"I never thought about it. Some people you take to; some people you don't."

"I'm not much for friends. Before I took to someone, I'd want to know why."

"It isn't a thing you can plan."

"It ought to be," he said. "That girl in the college library. How much better it would've been if you'd thought ahead."

"Why better?"

"You'd not have gotten friendly with that kind of person."

The sun was down now, drawing the last of the blue sky with it. From the highway, the lights of an occasional car scanned the Dunes, overshooting the vast scoops of darkness in the sand.

"What does all this have to do with Clara?"

"You go to lunch with her. She lends you books. She has you out to the ranch when Erskine isn't there."

"So?"

"And whenever I happen to be around, the talk's only about horses, grapefruit, and the *Press*—and then more horses."

"In other words, nothing important."

"Not that I ever get to hear."

"And you want to know what we talk about when you're *not* around?"

"That's reasonable enough."

"No, it isn't. You must think we have secrets."

"Haven't you?"

Turning her head, she studied him. "I'm slow," she said, "but are you implying that Clara's like the girl in Greeley?"

"Well, isn't she?"

"I never used this word before, and I'm not even sure what it means. You're *preposterous!*"

"It means contrary to common sense."

"You don't know beans about Clara, and you know even less about me. If she's *that kind*, as you put it, you must think I am too."

"That wouldn't make me preposterous."

"Wouldn't it? A while back, you were uneasy about me and Erskine. Now it's me and Clara."

"Which is it?"

237

The black sky was pinked with points of light. Taking up a fistful of sand, she tried to retain it, but the grains drained from her hand, and she was left with only a memory of their warmth.

"Neither," she said.

☙

Dear Connie:

By now, you probably have heard that I'm working for the *Imperial Valley Press*—as a reporter, no less! I like the job better than any I've ever had. It not only keeps me on the go, but it calls for using my head (such as it is). It's a far cry from peddling icky candy at the Five-and-Dime and mailing bills for Home Gas & Electric. Sometimes I get sent on a particular assignment, like covering a case at the Courthouse, or a parade, or a schoolboard meeting, but just as often I'm allowed to dream up stuff to write about, and that's what I like best—making something out of thin air.

We're into the real hot weather now. We had hot in Nebraska, but this beats anything I ever saw. Don't tell Mama—she'd fret—but food has no appeal, and I'm down to about a hundred pounds.

Only one place here is air-cooled, the Barbara Worth, a very ritzy hotel. It's five stories high and a block square, with a lobby you could play basketball in—and one big rug covers it all! There are lots of sofas and upholstered armchairs, and listen to this—the manager doesn't say a word when people come in just to set in the cool. The only trouble is, the heat seems worse when you go back out again.

Things aren't too good between me and Leonard, I'm sorry to say. In fact, they never were. We're different kinds, and we see things different, and while there's no real quarreling, there's also no real joy. I'd like to put things right, but I don't know how to go about it, or even whether I can. The other day I found myself wondering if a kid was the answer....

Dear Marg:

Don't do it!

Where two people aren't getting along, it's just plain dumb to think a kid will fix things. People should have a kid when they *are*

238

getting along. If they're not, a kid only makes things worse. And sure as life worse for the mother if push comes to shove and the father leaves. She's stuck with the kid.

Listen to old Connie. She has a wise head, baby sister.

Don't do it!

Don't even think it! (that's Daddy talking now)

☙

—*Whenever I ask myself what's wrong with him, I always get the same answer: nothing's wrong. But if nothing's wrong, why do I keep asking the question? Maybe my answer's as wrong as he is.*

—*There's no commotion in him; he's never offhand, amusing, playful, never surprising or surprised. He's slow to anger and slower to rejoice, and not being low or high, he's neither glum nor gay. He doesn't swear, drink, or eye other girls, but he might be less stagnant if he did: his blood might flow, his words might turn and tumble, churn and pour, But none of that will ever happen. He's surrounded by himself, he's landlocked, he's unaffected by the tides....*

☙

Calexico, a small town close to the Mexican border, was a dozen miles south of El Centro on California 99. From either side of the highway spread expanses of alfalfa, some of it cut and curing and sending out the savor of its sun-dried flowers. A paling of blue gums lined the pavement, and bars of light and shade were laid athwart the road. Ties, thought Marguerite, and she thought too of Clarks and of the U.P. tracks that ran through her childhood, thought of things now a long way back.

Erskine had sent her out to learn the details of a shooting at the International Boundary. On her return, she reported her findings to the editor.

"It won't be an easy one to write," she said.

"Write it hard, then."

"People are going to be hurt."

"That's what news does. Hurt 'em."

"But the man left a wife and kids."

"About a hundred words ought to do it," Erskine said, and he turned away.

239

Her story:

> Early today, Paul Mitchell, 34, of Brawley, was shot and killed by Frank Cooper as the pair came back from a fling in Mexico. Cooper fled the scene, taking off in the direction of Yuma. When caught near Gordon's Well, he had not yet rid himself of Mitchell's body. The man was dead of two bullet-wounds, one in the chest and one in the head.
>
> According to the Calexico police, Cooper has confessed to the crime. In his statement, he said that he and Mitchell had spent the night in a Mexicali whorehouse, where a dispute arose over the services of a girl that both had spoken for. She chose him, Cooper said, whereupon Mitchell tried to brain him with a beer-bottle. On their way past Customs this morning, the quarrel flared anew, and now with a fatal result.
>
> Mitchell is survived by his wife and two minor children. Cooper, 32, is a resident of El Centro.

"Well, you told me to hurt 'em," Marguerite said.
"And you did."
"Are you going to run the story?"
"Yes, after I change *whorehouse* to *bordello*."
"You'll be hurting me too."
"Or maybe I'll just say house of ill fame."

The Imperial Valley Irrigation District had brought suit against a Holtville rancher, alleging that he had taken water from a ditch in an illegal manner in order to avoid the payment of rates. Covering the trial for the *Press*, Marguerite was among the several in the courtroom audience, and she was listening to the testimony of a witness for the Irrigation District.

COUNSEL: ...Why did the District send you out to the defendant's property?
WITNESS: It didn't. My orders was to go to his *neighbor's* property.
COUNSEL: What for?
WITNESS: He reported they was a weak place in the errigation-ditch.
COUNSEL: And where was this ditch?

WITNESS: It run between the two properties.
COUNSEL: Did you find the weak place?
WITNESS: Yes. The embankment looked like giving way.
COUNSEL: What did you do about it?
WITNESS: I drove in some stakes and boarded up the break.
COUNSEL: And then what?
WITNESS: I'm near about finishing up when I see something paculia on the other side of the ditch.
COUNSEL: Meaning the defendant's side.
WITNESS: Yes, his side.
COUNSEL: And what was this peculiar thing?
WITNESS: Over there, they's a particula heady clump of reeds, and sticking out of them, they's the end of a hose. Kind of like a fire-hose.
COUNSEL: What did you do about it?
WITNESS: Like I say, it being paculia, I went over and took a closer look.
COUNSEL: And what did this closer look reveal?
WITNESS: They's a citrus grove over there, and I traced the hose back in a ways.
COUNSEL: To what, if anything?
WITNESS: Three-four rows back, hid under a tree, they's a water-pump....

She'd been taking shorthand notes of the testimony, but her attention flagged with the heat—flagged, she thought, as she stared at the colors drooping beside the bench....

Toward the end of an afternoon, Marguerite drove to the packing-plant, where Leonard was awaiting her, and they started for home. Above the sunburned road, the hot air writhed, and trees and houses and oncoming cars were seen as if through water.

"What faults do *you* find in *me*?" she said.
Giving her a glance, he said, "Sounds like it's *my* turn."
"I'm trying to find out whether you think it was a mistake to marry me."
"Mistake? It was the best thing I ever did."

"Don't string me along, Leonard."

"You can't really want to hear about your faults."

"Why else would I be asking?"

In the jellied air, the hills ahead seemed to be in the making, to form and reform, as if they were just then being thrown up from the earth.

"All right...," he said.

And she wondered what he'd say.

—You have a mind of your own. I can't call you stubborn, because you're not; mostly, you're very willing. But when it comes to something you believe is important, you won't give an inch....Also, though some mightn't think it a fault, you're private; you're the most private person I've ever met. There are places in your mind where even you seldom go....You don't talk much and almost never about yourself, which is part of the privacy, I suppose, but at times I get the feeling that I'm married to someone I hardly know....You don't seem to expect much of life. It's as if you could see it all from here, and what's in store for you is only more of the same....All you had was a high school education, and though you wanted a degree, you never got one. For those who were luckier, your respect is high, but let them show disrespect for you, and you're off them like a wet sock....And talking about dirt, I got used to a certain amount of it in the South. But you, you'll quit a restaurant for a fly-speck, you'll sleep on the floor if you suspect a bed, and as for using a public toilet...!

"Well...," she said.

"You have only one little fault."

"And what's that?"

"You don't love me," he said.

The heat subdued sound and retarded motion. The wind hardly stirred the blue-gum leaves, and far-off cars seemed even further away, and so did telephone bells, dog-bark, jostled crockery, and the engines of other lives. All day, the sun had cooked the air-space under the roof of the bungalow, and the rooms below it had been cooked in turn, until, though it was night now, their contents were hot still—metal, paper, flooring, fabric, each held a reminder of the day. Outside, in the rear yard, where Marguerite and Leonard lay on their mats, the sprinkler spun its slow circles, sowing seeds of warm water on the sunburned lawn.

"Marguerite," he said, "I want you to take a week in Coronado."
"By myself?" she said. "While you sweat it out in El Centro?"
"Both of us can't go."
"Then both of us stay. That's the fair thing."
"This time, fair is foolish. You're eating so little, you're getting so thin—and still you keep chasing stories. Tell the truth—what do you weigh?"
"A hundred."
"Never."
"Ninety-five, then—and that *is* the truth."
"I say you ought to get going right now."
"In the dark?"
"If you wait till it's light, it'll hot up before you get to the mountains."
"I feel like a deserter."
"You'll be a cool deserter, though," he said. "I'll call Erskine in the morning."
"What will you tell him?"
"That I insisted...."

She was on her way west within an hour, and it was still dark when she left Edgar Siding, where the road began its rise out of the valley. At a curve near Plaster City, she stopped the car to glance back at the clusters of light below, the sprawl of fallen stars that were Imperial and Brawley. Moving on, she was overtaken by dawn only when she'd reached Incopah Gorge. There, two thousand feet above the level of the Sink, it was cold air that came at her through the open windshield, and she breathed it deep.

At Boulder Park, she drew up at a diner and ordered a cup of coffee, but when it was brought, she ignored it, ignored as well the cars that passed, the hills rippling away toward Mexico, the sounds at the counter, the kitchen sounds. Her mind was forty miles back at an El Centro bungalow, where a few hours before she'd accepted a kindness with little more than a grateful protest. But somewhere along the road from there to here, the true nature of the give-and-take had begun to come clear, until, seeing it at last for what it was, she knew that her week of freedom had not been a gift so much as a sale—a limited stay in Coronado in return for a long one on the tether of gratitude. How, she wondered, how could she have failed to perceive that sooner?

The doors of the diner opened and closed as patrons came and went, and veils of smoke swirled, visible air, and sitting before a cup of luke-warm coffee, Marguerite watched a passing car headed for Jacumba and the Coast. She rose and left the diner, but the way she chose led back to the Sink.

Later in the day, when Leonard returned from the packing-plant, he found the car in the driveway and Marguerite awaiting him on the porch. "How come?" he said.

"I changed my mind."

"Why?"

"It wouldn't've been right to run out on you."

"So you said last night, but that isn't the real reason, is it?"

"No," she said.

Dear Marg:

First about the beauty shop. Its panning out fine like I knew it would. Its in a good location and after a couple of months of drop ins now we get the once a week kind and that means theres always something to count on.

So like I said when Midge made much of me for sending Mama and Daddy an anniversary present it really didnt strain me. The money wasnt doing any good under the mattress and its sure do-ing good where it went. Daddy being 65 he dont get work like he used to.

Stop blaming yourself for not being able to chip in. You want to and thats the main thing. As our *dear* sister in law Pearl Smith would say you cant get blood out of a turnip. Not that youre a turnip Marg.

Now about you and Leonard. You done dead right not taking advantage of his *kind* offer to stake you to a week on the beach. You said it yourself—you would of been obligated God knows how long for the *favor*. With something in the wind between you two you was being far sighted when you turned around and come back to El Centro. Remember you always got a home where I am baby sister. I know what youre going through. It was the same with me and John Roach before I up and quit him.

I enclose you a little spare change.

Im writing you at the newspaper like you wanted.

Pearl the Section Boss

Dear Section Boss:

There's four of us Smith sisters, and you're the best of the lot by far. It was good of you to send the ten-spot, but here it is right back. I'm working, and I have no intention of living off you. Living *with* you—that's another pair of shoes. So don't be surprised if one of these days, I....

Marg

One afternoon, when she called for Leonard at the packing-plant, he said, "Guess what, Mrs. Roberts. They gave your husband a raise."

"That's wonderful, Leonard," she said. "I'm glad for you."

"Aren't you going to ask how much?"

"I couldn't do a thing like that."

"You couldn't? Why not""

"It isn't my affair."

"The raise isn't your affair?"

"The raise, yes. But not how much."

"Well, anyway. It's paying for our dinner tonight at the Barbara Worth...."

The low-watt lighting of the hotel café seemed to cool the air all the more, and the heat in wait outdoors was forgotten in the pleasure of pain suspended. With most of the tables occupied, always an undertone could be heard, the constant drone of wordless speech, and food-smells and smoke filled the temperate intermission.

Afterward, they sat for a while in the two-story space of the lobby. Others were there, earlier diners and fugitives from the heat outside, some of them on the chairs and lounges and some on their feet. Lining the upper level of the walls was a mural illustrating the conquest of the desert by Man the Water-bringer.

"You know what I'm remembering?" Leonard said. "The first dinner we had together."

They were surrounded by scenes of stopped motion. Life-size figures, all of them stock-still, were shown at the work of tapping the Colorado for the irrigation of their fields and groves. It was as if they'd paused to be painted, and so posed, they'd been forever stayed: they'd never breathe again, the water would not flow, the greenery would grow no further nor would it fade.

"You got mad and walked home from Evans."

"Three miles, and in my stocking feet."

"Would you do that today?"

"If you made small of me again? I'd walk six."

"You get halfway mad just thinking about it."

"You still have no notion of what you did. It wasn't just me that you faulted with that eating-lesson; it was my family and their ways. Nobody can do that and expect me to squat for it."

"I'm not like that any more," he said. "I've changed."

He hadn't, she thought, and neither had she: he was as likely as ever to give offense, and she was as ready as ever to take it. They were stalled, both of them, like the symbols in the mural, like Man, Woman, and Water, like Fruits that would never ripen.

"It was wrong of me to do what I did," he said. "It was wrong to correct you in public."

He was picking at a scab that had formed over an injury, but he seemed not to realize that it was *her* injury and *her* scab. In her mind, she said to herself what she feared he was about to say: *I can see now how I must've embarrassed you. I should've waited till we were alone.*

"I'd just as soon hear no more about it," she said.

"But there's more to be said...."

He doesn't know where or how to stop, she thought. He'll go on till he says something outrageous (*It all came right in the end; you never needed a second lesson*), and the scab will break loose, and I'll bleed.

"It's time to go home," she said, and, rising, she moved toward the door.

She paused there to prepare for what lay in store in the street, and taking a final few breaths of the cooler air in the lobby, she went outside. It was as if she'd walked into a substance. There were dimensions to the heat; it felt more like a thing than a sensation, and it laid hold of her, contained her, submerged her in its embrace. Feeling sweat start anew, she regretted the respite she'd sought from torment; resumed, it seemed all the worse.

Overtaken by Leonard, she said, "I'm wet, and I've been out here hardly a minute. We'd've been better off sitting in the shower with a Coke."

There were nights when the whirler in the yard was merely a reminder of the heat that the earth had absorbed during the day and passed on down to the mains. Warm water came from the risers, playing in slow circles as if in a wearisome game. For Marguerite and Leonard, it yielded little, as did another of the measures they took to endure. An electric fan was trained on the open ice-chest in order to produce a blow-back of chilled air; but as the frozen block dwindled, so did the chill, and all too soon what blew back was the smell of food and warming zinc.

"There's Coronado," he said. "And the raise will pay for more than a week."

She shook her head, saying, "We still haven't tried sitting in the shower with a Coke."

Stripping away what little they were wearing, they uncapped their drinks, and sat themselves in the tile basin of the shower. It was a warm rain that fell upon them, but not quite as warm as the air, it let them fancy it cool.

"This was a good idea," he said. "Why didn't we think of it before?"

"It won't seem so good coming out. We'll dry ourselves, and the exertion will make us sweat some more, and then of course we'll need another shower....It's endless."

"The hundredth day will end it."

247

"When'll that be?" she said. "I haven't kept count...."

She did not hear his reply. Facing him through a beaded curtain of water, she thought of how like their marriage was to the small compartment that enclosed them—a four-by-four cabin in the universe. Here was her companion for life, she thought, here naked before her was the presence that, like the Hundred Days, she'd have to bear with to the end. She tried to remember when, if ever, they'd been of one mind, when they'd rejoiced together, when either had known loss as the other left a room. She could recall no such time; but how insistent her memory of their crisscross views, of aims pursued in contrary ways, of divisions!

He sat with his head tilted back and his eyes closed. Water played down upon him, making a skullcap of his hair, and while he let his cupped hands fill and spill over, still his eyes stayed closed. He was well-made and masculine, and for all his leanness and pallor, Marguerite knew him to be strong. Lean and pale, she thought (*Daddy would say he'd have to stand up twice to throw a shadow*), but it was his narrow-gauge mind that troubled her; like his body, it cast a pallid shadow.

Though her eyes too were closed, she saw him all the same, and describing him to herself, she found that few affirmatives came to mind; her appraisal in the blind conveyed largely what he was not. He wasn't unintelligent, she thought, he wasn't unattractive, and he was neither coarse nor mean. But what *was* he?, she wondered, why did he evoke negations?, why, after two years of marriage, did he so seldom seem to be there?

It might be, she thought, that he wasn't there now, and to verify the notion, she looked through the waterfall and took him in: his hair was worn neither short nor long, his nails were pared, and his feet were free of callus and corn, for all they'd known was sensible shoes. The word *precise* suggested itself to her, followed by *careful*, and finally *measured*: he was the kind that tried for the possible, never for the out-of-reach.

This trend, this train, where was it taking her, to what end? Was it some unforethought-of place, or was it the one that had always been just around a corner in her mind? She watched rills of water rinse his face, run the hills and dales of his body, serpentine his legs, and flow away. She studied the clear and nearby stranger, and quite as clearly could she see the distances beyond him—an expanse of dead-level living, featureless and lonely, a plane of empty years. Was it wrong, she wondered, to long for more? *Was* there more?

"There has to be," she said.

With his eyes still closed, he said, "What does?"

"More."

What was she looking for? Or was she merely looking elsewhere, anywhere away from the haunt called here?

When she returned from the newspaper office one afternoon, she told Leonard that they'd been invited by the Erskines for another Sunday breakfast. "And a swim," she said. "We're to bring our suits."

"A swim?" he said. "Where?"

"In a ditch, I suppose."

"But you don't swim."

"It's only three feet deep."

"Why don't *you* go?" he said. "I can get all the wet I want in the shower."

"I won't insist, but I'd've thought the people were more your kind than mine."

"Do you realize what you're saying?"

"I'd be a fool if I didn't. You *aren't* my kind."

"Why in the world would you think that?"

"Oh, come on, Leonard. We're as different as snowflakes."

"At the start, maybe. But wouldn't you say we're closer than we were?"

They were not, she thought. Unalike to begin with, unalike they'd remained. Worse, he no longer knew the extent of the diversity: through association, he seemed to believe, they were gradually becoming the same.

"If you object to my going," she said, "I'll stay."

"No," he said. "You like the Erskines, so go and have a good time."

And when Sunday came, she went.

"Me," Erskine said after breakfast, I'm taking my ease in that deck-chair."

"Good," Clara said. "I won't need my suit."

"I'll need mine," Marguerite said.

Erskine nodded. "I'd've bet as much. A private lady."

"In the Smith family, we didn't show up in a wrapper, much less naked as a jaybird."

"What would've happened if somebody did?"

"Mama would've taken a switch to somebody's behind."

"Were you ever the somebody?"

"I saw my sister Bijou get it. That's all the lesson I needed."

Walking through the grove to the irrigation ditch, Marguerite and Clara undressed in separate aisles, where they were concealed from each other by the foliage. When they reappeared, Clara too was clad in a bathing-suit.

"I didn't want to stun you," she said.

"Naked women don't exactly stun me."

"Naked women of forty-five?"

"A naked woman is a naked woman."

Clara laughed. "Wait till you get to be forty-five." At that hour, the bench beside the ditch was still in shadow, and indicating it, she said, "Let's sit for a while. It's pleasant here."

What sound came through the grove was small, a compound of far-away traffic, wingbeat, wind in wire, a humming as from the circulation of the blood. The heat evoked flavor from the damp earth, the leaves, the rind of ripening fruit, and the air was laden with citric savor. Birds worked the softened ground. Insects made arcs of travel, water moved past in the sun and shade.

"A while back," Clara said, "I asked if you were happy."

"That's so. You did."

"Well, I'm asking again."

"Why a second time?"

"To be frank, I didn't believe you. You're not happy at all."

"What makes you so sure?"

"I've been married to Jimmy for twenty years, and no matter where he goes—Yuma, San Diego, L.A.—I know when he's on his way back. I can feel him coming nearer. Can you say that about Leonard?"

In a clash among the reeds, two blackbirds flashed their red epaulettes. A water-spider skated a zigzag series on the ditch.

"No, I can't," Marguerite said.

"Jimmy and I never thought you could."

"Up to now, I haven't spoken of Leonard except to my family. I'm really what Jimmy said—a private person."

"A private *lady*, is what he said, and indeed you are. You're private in all your ways, and I admire that immensely. But your feelings aren't private, not any more. They're written all over you."

"You know a sight more about it than I do, but to my notion, marriage ought to change people, make them better or, if it so turns out, worse. But if they stay as they were, what did they get married for? One way or another, they simply have to change, and Leonard and I haven't. Nothing's happened to either of us, and nothing's going to....A dreary view—more of the same, always more of the same."

She reached down for a few pebbles and tossed them one by one at the ditch. As they struck the water, each made the same single chuckling sound.

"But there's more than one window," she said, "and I can change the view."

"If you go," Clara said," *when* you go, I'll miss you. We haven't seen much of each other, but some people—it's good just to know they're around."

"My Mama and Daddy have been married for more than forty years, and hard times are all they've ever known, but there never was a day when they would've split. They'll stay married till they die, and if I had what they do, so would I....Please don't think, though, that Leonard's no-account, because he isn't. He's aboveboard, he's kind, and he behaves well no matter what. It's odd, but things'd be better if he was worse: I could be angry instead of blank, I could work on him instead of sitting still and waiting for nothing....Mama and Daddy weren't out for the fine things and an easy life, and neither am I. But like you, I've got to know that something's on the way, that someone's coming near."

Clara rose, and for a moment she stood on the embankment, looking off into the baking grove, where gelatin air shook between the trees.

"Where will you go?" she said.

"To Los Angeles. I have a sister there."

"Are the two of you close?"

"Not in age. She's old enough to be my mother—and till I was five or six, she was just as good as. She brought me up."

"What'll you do in L.A.?"

"Get a job, of course."

"Jimmy's shown me everything you've written for the *Press*. You're good, and he'd give you a letter to a big-city paper. In fact, he said that's where you belong."

But Marguerite shook her head. "I have something else in mind. I'm thinking of trying a film studio."

"As what?"

"As anything, just so I get inside."

"Not as a typist, I hope. Start as one, you'll end as one."

"I didn't."

"That town up there is busting with people who want to get into a studio."

"And some of 'em do," Marguerite said.

"One in a thousand."

"I must be that one, then."

"What do you mean?"

"I picked the name of a company out of a directory and wrote them a letter. I didn't know who to address, so I just sent it to the company. And I got an answer! A man name of Wallace said to look him up if I ever got to L.A."

"You've must've written quite a letter."

"A dozen lines, is all, but it looks like they got me past the gate."

Clara studied her, and then she said, "Something tells me that once you're in, you'll stay there."

"I mean to."

She slept without nightclothes nor even a sheet for covering, and lying in a print of sweat, she was awakened at times by the weight of the heat: it had substance, she thought, it was material, and it freighted the air. Wetness came from her as though her skin no longer held her in; everywhere it wept, combining here and there to sidle down a slope of her body. From the out-of-doors, no sound could be heard, and to her fancy, all life lay crushed under the burden of breathing. Her mind wended to the other bedroom, and she wondered whether Leonard too was unable to sleep—and then she wondered why it mattered. When the summer ended, she thought, when the summer ended....

Early one afternoon, in the hope that there might be a sequel to the story she'd written about Carlos Fonseca, she made another visit to his junk-shop. It was a high-heat day, and the short run from the newspaper office was enough to convert the car into a kiln, and the wheel, the seat, and the pedals became so hot that they themselves seemed the source of the heat. Her hands drew it into her, her feet absorbed it through her shoes, and her dress, the only clothing she wore, was swaged with sweat to the leather she sat on, and climbing down, she had to peel herself loose.

She found Fonseca, listless amid his harvest of odds and ends, staring across the road at the railway yards. His stock, picked over again and again, had been relieved of all that was useful and reduced to what it had begun as on the Dunes, thrown-away trash.

"When they go open that road," he said. "Fonseca *el hombre de negocios*, he is kill."

"Don't talk like that, Mr. Fonseca," she said. "You're still a good businessman, and you'll find something else to do. You'll be rich."

"Where I find these kind business? Where I get stuff for to sell and no pay for it? In all the world, is not exist. Was perfecto, my business, and now is no more."

He gestured at the icing-depot across the road, where farm trucks were drawn up at the dock, discharging their hauls of produce for transfer into the waiting refrigerator cars.

"See all them fruits and vegables," he said. "They taking them away for sell in the big city, *pero* they no get there *fresco* if they no have ice. You think they giving ice free over there? No money, no ice—that is the way."

"I'm sorry you feel so bad, Mr. Fonseca, but you have good ideas. Starting this shop was one of them, and I'm sure you'll soon have another...."

But Fonseca was no longer listening. Much more intently than before, he was eyeing the depot, and she turned to follow his gaze. What had been mere activity on the unloading dock had become commotion. Their crates and hand-trucks abandoned, drivers and freight-handlers were swarming in a doorway. After a moment or two, a body was carried out through the crowd and laid on the planks of the platform....

☙

"I've got a story, Jimmy!" Marguerite said as she passed his room on her way to her desk.

At the Southern Pacific yards this afternoon, Jack Gannon, a driver for the Growers Association, died on the platform of the car-icing plant. He had just brought a load of produce from Heber for shipment out of the Valley.

According to those at the unloading dock, his behavior was strange. He spoke to no one, they say, and he seemed confused as to his whereabouts. But with stacks of perishable produce standing exposed to the heat, which was above 100°, no time could be devoted to Gannon, and he was left unattended.

His extreme pallor, his rapid breathing, and the absence of sweat—all these were symptoms of heatstroke, but they went unrecognized. Only when the man made a dash for the ice-room did others realize his true condition. Efforts to restrain him failed, for he broke loose and plunged into the freezer.

The quick drop in temperature was too great a shock for his system, and he collapsed almost at once. Carried out, he died before medical aid could reach the scene.

Born in Jefferson Barracks, Missouri, Gannon was 47 years of age. He leaves no immediate family.

"Who put you onto the story?" Erskine said.
"Nobody," Marguerite said. "I was there."
"The right place to be, if you're a reporter."
"I'm not going to be a reporter, Jimmy."

"So I hear from Clara. She says you have other things in mind."

"That's true, but if you'll let me, I'd like to stick around till Fall."

He was looking away through the window at tar-paper roofs, at radio aerials, at a line of distant blue gums, when he said, "You're a dandy girl, Marguerite. Clara and I, we think you deserve the best."

"Everybody does. I'm nothing special on a stick."

He turned from the window, saying, "Clara can't remember anyone she liked better, and neither can I. And one of the reasons is that you're so wrong about yourself. You think you're only a Little Miss Nobody, and the fact is, you're as rare as they come."

"You're embarrassing me, Jimmy."

"I'm saying what Clara surely said. We've talked you over more than once, and we never did think this was your last stop. Not down here, forty-five feet below sea-level. I had it in mind to pass you along to some-one I know on the *Herald-Examiner*, but Clara says you've got your eye on the movies...like half of Los Angeles."

"They're looking for miracles. All I want is a job. In time, maybe I could get to be a writer."

"This story of yours," he said, tapping the typewritten sheet before him. "There's no maybe about it."

The night was moonlit, and Marguerite and Leonard were in their rear yard, he lying on one of the straw mats and she, dressed only in a slip, standing in the slow-motion cast of the sprinkler. It was sowing seeds of water, she thought, as they struck her and broke, affixing a skin of cotton to her own. It clung, following her rounds and hollows and allowing pale colors to show, as though she were wearing a faded print.

The warm wind, passing through the blue-gum trees, made a sound like that of bygone fashion going by, of silken skirts, of silk on thighs. Far away up the Valley, a locomotive whistled twice long and twice short, but little other sound reached the yard, none of it enough to drown the patter of scattered water. Again, from further off now and further diminished, came the fanfare of the train, this time stirring the fancy, and Marguerite found herself thinking of the engine action, the track, and where the track ended.

"I hear that train every night," Leonard said.

"It's a produce train, reefers bound for Los Angeles."

"I thought it carried passengers—"

"Passenger trains don't depart in the middle of the night."

"—and sometimes I think it's carrying you."

Seating herself in a camp-chair outside the cast of the sprinkler, she looked down at Leonard, lying nearby and gazing at the star-shot sky.

"It's time we talked of such things," he said.

"Such things as what, Leonard?"

"Your leaving me."

"Am I going to do that?"

"Well, you've been thinking of it."

"To tell the truth, I have."

"Am I that bad a husband?"

"It isn't you, Leonard. It's us. We've been married for two years, and we're still where we started. Started! We never *did* start."

"I know that's what you've been thinking, and you're wrong. We started back in Loveland, and we've gotten as far as here."

"But here is the same as there."

"No, it isn't. Here is two years and several thousand miles from there."

"We could've been married twice as long and travelled twice as far, and still we'd just be fellow-passengers, no closer than before."

"No closer than we were at business college? No closer after two years of sleeping together, eating together, riding side-by-side in that crumby little car? How much closer can two people get, for God's sake?"

"We've done everything you say and more—and we're a million miles apart."

"I swear, Marguerite, I don't know what it is that you want."

"This'll surprise you, but I don't know, either. I know what I *don't* want, though—more of *this*."

"This. What do you mean by *this*?"

"What we have. Or rather what we *don't* have."

"Please, just once, tell me what that is."

"We don't love each other, Leonard."

The wind had died down for the moment, the train was too distant now to be heard, and in the quiet, the main sound was made by the whirled water as it struck the ground.

"What am I to say to a thing like that?"

"What comes to mind?"

"At this late day, am I really expected to declare myself?"

"Leonard, if you had anything to declare, I'd've heard it long ago and whenever I got near. But I've never declared myself, either, so we're even. We haven't fooled each other about how we feel."

"The word *love* comes easy to some people, but not to me. It's the hardest one to say."

"And it's the only one that nobody *has* to say. A look can say it. A person can say it just by coming into a room. It can flavor the air. Without it, marriage is just being together and doing things together—which seems to be your idea of it."

"What's yours?"

"I don't know, but why get married if that's all there is to it? We're no better than a team pulling a plow."

"I don't think of us as horses—or our marriage as a plow."

She could not have said what she desired of the relation; she knew only that she wanted more than it promised to be—a long passage across a level world. Coupled with Leonard, all she could see was a future as featureless as the past, a further flatness to be traversed to wherever it happened to end. Her longings had no more shape than vapor. They were blurs changing even as she tried to place and name them, but still, for all their incoherence, she felt that not forever would they be beyond her grasp.

"I can't believe you're calling it quits over a word."

"I could go all my life without hearing it if only I knew the feeling was there. It isn't, Leonard, and it never was. You asked me to marry you because you thought you were guilty, and I agreed because it seemed the thing to do. That was poor stuff to build a lifetime on. It's a wonder we lasted as long as we did."

"You read too much, Marguerite. Or you read the wrong thing. Marriage isn't all beer and skittles."

"I never did know what that meant."

"Enjoyment."

"But that's just what marriage *is*! A good one is all enjoyment."

257

"In a story."

"I'm not talking about stories. I'm talking about my Mama and Daddy. They never had it soft a single day of their lives. It's been donkey-work all the way. Swink without gain, owning nothing, living in dumps, raising a family they could hardly feed, sick at times, wore out, sore, and scanting themselves to provide for their kids—but, gracious life, they enjoyed every damn twist and turn of it, and they still do. Guess why, Leonard. Take a wild guess."

"I hope you're not going to tell me—"

"But I am. They love each other, those old-timers, and they always will. I know you find that hard to credit, and the reason is, you never saw the like in your home."

"That's a cruel thing to say. You hardly know my people."

"It's a true thing, though, and that's why the word *love* gets stuck in your throat. It's why your brother Baxter is a high-toned bastard. It's why your mother can't stand the sight of me. And it's why your father, the best of you all, walks around in a daze."

He raised himself now to sit crosslegged on the mat, and drawing a hand across his chest, he left five swathes in the sweat and dust.

"You say I don't love you because there's no love in my family. Why don't you love me, then, if there's so much of it in yours?"

Why, she wondered, was she thinking of the saleslady in Grand Junction? Hilda Nielsen—was that her name, and why had the last words she'd spoken come again to mind? She'd expressed a wish for Marguerite, and though she'd never be seen or heard from again, she became part of the portfolio of memory. The woman herself was dim and indistinct, a snapshot underexposed, but her voice clear still, after a year on the air, and it was saying *Have a good life* to one who was seeking it, that and nothing more.

"*Have a good life*, she said."

"Who said?"

"That woman in the dress-shop at Grand Junction."

"Her again—the Swede?"

"When we said goodbye, she wished me a good life, and all at once it seems to answer your question."

"How?"

"I'm not *having* a good life."

"What would make it good—more clothes, more money, more this, more that?"

"You weren't listening, I guess, when I told you about Mama and Daddy. They never had any this and that, but they couldn't've *had* a better life....Is that what you think I want—more things?"

"When people talk of a good life, that's what they generally mean."

"Not me, Leonard. I'd settle right now for what my folks had—which was nothing but each other."

He stood up now, looking roundabout him as though he found the place strange and disturbing, but the strangeness was within him, and his disquiet remained.

"Is there nothing I can do to change your mind?" he said.

How could she reply?

Could she say *Transform your face, alter your voice, and see the world with a different eye?*

Could she say *Make me rejoice that we came to this place the earth at the selfsame time?*

Could she say *Feel and act for once in an unaccustomed way, arrive late for a change, be imprecise, forget to button your fly?*

Could she say *Use a wrong word or misspell the right one, complain, be rude, pick a fight with a stranger, even if the stranger is I?*

Could she say *Put history behind you, dismiss it from your mind, live among the living instead of the dead?*

Could she say *Stop being what you are?*

She said, "You'd have to be someone else."

"Someone in particular?"

"No, just someone who isn't you."

He went into the house, and she stayed outside, listening to the circular scatter of the sprinkler. After a moment or two, he returned with a damp towel and a pair of her slippers, and kneeling before her, he wiped her feet clean.

"You're thoughtful, Leonard," she said. "You're a kind man."

"I wish kindness was enough."

"It ought to be. But people want too much from people, more than they can give."

"After you leave, I don't think I'll be able to stay here. It'll be too lonely."

"Where would you go?"

"Back to Greeley, maybe. It won't matter, not if you aren't there."

"I didn't know I meant that much to you. You're so quiet, so—what's the word?—controlled, that you don't seem part of what's going on, like a witness."

"You were always important. I've known that since the first time I saw you, and I'd've spoken to you then if I hadn't been so—controlled, as you say. But the control came from outside. I was born controlled, and I'll die the same way. I try, but I can't shake it, and some day—the day you go away—I'll stop trying....Will you be coming in now?"

"In a little while, Leonard," she said, and she watched him turn away toward the door, and he'd almost reached it when she said, "If you like, I'll come to your room."

He paused and looked back, his expression obscure in the dimness, and he said, "Thanks, Marguerite, but we've already said goodbye."

He entered the house, and as the screen-door swung closed behind him, she heard the stutter of its springs. He was right, she thought: they *had* said goodbye.

THE VIEW FROM AFAR OFF

1931: Viele Pond, N.Y.

He's been a lawyer for more than two years, but apart from a few ap-pointments as a public defender, he has yet to practice law. His only inter-est is literature, and when Natchie Weinstein ("I'm writing a book") proposes that they pull up stakes and head for the woods with their stalled manu-scripts, they take off, one of them with Miss Lonelyhearts *and the other with* The Water Wheel. *They wind up in the Adirondacks in a cabin rented from a Warrensburg banker. With it come twelve hundred acres of* *forest and a trout-stocked pond, and there they spend a summer that will reshape their lives. Particularly will it change the lawyer's, for, based on a story told by the banker, he'll write his second novel.* In time, the book will take him west to the Paramount Studios, where the young woman he's destined to meet is destined to be employed.*

THE END OF THE HUNDRED DAYS

On another evening, again they sat in the darkness of the yard, their talk small and broken by long silences, as though they'd already spoken and disposed of consequential things. As usual, a hot wind blew, tempered not at all as it passed through the curtain of irrigation flown by the whirler. In the heat, sweat seemed less to exude on its own than to be sucked through the skin, and it glistened in the starlight as it gathered and ran.

"What do you weigh?" he said.
"Why do you want to know?"
"Last time I asked, you were down to ninety-five. I think you're down even further."
"I'm eighty-five."
"You look like a dress on a hanger."

The wind seemed to be an exhalation of the earth, rising through pavement and greenery, through water, wood, and wire, and, warm to start with, it was warmed still more by whatever it touched, until, reaching the sprayed yard, it was a thing of dimensions, an element as tangible as any other.

"I think it's time you cleared out," he said.

But her attention was elsewhere, and his voice reached her drained by distance, like an echo. She'd been distracted by a change in the quality of the air. It was almost imperceptible, but it seemed to her that the warmth of the wind had abated for an instant—faltered, she thought—and then resumed. She waited, wondering whether she'd been mistaken, but after a moment, another weakness came, this one more pronounced and longer-lasting than the other.

The Old Man's Place, 1935   261

"Did you feel that?" she said.

"Yes," he said, "and I'm afraid I know what it means."

THE VIEW FROM AFAR OFF

1929: West End, N.J.

No photo of him has survived that summer; there's only a single shot of that summer's girl, a black-haired beauty. Years later and married to another, still he'll recall and warmly write of the spell he was under during those days and nights at the shore.

She'd await him on the hotel porch, he'll say, and on his way to join her, he'll hear talk, music, and laughter from the ballroom, but sight will soften sound, he'll say (the white gown, the black sash, the red rose), and almost through silence, he'll move toward the pleasures of the season. It was the season of sin, he'll say, and its pleasures wore crepe de chine, a velvet sash, and a red red velvet rose.

He'll show his wife what he'd written, and she'll say, "I'm so glad you remember her, John. It proves you'll remember me."

1926-1927

A TRAIN-RIDE TO THE FUTURE

From the rear platform of the three-car local, she watched the El Centro depot grow smaller, and Leonard with it, and she continued to watch until they disappeared in the offing. Briefly she'd fancied that they were in motion, not she, that in their retreat they were drawing the rails and ties from under her feet; they were stranding her, she thought, and she was standing still....

LEONARD: It's painful to talk about this, but there's no help for it. When you get to Los Angeles, are you going to...well, see a lawyer?

MARGUERITE: There's no particular hurry. I have no one else in mind.

LEONARD: Some day, though, you will.

MARGUERITE: And you'll have other girls.

LEONARD: Yes, but that's all they'll be—other girls.

The roadbed of the branch line ran through the towns of Brawley and Calipatria and mile after mile of citrus groves and melon fields, all of it overlaid with a grid of irrigation. At Niland, there was a junction with the main line, and from there the right-of-way lay across the instep of the Chocolate Mountains close by the shore of the lake called Salton Sea....

LEONARD: I'll stop by the bank tomorrow and get you a cashier's check for half of what we have.

MARGUERITE: Half?

LEONARD: In California, it's yours by right.

MARGUERITE: I don't care a rush about rights. All I want is train-fare and a ten-dollar bill.

LEONARD: You're being foolish. Whatever we have we made together, and half of it belongs to you.

MARGUERITE: You keep it, Leonard. And as long as we're settling up, keep the car too.

LEONARD: But we bought it out of what we made on the pearls.

MARGUERITE: You'll need a car; I won't.

Seated now against a window, Marguerite took little note of the view— the slopes and gullies at the one hand and the vast landlocked expanse at the other. The lifeless water did not stay her eye long nor did the rucks of the mesquite. She was scarcely aware of the dust devils spun up by the speeding cars, and she did not dwell on the smoke trees they passed, their delicate flowers like clouds of gray gas....

MARGUERITE: I'd like it if you wrote to me now and then.

LEONARD: Would you? Why?

MARGUERITE: I want to know how you are and how things are going for you.

LEONARD: I'd not have thought it mattered.

MARGUERITE: Do you really suppose I'm that cold?

LEONARD: Well, when a wife leaves....
MARGUERITE: The past goes along. Life isn't a calendar.

Her mind was on what couldn't be seen—events still in the making, roads yet to be travelled, the faces and places and choices to come. She was thinking far beyond the light Pacific at the head of the train, further even than the City of the Angels at the end of the line—for that end, she knew, would be only her beginning....

MARGUERITE: You say you might be going back to Greeley. Would you take some advice?
LEONARD: From you? Any time.
MARGUERITE: Stay away from that drug store.
LEONARD: All I ever did was help my father once in a while.
MARGUERITE: Let Baxter help. He doesn't do much else.
LEONARD: Why so strong about the store?
MARGUERITE: Because you're a good accountant. If you stick with it, you're bound to pick up a clientele.
LEONARD: Maybe I should've stuck to it in the first place. We might've....
MARGUERITE: I don't think so, Leonard.

Along the rim of the Salton, many a siding lay, each with a name she'd never before heard—Mundo and Wister and Frink, she read, and then Bertram and Durmid—but never was a town to be seen, and not until Mecca was reached did the empty landscape change. Now there were date gardens and vineyards, and a far way beyond them reared the San Bernardinos, a crest here and there capped with yesteryear snow....

LEONARD: Your train leaves at noon. I'll drive you to the depot and put you aboard.
MARGUERITE: Will the plant let you off?
LEONARD: What can they do—nail me to the floor?
MARGUERITE: I could arrange for a taxi.
LEONARD: I'll take you. I won't believe you're gone till I see you go.

Beyond Indio, the right-of-way ran through an orderly forest of date palms in which, just below their spray of fronds, hung clusters of fruit, each swathed in cloth against the nighttime chill of the desert. Women holding their children, she thought, a troupe of long-legged women....

LEONARD: There's a bench over by that baggage-truck. You can sit down till your train comes.

MARGUERITE: It won't be long. I think I heard it.

LEONARD: Looks like no one else'll be getting on. It'll be a special train for you, compliments of Southern Pacific.

MARGUERITE: You're being very good about all this, Leonard. I'm glad there's no bad feeling.

LEONARD: There is, though. It's inside, and it doesn't show—

MARGUERITE: I said a foolish thing. I feel bad too.

LEONARD: —and I'm going to keep on feeling bad for a long long time.

MARGUERITE: I'm sorry.

LEONARD: I wish you well.

For some way now the route had been bearing toward the mountains, and though they were still distant, she could see where the desert was halted by an overflow of greenery down the ridges. The highest of the summits wore pompadours of snow....

MARGUERITE: Well, it's time to say goodbye, Leonard.

LEONARD: I can't speak the words. I simply can't.

MARGUERITE: Will you let me kiss you, then...?

1927

1452 W. 39TH ST.

In Los Angeles, at the Central Avenue terminal of the Southern Pacific, Marguerite took a taxi to her sister's address. It was on a quiet street of small houses, nearly all of them turkey-tail bungalows much like the one she'd just quitted in El Centro. Each was single-story and had a porch shaded by a broad roof, and at either side, as if with outspread wings, the roof also overhung the walls. There were lights within, and for a moment Marguerite stood before the screen, listening to familiar voices, to supper-sounds, to the simmer of the surrounding city.

And then she called through the mesh, saying," Save some of that for me."

"Baby sister!" Pearl said as she came away from the table and hastened toward the door....

The Depression, 1929-1939

THE COLOR OF THE AIR

They're all right, Jack

During a panic, nothing is being lost but money.
—John Galbraith

True, Jack, but it's you who lost the money, not the rich; they haven't lost a pistareen. Gone your green and your last red cent, but they still dine on best-year wine and larded snipe while you line up for stale bread and garbage soup. It's you, Jack, urgent with apples at every crossing of two streets, and it's they in the sun on a Ligurian beach. It's they who sleep between sheets, Jack, and you who make do with doorways and shanties in the park. Your soles touch the ground through the holes in your shoes, your teeth are loose and your sight's sour, and at times you bring up blood: you're half-dead on your feet, Jack, and one day you'll be all-dead in a ditch.

You ought to be able to see that, Jack, even with those conjunctive eyes. They know that they're the few and you're the many—why in the world don't you? When will you realize that what you gave them through the ages you can take back in an hour? When, Jack, when will you use your numbers and your power to impoverish the rich?

They gave you the make-work job of raking fallen leaves, and as

266

they speed past and scatter them, they laugh up their sleeves: you come cheap, Jack; you get the dollar-bills, and they keep the Clevelands. Until you learn, Jack, there's more of the same in store for you. You'll go on laying stones in homocentric circles, you'll swab the tiles in public toilets, and as before, you'll pile a billion leaves....

1936

THE WRITERS BUILDING AT PARAMOUNT

Four stories below her window, a gardener was tending a small plot of grass in the courtyard. Though he worked in plain sight, her look was fixed on nothing, and she saw him only as a blur in slow motion. Through a wall, she could hear the firing of a neighbor's typewriter, a burst of words followed by a silence, as though his brain had grown hot and jammed. Turning from the window to her desk, idly she scanned what lay upon it—a telephone, a dictionary, a tray of pencils, the green square of a blotter, a pair of porcelain figurines.

These last were her own. They'd been given to her by a man she'd once known, a man whose image, like that of the gardener in the yard, dispersed even as it came within view. Gone now the giver, but his gift remained—two pieces of blue-white china in the shape of dancing girls poised with arms outflung and skirts aswirl. Where she went, there went they: her only personal possession here, they'd been brought from one impersonal room to another, and when she quitted this one, they'd go with her to the next. Others might've assumed them to be the last memoranda of a past attachment, but in truth they were souvenirs of nothing and no one; they were merely a pair of graceful figurines.

Thirty-one years of her life were behind her, and she had no wish to relive them, least of all in her mind. The relics of bygone times--the correspondence, the inscribed volume and the pressed flower, the dance-favor with the same name on every line—none of these had she pre-served; they belonged, she thought, with the dead. But even so little as a dismissal of the past had been enough to awaken it, and like sediment disturbed, it rose from the bottom of memory.

Teddy Simmons, she thought, and through beclouded time, she saw

267

the tow-headed boy usually to be found in her wake, tied, it seemed, like a dinghy. Now and again, she'd forget he was there, and turning around, she'd collide with him. They'd been in the same class at grade school, they'd played together on the grounds, and they'd walked with each other on their winding way home; but for all their childhood in company, she could recall none of the countless words they'd spoken: the scenes came back without sound.

Creatures she'd loved came to mind: the Dalmatian Jack that had taught her to walk; the bullcalf Bolivar; the raccoon that slept in a dresser drawer. And she thought of Croppy the burro and a slew of horses: a team of wind-broken Clydesdales, a high-stepper, a roadster, a cow-pony named Buck. And then she thought of Leonard, for he too was a creature, though one she'd never loved.

Leonard, she thought, and she saw him as in a faded photo, vague in outline and lacking detail, and it surprised her that he'd so soon become indistinct: their years apart had nearly erased their years of marriage. How could that have happened?, she wondered, how could he be so close to extinction that she could hardly remember his voice, his taste, his touch, his presence in any room? How could it have come to pass that he'd make so slight an impression on the mind?

She glanced at the letters and numerals on the keys of her Royal, at the blank sheet on the pitted platen, at a box of carbons, and then her gaze strayed to an armchair that she rarely used, to walls bare save for a calendar of black and red days. There was little to be seen here, she thought, nothing, really, except herself. In the hall, a figure cast a passing shadow on the glass panel of the door.

Names now came to her, those of the men she'd known since her parting with Leonard, and like the shadow on the door, they too were dim and fleeting. Wallace, Wiggins, Ives, she thought, and through the blear of time, their faces reappeared. Wallace: quiet and courtly as a rule, but menacing in the face of an affront, one such having been the wish she expressed to leave him. Wiggins: capricious and explosive, a Canadian wounded in the Great War and walking around since with a plate in his skull. And Ives, born Ivello: a five-and-dime thief, a flim-flammer, a raiser of checks, a liar by choice, and a reckless knave. How had she come by these queer sticks? Was she worthy only of the violent, the light-fingered, the second-rater? Was there something about her that warned their betters away?

Dispirited, again she let her eyes take her on a tour of the room. This time, though, they saw nothing but the calendar, and in fancy, as in a trick shot, it suddenly seemed to shed its leaves, a gust of numbers stopping on the last day of October. Her own fancy had produced the illusion, but she was all the more depressed by the number she'd made herself face—her age.

She broke her flow of thought by turning once more to the window and the yard below: the gardener had gone, and no one else was to be seen. Leaving the room now, she walked along the hall toward the elevator. The doors were being held open for her by a writer named—March, was it, Joseph March?—and standing beside him was someone she did not know....

1936

☙ **AFTERWORD** ☙

On the fourth floor of the Writers Building at Paramount, you and Joe March were awaiting the arrival of the elevator from the levels below. Through the shaft came the pulsing drone of the motor, but your mind was elsewhere, and you scarcely heard the sound. You were listening to other sound, cadenced and precise, but it was in your fancy only and recalled from other times: the sound of footsteps on the hallway tiles.

At midmorning each day, someone would approach your room, pass a shadow across the glass panel of your door, and move away. You'd try to imagine a face and figure for the person going by, but able to visualize nothing, you'd be left with disembodied footfalls in transit along the hall.

Noting your abstraction, Joe said, "Still listening for her?"

"Listening *to* her. I keep thinking of the way she walks."

"Be bold. Knock on her door and ask her to join us."

"I've never spoken to her, never even seen her."

"Jack," Joe said. "It's only for a cup of coffee."

"I know, but what if she refuses?"

"Nobody refuses a cup of coffee. Nobody."

"What if I don't like her looks?"

"Or worse—what if she doesn't like yours?"

You heard footsteps now, a series taken at the customary pace, steady, resolute (rhythmical, you thought)—but were they old sounds recalled, or were they being newly made...?

"Miss Roberts," Joe was saying, "meet John Sanford."

You turned, and she was there.....

☙